Native-Speakerism in Japan

MULTILINGUAL MATTERS
Series Editor: John Edwards, *St. Francis Xavier University, Canada*

Multilingual Matters series publishes books on bilingualism, bilingual education, immersion education, second language learning, language policy, multiculturalism. The editor is particularly interested in 'macro'-level studies of language policies, language maintenance, language shift, language revival and language planning. Books in the series discuss the relationship between language in a broad sense and larger cultural issues, particularly identity related ones.

Full details of all the books in this series and of all our other publications can be found on http://www.multilingual-matters.com, or by writing to Multilingual Matters, St Nicholas House, 31-34 High Street, Bristol BS1 2AW, UK.

Native-Speakerism in Japan
Intergroup Dynamics in Foreign Language Education

Edited by
Stephanie Ann Houghton and Damian J. Rivers

MULTILINGUAL MATTERS
Bristol • Buffalo • Toronto

Library of Congress Cataloging in Publication Data
A catalog record for this book is available from the Library of Congress.
Native-Speakerism in Japan: Intergroup Dynamics in Foreign Language Education/Edited by Stephanie A. Houghton and Damian J. Rivers.
Multilingual Matters: 151
Includes bibliographical references and index.
1. Linguistic informants--Japan. 2. Language and languages--Study and teaching--Japan. 3. Language teaching--Japan. 4. Second language acquisition--Japan. 5. Linguistics--Study and teaching--Japan. 6. Japan--Languages. I. Houghton, Stephanie, 1969- II. Rivers, Damian J.
P128.I53N38 2013
418.0071'052--dc23 2012036459

British Library Cataloguing in Publication Data
A catalogue entry for this book is available from the British Library.

ISBN-13: 978-1-84769-869-8 (hbk)
ISBN-13: 978-1-84769-868-1 (pbk)

Multilingual Matters
UK: St Nicholas House, 31-34 High Street, Bristol BS1 2AW, UK.
USA: UTP, 2250 Military Road, Tonawanda, NY 14150, USA.
Canada: UTP, 5201 Dufferin Street, North York, Ontario M3H 5T8, Canada.

Copyright © 2013 Stephanie Ann Houghton, Damian J. Rivers and the authors of individual chapters.

All rights reserved. No part of this work may be reproduced in any form or by any means without permission in writing from the publisher.

The policy of Multilingual Matters/Channel View Publications is to use papers that are natural, renewable and recyclable products, made from wood grown in sustainable forests. In the manufacturing process of our books, and to further support our policy, preference is given to printers that have FSC and PEFC Chain of Custody certification. The FSC and/or PEFC logos will appear on those books where full certification has been granted to the printer concerned.

Typeset by Ditech
Printed and bound in Great Britain by Short Run Press Ltd.

Contents

Tables and Figures viii
List of Acronyms ix
Acknowledgements x

Introduction: Redefining Native-Speakerism 1
Stephanie Ann Houghton and Damian J. Rivers

Part 1: Native-Speakerism: Shifting to a Postmodern Paradigm

1 'Native Speaker' Teachers and Cultural Belief 17
  Adrian Holliday

Part 2: 'Native Speaker' Teachers in Workplace Conflict

2 (Dis)Integration of Mother Tongue Teachers in Italian Universities: Human Rights Abuses and the Quest for Equal Treatment in the European Single Market 29
  David Petrie

3 Kumamoto General Union vs. the Prefectural University of Kumamoto: Reviewing the Decision Rendered by the Kumamoto District Court 42
  Kirk Masden

4 The Overthrow of the Foreign Lecturer Position, and its Aftermath 60
  Stephanie Ann Houghton

5 Institutionalized Native-Speakerism: Voices of Dissent
   and Acts of Resistance   75
   Damian J. Rivers

6 Negotiating a Professional Identity: Non-Japanese Teachers
   of English in Pre-Tertiary Education in Japan   92
   Joe Geluso

7 Forming Pathways of Belonging: Social Inclusion for
   Teachers Abroad   105
   Joseph Falout

Part 3: Employment Policies and Patterns in Japanese Tertiary and Secondary Education

8 Communicative English in Japan and 'Native Speakers of
   English'   119
   Ryoko Tsuneyoshi

9 Hiring Criteria for Japanese University English-Teaching
   Faculty   132
   Blake E. Hayes

10 On the (Out)Skirts of TESOL Networks of Homophily:
   Substantive Citizenship in Japan   147
   Salem Kim Hicks

11 The Construction of the 'Native Speaker' in Japan's
   Educational Policies for TEFL   159
   Kayoko Hashimoto

12 The Meaning of Japan's Role of Professional Foreigner   169
   Evan Heimlich

Part 4: Native-Speakerism as a Multi-Faceted and Contemporary Social Phenomenon

13 Scrutinizing the Native Speaker as Referent, Entity and
   Project   183
   Glenn Toh

14 Racialized Native Speakers: Voices of Japanese American
    English Language Professionals   196
    Ryuko Kubota and Donna Fujimoto

15 Native-Speakerism through English-Only Policies: Teachers,
    Students and the Changing Face of Japan   207
    Jennifer Yphantides

Part 5: Native-Speakerism from Socio-Historical Viewpoints

16 Changing Perceptions? A Variationist Sociolinguistic
    Perspective on Native Speaker Ideologies and Standard
    English in Japan   219
    Robert M. McKenzie

17 Ideologies of Nativism and Linguistic Globalization   231
    Philip Seargeant

18 The Native Speaker Language Teacher: Through Time
    and Space   243
    Martine Derivry-Plard

    References   256

    Index   282

Tables and Figures

Tables

Table I.1: Definitions of sexism, orientalism, racism and ethnocentrism by Oxford Dictionaries online — 4

Table 5.1: Demographics of the people employed in the EC during 2010-2011 — 77

Table 8.1: Foreign researchers by selected departments at the University of Tokyo (2007) — 127

Table 8.2: Number of courses in English at the University of Tokyo (2006-2007) — 129

Table 9.1: Benefits and constraints for Japanese in the hiring process — 137

Table 9.2: Benefits and constraints for non-Japanese in the hiring process — 138

Table 9.3: Racialized and gendered benefits and constraints — 138

Figures

Figure 7.1: Forming pathways of belonging — 115

Figure 12.1: The no/EFL eddy, swirling where the pro-communication-with-foreigners current runs adjacent to its opposite current — 177

Figure 12.2: Japan's employment-of-foreigners eddy, swirling where the pro-inclusion-of-foreigners current runs adjacent to its opposite current — 178

Figure 16.1: The native speaker/non-native speaker linguistic continuum — 221

List of Acronyms

Assistant English Teacher	AET
Assistant Language Teacher	ALT
Coordinator of International Relations	CIR
Council of Local Authorities for International Relations	CLAIR
English as a Foreign Language	EFL
English as a Lingua Franca	ELF
English as a Second Language	ESL
English as an Additional Language	EAL
English as an International Language	EIL
English Language Teaching	ELT
English Language Teachers	ELTs
European Court of Justice	ECJ
Japan Association for Language Teaching	JALT
Japan Exchange and Teaching Programme	JET
Japanese Teacher of English	JTE
Kumamoto Nichinichi Shinbun	KNS
Ministry of Education, Culture, Sports, Science and Technology	MEXT*
Ministry of Internal Affairs and Communication	MIC
Ministry of Foreign Affairs	MOFA
Ministry of Health, Labour and Welfare	MHLW
Native English Speaker Teacher	NEST
Native Speaker of English	NSE
Native Speaker of Japanese	NSJ
Non-Native English Speaker Teacher	NNEST
Non-Native Speaker of English	NNSE
Sports Exchange Advisor	SEA
Teaching English as a Foreign Language	TEFL
Test of English for International Communication	TOEIC
Teaching English to Speakers of Other Languages	TESOL
Times Higher Education Supplement	THES

Note: *Until January 2001 the 'Ministry of Education, Culture, Sports, Science and Technology' (MEXT) (*Monbukagakushou*) was known as the 'Ministry of Education' (MOE) (*Monbushou*). However, for the purpose of clarity, throughout this volume the modern MEXT acronym will be used even when referring to events that preceded the 2001 name change.

Acknowledgements

We would like to offer our sincere thanks to the Research Centre for Cultural and Linguistic Practices in the International University (CALPIU) in Roskilde, Denmark for providing a supportive environment in which the ideas leading to the conceptualization of this volume were initially formulated (Houghton, 2008) and later advanced upon (Rivers *et al.*, 2012). We also offer our sincere thanks to Robert Phillipson, Tove Skutknabb-Kangas and Alan Davies for their guidance and feedback in the early stages of this project, as well as to the editorial staff at Multilingual Matters for their unwavering professionalism. Finally, we would like to express our deepest gratitude and admiration to all contributing authors who have demonstrated their courage and a commitment to professionalism in attempting to tackle, from a variety of standpoints, the quandary that is native-speakerism.

Stephanie Ann Houghton and Damian J. Rivers
Fukuoka and Osaka, Japan
26 June 2012

Introduction: Redefining Native-Speakerism

Stephanie Ann Houghton and
Damian J. Rivers

> Native-speakerism is a pervasive ideology within ELT, characterized by the belief that 'native-speaker' teachers represent a 'Western culture' from which spring the ideals both of the English language and of English language teaching methodology.
>
> Holliday (2006: 385)

This definition of native-speakerism, first advanced by Holliday in 2005 and recognized soon after as a *Key Concept in ELT* by the *ELT Journal* in 2006, reflects a traditional orientation towards English language education rooted in dichotomous 'us' and 'them' dynamics in which 'native speakers' of English are considered the norm, the owners of the English language and its naturally endowed teaching experts, in contrast to 'non-native speakers' of English who are generally considered deficient, an ideology otherwise termed cultural disbelief (Holliday, Chapter 1).

In this culturally reductive politics of Self and Other, Holliday argues that non-native speakers of English are confined by an ideology of deficiency through which the vested interests of native speakers (and their predominantly Western Inner Circle in-groups) are promoted, while non-native speakers and their respective groups are systematically stripped of cultural value as inferior out-group members. Furthermore, academic analysis of these intergroup dynamics *also* tends to be marked by dichotomy as native speakers are cast predominantly as perpetrators, while non-native-speakers are cast as the only group worthy of authentic victim status (Rivers, Chapter 5). And the ELT labour market in Japan, for example, is itself 'dichotomized as Japanese/non-Japanese' (Hayes, Chapter 9), which overlaps native-speakerism as nationality is often conflated with native speaker status, and indeed, Heimlich claims that in Japan '[f]oreignness of the worker is the qualification of the [native-speaker] role' to 'firewall Japaneseness from hybridization' (Heimlich, Chapter 12).

Given the often *politically* motivated nature of the native speaker status ascription process, the primary concern when addressing native-speakerism in this book is 'not with who is and is not a "native speaker", but with the ideological associations of the distinction' (Holliday, 2005a: 6), and its impact upon 'many aspects of professional life, from employment policy to the presentation of language' (Holliday, 2006: 385). The promotion of learner-centred ELT methodology, for example, has been characterized as a native-speakerist system of control that denies the identities of students and teachers from outside the English-speaking West 'especially when they have difficulty with the specific types of active, collaborative, and self-directed "learned-centred" teaching–learning techniques that have frequently been constructed and packaged as superior within the English-speaking West' (Holliday, 2006: 385).

Holliday suggests that 'this cultural reduction, or culturism, falls within the broader *chauvinistic* [emphasis ours] narrative of Orientalism (Said, 1978)' (Holliday, 2006: 386) through which the behaviours of 'non-native speakers' are 'corrected' by 'native speakers' through English language education as part of what Holliday calls their 'moral mission' to bring a 'superior' culture of teaching and learning to students and colleagues who are perceived not to be able to succeed on their own terms (Holliday, 2006: 386), praising the way in which Phillipson's discussion of linguistic imperialism placed 'the possibility and potential of imperialism in TESOL firmly on the TESOL agenda in the English-speaking West' (Holliday, 2005a: 10).

In taking a more focused look at the notion of culturism, it represents a position borne from the combination of four contributing domains that include an essentialist view of culture, colonialist ideology, politics of the Self and Other and reification according to Holliday (2005a), and when applied to the specific field of TESOL, it is realized as native-speakerism. While the terms *imperialism* and *colonialism* tend to invoke images of Great Britain's colonial past, Tsuneyoshi (Chapter 8) is quick to remind the reader that '[b]eing a colonizer, Japan has never been colonized by a foreign power; though it experienced a period of occupation by the United States after World War II, even then, English was never forced upon the public'.

Interpreting native-speakerism, then, primarily in terms of imperialism or colonialism, and thus ideology, can only limit the analysis in ways that obscure the complexity of native-speakerism as a global, and very contemporary, social phenomenon. Taking a broader view, the focus here is placed in this introduction upon *chauvinism*, an overarching umbrella term that encompasses other 'isms', including imperialism and colonialism. *Chauvinism* is defined in Oxford Dictionaries Online as 'excessive or prejudiced support for one's own cause, group, or sex' (http://oxforddictionaries.com/definition/

chauvinism?q=chauvinism), a definition that highlights connections between *native-speakerism* and *ethnocentrism, racism* and *sexism* through the concept of *culturism*, and by extension with *orientalism*.

Such discrete prejudices may, however, intersect and overlap in real life flavouring and influencing one another as multitudes of differing social situations come into being and then dissipate or persist throughout daily working life. Hayes (Chapter 9) shows how the inequalities characterizing the native speaker status intersect particularly with gender, race and age in complex and nuanced ways in the Japanese context, while Hicks (Chapter 10), also focusing on the native speaker as a gendered status, explores how various ideologies and structures come into play to present eight additional barriers to native speaker women. By way of contrast, and adding further complexity into the mix, Kubota and Fujimoto (Chapter 14) illustrate how the 'complex manifestations of racial exclusion and Othering experienced by Japanese American native English-speaking teachers in Japan' work together to exclude them in ways that are 'based on a racial hierarchy of power is entrenched in contemporary Japanese society'.

While there are no entries for *culturism* or *native-speakerism* in Oxford Dictionaries Online, a cursory glance at the definitions of sexism, orientalism, racism and ethnocentrism presented in Table I.1 highlights the ways in which specific prejudices can target specific groups, involving intergroup dynamics rooted in antagonism, prejudice and stereotyping that can potentially result in discrimination as power struggles unfold that are entrenched in the conscious or sub-conscious desire for one's own group to dominate another. Notably, however, while perpetrators and victims are to be found in any power struggle, they are not necessarily implied by the terms themselves. For example, it can be seen in Table I.1 below that the typical victims of sexism and orientalism are specified in the definitions themselves (i.e. women and Asians), but for racism and ethnocentrism, they are not.

When using pre-determined terminology to discuss different kinds of prejudices, the perpetrators and the victims may or may not be implied by the terms themselves, with the obvious danger being that the mere use of any given term (especially terms such as orientalism, sexism, male chauvinism and feminism) may accuse a certain group by automatically suggesting in the minds of people *who* are the perpetrators (in need of challenge) and *who* are the victims (in need of protection). And the same can be said of *native-speakerism*, a term which, within its present (albeit rather recently coined definition) *primarily* casts 'native speakers' from the English-speaking West as the perpetrators of native-speakerism (the subjects of the verb) and 'non-native speakers' from the English-speaking West as the victims (the objects of the verb). The objectification of native speakers is analysed by Toh (Chapter 13) who explores how '(1) the native

Table I.1 Definitions of sexism, orientalism, racism and ethnocentrism by Oxford Dictionaries Online

Sexism	• prejudice, stereotyping, or discrimination, typically against women, on the basis of sex (http://oxforddictionaries.com/definition/sexism)
Orientalism	• the representation of Asia in a stereotyped way that is regarded as embodying a colonialist attitude (http://oxforddictionaries.com/definition/orientalism)
Racism	• the belief that all members of each race possess characteristics, abilities, or qualities specific to that race, especially so as to distinguish it as inferior or superior to another race or races; • prejudice, discrimination, or antagonism directed against someone of a different race based on the belief that one's own race is superior (http://oxforddictionaries.com/definition/racism)
Ethnocentrism	• evaluating other cultures according to preconceptions originating in the standards and customs of one's own culture (http://oxforddictionaries.com/definition/ethnocentric)

speaker as a construct can, in different instances, be discursively represented, essentialised and "Othered" in the Japanese situation, and (2) how native speakers as people entering Japan come then to be employed, deployed, typified or otherwise looked upon the way they are'.

> [While] native-speakerism originates in a very particular set of educational and development cultures within the English-speaking West and is an easy position for those who conceptualise themselves as 'native speakers', it has had a massive influence and exists to a greater or lesser degree in the thinking of all ESOL educators. (Holliday, 2005a: 7)

The quotation above gives due recognition to the fact that native-speakerism can reside in the minds of 'native speakers' and 'non-native speakers' alike – *all* ESOL educators – and Holliday *does* recognize that not all English-speaking Western colleagues are native-speakerist. Nonetheless, inherent to the term native-speakerism *itself* is the implication of native-speaker as subject, and non-native speaker as object, a point with which this book takes serious issue for it renders present understandings of native-speakerism not only partial but also over-simplistic and biased. It has yet to be investigated empirically whether or not native-speakerism resides 'largely within the sphere of English-speaking Western TESOL' (Holliday, 2005a: 8), but most certainly 'TESOL is configured within government policies and institutional structures within particular countries, which in turn gives rise to particular professional cultures and discourses' (Holliday, 2005a: 8), and native-speakerism may manifest itself in different ways in different cultural contexts.

In a bid to release non-native speakers of English from the ideology of deficiency mentioned at the start of the introduction, Holliday (Chapter 1) argues that 'it is possible to counter cultural disbelief by means of a subtle but significant professional shift to cultural belief, but that this also requires a shift from a modernist, positivist to a postmodern paradigm'. As part of this proposed shift, Holliday explains, the notion of the objectivity of the native – non-native speaker criterion is to be rejected in favour of a deep recognition of the subjectivity of the ascription process, whose insidious nature necessitates systematic consideration of the ways in which discourse serves ideology, while also being driven by it, in the construction of social reality.

To this end, following Fairclough (1995), Holliday recommends the use of critical discourse analysis to expose 'the hegemonic discourse of native-speakerism. It explores the ways in which its prejudices and politics are deeply embedded in every aspect of practice' (Holliday, 2005a: 10). Indeed, Hashimoto (Chapter 11) uses critical discourse analysis to interrogate the bi-lingual Japanese and English discourse of the Japanese government on the role of native speaker teachers played in Japan, revealing subtle, yet significant, differences between them that show how the term serves to restrict the functions of native speakers within the Japanese education system at least at the high school level. Notably, Hashimoto exposes how native speakers are viewed by the Japanese government not as teachers, but rather as *resources* to be utilized by teachers (i.e. Japanese teachers of English) for the purposes of TEFL. The Japanese government's (MEXT, 2006) comparative analysis of the relative value of English language education of native speakers and Information Communications Technology (ICT) (see Hashimoto, Chapter 11) not only further illustrates the objectification (and, indeed, dehumanization) of native-speakerism mentioned earlier but also undermines Holliday's definition of native-speakerism presented at the start of the introduction, which clearly rests upon the view that native speaker teachers are sought for their English language and teaching methodology.

Describing NSEs as resources to be utilised is a common practice in both the private and public sectors in Japan, and the rhetoric of 'utilisation of native speakers' is predominant throughout the government documents produced by the Cabinet, the MEXT and the MIC. (Hashimoto, Chapter 11)

Also notable in this regard is that while Holliday (Chapter 1) claims that the concept of the superior native speaker teacher originated in the 1960s when the concept was constructed as a saleable product to support American and British aid trajectories (Holliday, Chapter 1), Seargeant (Chapter 17) traces the conceptual origins of the term further back to the Romantic era in Europe to 'ideas that flourished during that period concerning the identity of nation, culture and language', a point echoed by Derivry-Plard (Chapter 18) who seeks to 'enlarge the notion of the native speaking English teacher to a broader one: the native speaker language teacher'.

Throughout time and space, native-speaker teachers of foreign languages have not always been in high demand, as demand is linked to the dominant diplomatic and economic powers of the time (e.g. Chinese in Asia with the spread of Chinese characters in ancient times, French in 18th-Century Europe and English in the 21st-Century global world). (Derivry-Plard, Chapter 18)

Of particular importance to the current volume, then, is the acknowledgement that although originating largely in Western and particularly European discourse, native-speakerism can also thrive within non-Western, non-English speaking contexts necessitating a far broader definition of the term that Holliday allows. And indeed, the negative impact of native-speakerism may extend far beyond the resident population of native speaker teachers to oppress other racial groups in the process through the imposition of racial hierarchies in society as a whole under the ostensibly positive guise of internationally-friendly English language education. This point is advanced by Tsuneyoshi (Chapter 8) who suggests that naïve understandings of language and culture implemented through English activities in Japan can 'work to disadvantage the colonized populations in Japan in preference of those from English-speaking countries'.

Another limitation of Holliday's notion of cultural belief becomes apparent when one considers that for a 'native speaker' to have cultural belief in a 'non-native speaker' necessarily requires that person first to categorize the SELF as a 'native speaker' and the OTHER as a 'non-native speaker' before actively engaging in the act of cultural belief. Insofar as the continuation of this mental activity rests upon the ongoing perpetuation of an 'us' and 'them' distinction in the mind of the person concerned, there can be no ultimate release from this dynamic unless this cycle is allowed to break in recognition of the strengths and weaknesses of the individual human beings with whom one interacts.

And when this cycle *does* break, what one witnesses is something akin to the situation described in the conclusion of Masden's chapter in which the President of the Prefectural University of Kumamoto (PUK) was blaming 'differences in cultural background between Japanese people and people from English-speaking countries' for workplace conflict revolving upon accusations of discrimination on the basis of nationality, while over 10,000 Japanese people were simultaneously supporting the foreign complainants in a petition opposing the university's treatment of them. It seems that to some extent, while the President of the university was psychologically trapped in 'us' and 'them' dynamics, those who signed the petition were not.

While Holliday's (2005a) definition has been useful in providing a foundation for new theoretical direction through which to forward explorations of issues concerning the dimensions of native-speakerism in foreign language education, we see this definition as now being limited in its ability to capture the multitude of intricate ways that native-speakerism, embedded within the fabric of the TESOL industry, is reflected through daily pedagogical practice, institutional and national policy, as well as legal frameworks which centre around issues of prejudice, stereotyping and/or discrimination.

Resisting Native-Speakerism

From a comparative perspective, the relative status of native and non-native speaker language teachers within educational institutions has long been an issue worldwide, but existing work to date has tended to focus upon the position of non-native teachers and their struggle against unfavourable comparisons with their native speaker counterparts (Braine, 1999; Llurda, 2005; Medgyes, 1994), as exemplified by the formation of NNEST, a politically oriented professional organization which has as one of its principles 'to create a non discriminatory professional environment for all TESOL members regardless of native language and place of birth' (Holliday, 2005a: 6). However, while '"non-native speakers" are certainly victims of prejudice and discrimination at the pre-employment stage, "native-speakers" are also victims of prejudice and discrimination at the post-employment stage' (Rivers & Ross, forthcoming), and in response to this trend, native speaker language teachers have been increasingly placed in the academic spotlight as interest grows in native-speakerism especially in EFL education (Houghton, 2008; Kabel, 2009; Modiano, 2009; Rivers *et al.*, 2012; Waters, 2007).

Until recently, however, the voices of such teachers articulating their own concerns within the Japanese context have been rare due in part to the observation that native speaker teaching in Japan is shrouded in a cloak of silence that can be broken only at the risk of being fired (Bueno & Caesar, 2003), and this situation is long-standing despite the importation of thousands of native speaker English language teachers to Japan on the JET Programme in order to kick-start the national development of communicative competence in a country that was, and still is, struggling to move away from a reliance on the grammar-translation methodology. This mass importation has resulted in the creation of many intercultural workplaces in Japan in which such teachers are employed from primary through high school to university level, as well as in the thousands of private English conversation schools scattered across the country. And the perceived need for native speaker teachers is likely to only increase as English is introduced at the primary school level (see Hashimoto, 2011) and as the medium of instruction in the English language classroom at the high school level as a matter of national policy in 2013. Nonetheless, no matter at what level the native speaker language teacher temporarily resides, the institutional expectation that all forms of criticality, dissent, questioning and resistance remain silent is persistent and powerful.

In their recent work, Willis and Rappleye (2011) present a persuasive argument for the need to re-imagine what is known about the Japanese education system. Through a series of chapters, they stress the need to focus on the conflicts and contradictions created by that which is real and that which is imagined, especially in relation to conceptualizations of the self and the other. Despite this timely volume, however, Japan's socio-historical dependence upon native speaker models in foreign language education remains as steadfast as it was over a century ago with no indication that alternative solutions to the controversial native speaker position will ever be forthcoming. Therefore, we see the concept of the native speaker as one domain in which research focusing on the deconstruction of former and the reconstruction of future bodies of knowledge is urgently required. That is, explorations concerning the native speaker should represent an integral part of the re-imagination process due to the native speakers' position at the crossroads created by the real, the imagined, the self, the other, the former and the future.

Overview of the Volume

This book is divided into five main sections focusing predominantly upon native-speakerism in Japan, while also identifying links with the current situation in Italian tertiary education. Part 1 opens with a chapter by Holliday to review ways in which native-speakerism has been conceptualized and empirically investigated to date. Through consideration of the dual concepts of cultural disbelief and cultural belief in relation to native-speakerism, the need for a shift from a modernist, positivist to a postmodern paradigm is explained and justified in terms of releasing non-native speakers of English from the ideology of deficiency, mentioned at the start of this introduction, through the application of critical discourse analysis 'as a means for laying bare what is concealed between the lines of day-to-day professional talk and text' (Holliday, Chapter 1). By laying out a principled research agenda at the start of this book, and despite the special consideration given by Holliday to the problems facing the so-called non-native speakers within it, this opening chapter provides important conceptual and methodological foundations that can help readers to understand and interpret the wide-ranging chapters that appear later in the volume. Furthermore, it can also empower researchers interested in native-speakerism, as it affects teachers of *any* background, with tools with which to conduct incisive research that can get to the bottom of ideology and discourse as Holliday suggests.

The emphasis then shifts specifically to problems facing those teachers categorized as native speakers, and there it remains for the rest of the volume. In Part 2, a series of six chapters are presented that showcase contrasting, yet complementary, examples of 'native speaker' teachers resisting native-speakerism either directly with their employer by making use of legal mechanisms involving collective bargaining through labour unions and/or court action or indirectly by engaging in academic forms of protest, principled dissent or resistance.

The first three chapters in Part 2 showcase *direct* forms of resistance against native-speakerism by language teachers employed on the basis of their mother tongue in Italy, where ' [o]n six occasions, between 1989 and 2008 the ECJ ruled that Italy was infringing EU laws prohibiting discrimination based on nationality with regard to non-Italian workers employed in its universities. This chapter deals with the biggest case of mass discrimination based on nationality in the history of the EU: foreign lecturers working in Italian universities' (Petrie, Chapter 2). Next, Masden (Chapter 3) reviews the decision rendered by the Kumamoto District Court in the case of Kumamoto General Union vs. the Prefectural University of Kumamoto in which the termination of two teachers was (ultimately unsuccessfully) challenged through the court system, and the real-time unfolding of which directly influenced the overthrow of the 'foreign lecturer' position through labour union negotiations at a nearby university in southern Japan (Houghton, Chapter 4). Taken as a set, these three chapters expand potential thinking on native-speakerism beyond domestic national legal frameworks to the supranational level of European law, showing how *even* at this level (which does not exist in Asia) there can be more barriers than solutions, not only because the prejudices are so deep-rooted but also because the law itself, national, international or supranational, seems ill-equipped to deal effectively with the problems posed by native-speakerism.

The second of the three chapters in Part 2 showcase *indirect* forms of resistance against native-speakerism by language teachers in Japan and deal more readily with the interpersonal costs of offering resistance to the cascading torrent of fixed parameter norms present within the Japanese TESOL context. The chapter by Rivers (Chapter 5) presents a context-specific example of the *eikaiwa*-ization of EFL education at the tertiary level by recounting various struggles encountered within an institution functioning upon deeply entrenched ideologies of native-speakerism. Through sharing a small number of rarely heard minority voices, and detailing through professional experience, how acts of principled resistance can lead to conflict with figures in authority intent on maintaining the status quo, Rivers (Chapter 5) argues that those teachers burdened with the 'native-speaker' English teacher status label must 'become more actively engaged in the fight to transcend the limitations of their conditioned status without fear of being labeled as an in-group deviant, losing position within the social hierarchy, not having a contract renewed, or being fired'. The next chapter by Geluso (Chapter 6) widens the scope of non-Japanese teachers voicing their own professional identity concerns and explores a variety of issues pertaining to an existence on the periphery of mainstream education, highlighting how 'while it is true that NESTs enjoy many opportunities for employment as language teachers in Japan, the positions made available to them are located on the periphery of the institutions in which they teach'.

Finally, Falout (Chapter 7) takes a less critical stance in seeking ways in which those teachers who feel excluded and marginalized can take active steps toward maintaining and increasing psychological well-being and work-related satisfaction. Falout highlights how foreign language teachers 'may be at risk of not fulfilling the fundamental psychological need of frequent contact with several people in ongoing relationships of mutual care', concluding that 'when feeling socially excluded, most cognitive, emotional, and behavioral reactions that arise exacerbate social withdrawals, lead to wider detachments, and block formation of potential alliances'. This chapter provides a useful foundation for those teachers in Japan primarily looking to retain a sense of well-being under challenging conditions marked by interpersonal isolation, strategically maintained cultural difference and professional stagnation.

After showcasing six examples of 'native speaker' resistance to native-speakerism in different ways and different contexts, Part 3 of this volume then takes a critical step back from the turmoil of workplace conflict to present a series of five chapters that provide analysis of employment policies and patterns in tertiary and secondary education in Japan through empirical research and/

or informed social commentary formulated by professionals socialized in Japan (both Japanese and non-Japanese). Focusing on patterns in the employment of foreigners at the University of Tokyo, Tsuneyoshi (Chapter 8) claims that '[m]any of the foreign faculty are specially appointed researchers (*tokutei yuuki*), often hired for a certain purpose (e.g. participating in a certain project) and on a limited term'. Importantly, Tsuneyoshi suggests that 'a major axis of differentiation ... among the foreign faculty is whether one's role is language-based or discipline-based' with the former group of foreigners (i.e. the native speakers of English) being the most likely 'object of native-speakerism' since they are identified *not* for their disciplinary knowledge but for their language.

Taking a more general view, and through empirical research, Hayes (Chapter 9) explores some of the evaluation criteria applied in practice in the hiring of Japanese and non-Japanese teachers for language-related positions at universities in Japan exposing racialized and gendered benefits and constraints for each population. Also viewing the native speaker as a gendered status, Hicks (Chapter 10) places the spotlight upon additional barriers facing native speaker women that include stereotypical views of the male as breadwinner, 'informal homophilic networks linked to nepotism in hiring; social and professional isolation and exclusion; and permissive attitudes towards power and sexual harassment'.

Houghton's (Rivers *et al.*, 2012) cross-cutting analysis of chapters in this volume that relate to employment policies and practices highlights the various ways in which the language barrier can function in Japanese educational institutions both public and private. According to Tsuneyoshi (Chapter 8), in a 2008 survey by Tokyo University's Division of International Affairs of the foreign scholars at the university, the largest work-related obstacle mentioned was the Japanese language-centred environment mainly because of the use of formal, bureaucratic Japanese in committee meetings combined with a general lack of secretarial support. The language barrier seems to be used to block the pathway into this environment at different stages of the employment process, and in different ways. At the hiring stage, Hayes (Chapter 9) found through empirical research that when non-Japanese are hired, functional Japanese is usually considered by selection committee members to be sufficient for non-tenured positions, but since Japanese language skills are largely conflated with Japanese *nationality*, the Japanese language skills of non-Japanese applicants are often automatically assumed to be insufficient for tenured positions. This point is borne out by Houghton (Chapter 4) who shows how at one university, Japanese language ability and officially ascribed native speaker status serve as dual grounds for employment distinction between tenured and non-tenured full-time foreign language teachers (English and Korean), ostensibly without any genuine regard for the *actual* Japanese language ability of the individuals concerned.

Furthermore, in managerial decision-making processes, Houghton (Chapter 4) shows how in the absence of a clear standard, the arbitrary application of 'Japanese language ability' as an evaluation criterion in both educational and administrative matters can play a role in oppressive backlash dynamics set in motion by lower and middle management members in response to greater inclusion of foreigners into the community of the tenured university professoriate, and Heimlich (Chapter 12) further illustrates how *backlash dynamics* can come into play in the workplace as 'impetus towards segregation counter[s] the impetus towards racial integration'. Notwithstanding the obvious need for sufficient Japanese language to perform administrative duties in Japanese, and the need for cooperation on both sides, the language barrier can – if insufficiently defined and systematically applied in practice – be raised arbitrarily to suit the circumstances and the particular individuals involved on a case-by-case basis, and if it no longer serves because the Japanese language ability of the individuals concerned is so very high, 'the language barrier' may be ditched as an excuse altogether, leaving the barrier itself in place without proper justification.

The hollowness of the employment criterion of 'Japanese language ability' echoes deeply in Hashimoto (Chapter 11) who draws attention to the 'systematic exclusion of foreigners from full-time employment in the public education sector: the central government's advice to local boards of education to limit the employment of Japanese-speaking Korean nationals is a well-known case in point (MEXT, 1991)'.

> Teaching qualifications and Japanese proficiency are deliberately not sought in the selection process for ALTs, precisely because these would render them equal to or better than JTEs. It could be said that this constitutes Japan's answer to the 'monolingual fallacy', the 'native speaker fallacy' (Canagarajah, 1999; Phillipson, 1992), or the 'inferiority complex' to NSE (Jenkins, 2000). (Hashimoto, Chapter 11)

The tactical use of language policy and proficiency requirements (or non-requirements) as a tool of exclusion also extends to the implementation of English-only policies which native English speaker teachers are often expected to follow in the workplace. In such instances, like with ALTs and teachers employed at English conversation schools, Japanese language proficiency is often ignored as teachers in contexts such as that described by Rivers (Chapter 5), are simply not expected, required or welcome to play any part in the day-to-day functioning of the institution. Instead, they are shunned to the sidelines, restricted to an existence within foreign enclaves crafted for purpose in a manner that reaffirms their symbolic role as authentic foreigner, employed not to educate, but to construct a marketable atmosphere of exoticness and a visual token of internationalization.

Part 4 of this volume features three chapters that take a further step back to view the contemporary social phenomenon of native-speakerism from different angles highlighting some of its contrasting facets. Toh (Chapter 13) provides a thorough dissection of the definitional parameters used in identifying and dealing with the native speaker in the Japanese context by reflecting on 'discourses surrounding the native speaker phenomenon and how this is played out in various discursive spaces in Japan and in particular, how conversations referencing the native speaker are staged in professional spaces and real life contestations.' Drawing to a close a compelling and persuasive argument, Toh concludes that 'the aura and persona of the native speaker remains one powerful construct ... problematic as the term may be, its use in everyday as we all as professional parlance is, to be realistic, unlikely to show signs of abatement any time soon.'

Kubota and Fujimoto (Chapter 14) examine the native speaker in specific relation to issues of race and racialization by application of Critical Race Theory (CRT). Through a selection of narratives from Japanese – American teachers, the authors show how within the specific context of Japan 'native speakerness is a proxy of whiteness', further highlighting how consequently, teachers of Japanese – American ancestry face 'complex manifestations of racial exclusion and othering'. Kubota and Fujimoto end their chapter with a call for teachers and other language education professionals to 'engage in situated ethics of anti-oppression in second language education'.

In the third chapter of Part 4, Yphantides (Chapter 15) provides a broad social analysis of the aforementioned English-only language policies and their role in perpetuating native-speakerism. In considering the English-only myth and the associated costs and benefits of strict monolingual language policy implementation, Yphantides makes important conceptual links to the changing demographics of Japanese society. With reference to the increasing population of minority group students in Japanese education, Yphantides argues that 'if native or near native students are forced to use English-only, they run the risk of being cast as essentialized objects of cultural and linguistic perfection that their peers need to emulate'.

In Part 5, socio-historical and sociolinguistic views of native-speakerism are presented to show not only how the present preferences for native speaker teachers and certain kinds of English came about, but also how such preferences appear to be changing in response to globalization. Exploring the changing sociolinguistic position of English in Japan, and recognizing Japan's traditional and highly institutionalized dependence upon the native speaker model in response to long-standing policy of the recruitment of native speakers throughout the Japanese educational system, McKenzie (Chapter 16) suggests that language attitudes towards (speakers of) native and non-native varieties of English may be changing in response to the global spread of English, and the subsequent growth of English for international communication. This theme is developed by Seargeant (Chapter 17) who explores ways in which traditional identity categories (including that of the native speaker) are challenged as predominantly local-based group identification shifts to more dispersed global networks of affiliations through globalization processes.

Finally, echoing Houghton's call (Chapter 4) for the development of intercultural communicative competence in foreign language teachers more generally, Derivry-Plard (Chapter 18) argues that as professionals, language teachers must set aside the kinds of essentialist and reductive images of identities represented by the term 'native speaker' in order to conceptualize anew their professional language teaching field as 'a truly intercultural communicative space where binary oppositions like native/non native, exclusion/inclusion' not only can but *should* also be overcome as they represent 'an undeniable political injustice at a deep and psychological level' (Holliday, 2005a: 23).

It is in this spirit that we endorse Holliday's (2005a) call for forging a new common identity among global TESOL educators, while also insisting in the light of the chapters contained in this book upon considerable *reworking* and *expansion* of the definition of 'native-speakerism', which was specifically coined for that very purpose. It is only by actively striving to protect all the potential victims from the chauvinism of native-speakerism, regardless of language background, can mutual trust, respect and the development of a shared yet diverse professional identity be nurtured. It is to that end that we propose a revised definition of native-speakerism grounded in respect for human rights that is fit for the new millennium:

> *Native-speakerism* is prejudice, stereotyping and/or discrimination, typically by or against foreign language teachers, on the basis of either being or not being perceived and categorized as a native speaker of a particular language, which can form part of a larger complex of interconnected prejudices including ethnocentrism, racism and sexism. Its endorsement positions individuals from certain language groups as being innately superior to individuals from other language groups. Therefore native-speakerist policies and practices represent a fundamental breach of one's basic human rights.

Part 1

Native-Speakerism: Shifting to a Postmodern Paradigm

1 'Native Speaker' Teachers and Cultural Belief

Adrian Holliday

Introduction

Teachers who have traditionally been labelled 'native speakers' have much to offer. However, their potentially positive contribution has been marred by the ideology of native-speakerism which promotes the belief that they represent a 'Western culture' from which spring the ideals both of English and of the methodology for teaching it (Holliday, 2005a). This in turn derives from Phillipson's (1992) well-known linguistic imperialism thesis that the concept of the superior 'native speaker' teacher was explicitly constructed in the 1960s as a saleable product to support American and British aid trajectories. Inherent to this ideology is a conviction that 'non-Western' cultural realities are deficient, which I term cultural disbelief. I will, however, take a positive line and argue that it is possible to counter cultural disbelief by means of a subtle but significant professional shift to cultural belief, but that this also requires a shift from a modernist, positivist to a postmodern paradigm.

I will first look at the importance of associating native-speakerism with cultural disbelief, and then consider what it takes to shift to cultural belief.

The Danger of Domesticating the Issue

It is now fairly well-established that there is little linguistic support for a native – non-native speaker distinction (Braine, 1999; Canagarajah, 1999a; Jenkins, 2000). Nevertheless, much of the research into the distinction continues to revolve around the linguistic factor, the attitudes of language learners to 'native' or 'non-native speaker' exposure and the self-perceptions or special contribution of 'non-native speaker' teachers (Moussu & Llurda, 2008). These are important discussions which run deeply into the day-to-day lives of teachers and language students. They have led to an acute awareness across the profession of employment discrimination against 'non-native speaker' teachers, and to affirmative action in the constitutions of professional bodies such as TESOL (Moussu & Llurda, 2008).

However, taking affirmative action against discrimination on linguistic grounds can easily lead to the native – non-native speaker issue being domesticated, i.e. demoted to an everyday professional concern, and to a feeling that the problem has been solved. Over the past two years, my British masters' students have been telling me that discrimination against 'non-native speaker' teachers is a thing of the past and could not happen now. In contrast to this statement of optimism, there is evidence of a sustained, tacitly held cultural chauvinism. A recent qualitative study reveals that British teachers consider it their 'birthright' to criticize, albeit without foundation, not only the linguistic and pedagogic performance but also the cultural background and proficiency of their 'non-native speaker' colleagues, and that this chauvinism is deeply rooted and goes unrecognized in everyday professional discourses (Aboshiha, 2008; also cited in Holliday & Aboshiha, 2009). Moreover,

> The profession seemingly does nothing to examine these 'loaded discourses' either at the beginning of teachers' careers or during them, so in this way it is possible for such discourses to be unendingly perpetrated and the superior identity of the 'native speaker' teacher endlessly reinforced throughout the teachers' careers. (Aboshiha, 2008: 149)

There is therefore something deep within the profession everywhere which makes it possible for 'native speaker' and 'non-native speaker' to continue as a basic currency not only for labelling teachers but also for judging them through forms of chauvinism of which we are largely unaware and easily put aside. I say 'everywhere' because, as with other successful ideologies, native-speakerism has travelled and taken root beyond the group that instigated it. Discrimination against 'non-native speaker' teachers is evident in employment practices and customer preference far beyond the English-speaking West (e.g. Ali, 2009; Holliday, 2005a; Shao, 2005). White Western teachers can themselves be caught up in employment practices where they are used by schools to foreign governments because of their perceived speakerhood rather than other professional attributes they may possess (Kumaravadivelu, 2012: 22, citing Widin).

Discourses, Ideology and Paradigms

To understand, and then to act against, this hidden cultural disbelief, it is necessary to look at the tacit ways in which ideas about professional identity are organized and expressed through discourses, and at the ideologies which drive these discourses. A definition of discourse which is meaningful here is 'a group of statements which provide a language for talking about i.e., a way of representing a particular kind of knowledge about a topic' (Hall, 1996: 201, citing Foucault). In this respect, the 'kind of knowledge' is governed by the ideology, which the discourse thus serves. A definition of ideology which I find useful is 'a set of ideas put to work in the justification and maintenance of vested interests' (Spears, 1999: 19). Looking at the 'native speaker' issue in terms of discourse and ideology requires moving away from a practical, modernist preoccupation with what is the most efficient way to teach language, and into a postmodern understanding that what may appear most efficient (i.e. a 'native speaker' or a 'non-native speaker' mode) is itself always ideologically driven. Risking grave over-simplification from a very broad literature of views, these two paradigms can be summarized as follows, my most helpful sources being Guba and Lincoln (2005), Usher and Edwards (1994) and Berger and Luckmann (1979). The *modernist* paradigm states that social reality is definable and measurable in an objective, neutral manner. A positivist research methodology is aligned with this in its presumed ability to find objective truth. The *postmodern* paradigm, in contrast, states that science cannot escape from being subjective and ideological. A constructivist research methodology is aligned with this in its focus on how social reality is constructed through discourses. Dichotomizing professional thinking into these two paradigms may seem hypocritical, as it may appear as essentialist as defining cultural behaviour as either individualist or collectivist, which I critique below. There is, however, an important difference. I am not claiming, as the modernists tend to, that the categories are neutral and that one is not favoured over the other. Indeed, it is my intention to favour postmodernism and to Other modernism; and I do this openly *from* the position of postmodernism. Moreover, I believe that Othering modernism is justified because it has sufficient social and academic capital to bear it. As this chapter develops, I also Other the West because it has sufficient cultural capital to bear it. In places, I also take the liberty of imposing the postmodern label on researchers who might not themselves buy into it. In such cases, I take full responsibility for interpreting their work in this manner.

The two paradigms impact on the labelling of the native – non-native speaker division. The modernist, positivist paradigm suggests that categories such as 'native speaker' can be objective and neutral and relate to real domains, but that their definitions need to be researched, refined and made more accurate. The postmodern, constructivist paradigm, in contrast, maintains that such categories are blurred, negotiable and constructed by ideologies and discourses. This means that, at the risk of annoying the reader, it is necessary always to use inverted commas for the terms 'native speaker' or 'non-native speaker' to emphasize that they are always 'so-called'. It also means that the trend, followed by several journals, of using standardized acronyms such as NNS can lead us to forget that they are 'so-called', thus contributing to domesticating them as 'normal', routinized aspects of our professionalism. It would be better not to use the terms at all, but we do not yet have a suitable language to do this appropriately unless we simply refer to 'teachers'.

Somewhat connected with the postmodern view of labelling, although there is some geographical connotation, I use 'the West' and 'Western' as ideological concepts implying 'superior', 'developed' and 'modern' (Hall, 1996), which are closely associated with the notions of Centre, as a source of power which defines the rest of the world, and Periphery, which is the victim of Centre definition (Hannerz, 1991). The use of 'White', while implying skin colour, is similarly associated with the 'supremacy' of the West (Kubota & Lin, 2006). All of these terms are capitalized in common usage to indicate that they are more than neutral indicators of place or colour.

The Architecture of Cultural Disbelief in English Language Education

Cultural disbelief within native-speakerism connects with a broader ideology of neo-racism within Western liberal multiculturalism. According to the postmodern, critical cosmopolitan stance, discourses of cultural difference, though they may appear 'inclusive' and 'celebratory,' in effect reduce non-Western cultural realities and hide racism (Delanty et al., 2008; Hall, 1991a; Lentin, 2008; Spears, 1999).

In English language education, racism is revealed increasingly where the discrimination against 'non-native speakers' is connected to skin colour. Hence, non-White teachers are taken for 'non-native speakers' even if they were born and brought up with English as a first or only language; and White teachers who do not have this background can pass easily as 'native speakers' (e.g. Kubota et al., 2005, citing Connor; Kubota & Lin, 2006; Shuck, 2006). Yet, it is argued, this racism remains hidden beneath an 'inclusive' professional veneer (Kubota, 2002a), which, I would like to argue, as in Western multiculturalism, is promoted by an apparent celebration of cultural difference within the modernist, positivist paradigm, which would deny cultural disbelief (Holliday & Aboshiha, 2009).

Although the modernist paradigm will claim that national cultural descriptions are neutral and indeed celebratory of cultural difference, as long as they are carefully researched, the postmodern view is that the boundaries between cultural realities are blurred and negotiable and that descriptions of cultures are ideological (Beck & Sznaider, 2006; Hall, 1991b). The claim that, for example, the commonly stated descriptions of individualist and collectivist cultures are objective and neutral (Hofstede, 1991; Triandis, 2006) is thus refuted on the grounds that they are Western ideological constructions which represent an idealized Western Self and a demonized non-Western Other, respectively (Holliday, 2011; Kim, 2005; Kumaravadivelu, 2007; Moon, 2008). This view is borne out by the always positive, individualist descriptions of 'native speakers' as possessing self-determination and the ability to plan and organize, and the always negative, collectivist descriptions of 'non-native speakers' as being deficient in these areas (Holliday, 2005a; Kubota, 2001; Kumaravadivelu, 2003; Nayar, 2002; Pennycook, 2000).

Cultural disbelief thus *imagines* that while 'other cultures' have the right to be themselves, they present a 'problem' by not being very good at taking part in activities which require an *imagined* Western world view. In English language education, this ideology is translated into a powerful professional discourse which perpetuates the fallacy that 'non-native speaker' teachers and students have 'problems' with the 'autonomy', 'critical thinking' and educational 'contexts' necessary for effective language learning, and hijacks and claims exclusive rights to these concepts, and which makes them look, mistakenly, as though they are Western products.

A well-known example of this imagining of 'problem' concerns Chinese or East Asian students (Reid et al., 2009), even though there is considerable evidence that the cultural profiling, which often focuses on a perceived lack of autonomy and communicative ability, has been shown in a number of cases to be unfounded (e.g. Cheng, 2000; Clark & Gieve, 2006; Grimshaw, 2010; Holliday, 2005a; Kubota, 1999; Ryan & Louie, 2007). This preoccupation with 'autonomy' and 'critical thinking' within English language education is not dissimilar to the preoccupation with Islam within the wider West – non-West cultural politics, which has become a 'symbolic battleground' of cultural identity (Delanty et al., 2008).

The Need for Action

Action needs to be taken to convert this cultural disbelief into cultural belief. While *cultural disbelief* finds the cultural background of 'non-native speaker' teachers, and indeed students, deficient and problematic, *cultural belief* perceives the cultural background of *any* teacher or student to be a resource. The nature of the 'problem' would therefore shift to how to capitalize on the cultural richness and experience which teachers and students bring with them. There are three important factors to note about the feasibility of this shift.

The potential to leave ideology behind

Because native-speakerism is an ideology, it does not have to be bought into; and certainly by no means all the teachers who have English as their mother, and perhaps only, tongue, who are 'White', and born and brought up in the English-speaking West, subscribe to native-speakerism or the prejudices which it involves. However, they find themselves caught up in an educational methodology which is shot through with native-speakerist discourses, which, since its roots are in audiolingualism, has been a major driving force of their professionalism. There is much which is positive stemming from the immense experience and good intention which originates in the English-speaking West, *if* it can be liberated from cultural disbelief. In this sense, cultural disbelief can be cast as a form of false consciousness (Holliday, 2011).

While this may be particularly the case with White teachers, who are implicated in the far deeper cultural disbelief of the Western society within which they are located, it can be argued that false consciousness is also evident among a large number of people in all sectors of the profession, who have bought into cultural descriptions which in effect marginalize them (Kumaravadivelu, 2006).

Hidden cultural potential

Another aspect of the postmodern, critical cosmopolitan view of culture is that Centre-Western imposition of cultural theories leads to the cultural potentials of the non-West remaining unrecognized, within what might be called top-down globalization (Hall, 1991b). The same view maintains that the attributes which the West claims for itself, such as 'autonomy' and 'critical thinking', can be found everywhere (Kubota, 2001). The process of shifting to cultural belief therefore requires being positively open to the total proficiency of any cultural realities which may not be evident because of the manner in which we have grown used to looking at things. Elsewhere, influenced by interviews with 32 informants from across the world (Holliday, 2011) and reconstructed ethnographic narratives, I have described often unrecognized underlying cultural processes which involve universal skills and strategies through which all parties, regardless of cultural background, negotiate their individuality in dialogue with national structures. Creating discourses of and about culture and imagining narratives of Self and Other are all part of this, revealing such concepts as 'collectivism' and 'individualism' to be cultural narratives or discursive constructions rather than descriptions of how cultures are.

Enhanced cultural experience

Underlying universal cultural processes and the promise of unrecognized cultural richness implies that when people, from whatever cultural background, encounter unfamiliar cultural realities, the prior cultural experience that they are able to draw on will provide a rich resource. This resonates with the fairly old notion of communicative language learning building on the communicative competence which language students bring with them from their existing linguistic experience (Breen & Candlin, 1980; Holliday, 2005a).

Hence, whereas cultural disbelief has tended to frame 'non-native speaker' teachers and students as somehow confined and restricted by their collectivist cultures, cultural belief makes special effort to capitalize on the cultural experience that people bring with them, whoever they may be. Cultural travel in particular must be appreciated as an immense resource because of the greater diversity of experience it implies. The diverse experience which people bring from different cultural backgrounds may contribute in a variety of ways, with the potential to change and enrich both the nature and use of English and the way in which it is taught and learnt. Whereas cultural disbelief attempts to contain, define and pin down the foreign culture, cultural belief seeks to open up possibilities within a critical cosmopolitan climate in which all cultural practices are open to contestation (Delanty, 2008).

Research Agenda

The research required to support the cultural belief agenda, whether it be published or personal investigation to inform teaching and curriculum management, needs to search deeply both for the contributions which students and teachers bring with them and to recognize the established native-speakerist practices and beliefs which inhibit them.

Researching native-speakerism

Researching native-speakerism, wherever it may occur, requires getting to the bottom of ideology and discourse. Critical discourse analysis springs immediately to mind as a means for laying bare what is concealed between the lines of day-to-day professional talk and text. Good examples of this are the work of Baxter and Anderson, cited at length by Holliday (2005a). The postmodern, ethnographic approach to research demands that we must acknowledge the inevitable, subjective involvement of the researcher and that research is not free of ideology. This requires a break from the established, modernist view that interviews and survey research which claims objective neutrality, as advocated by Moussu and Llurda (2008), because it is not equipped to dig deep between the lines of what people say about their professional and educational experience (Holliday & Aboshiha, 2009; Kumaravadivelu, 2012).

Reading between the lines requires making creative connections beyond the text of what people say. An example of this is Aboshiha's (2008) doctoral study of seven White 'native speaker' teachers already cited above. Following the ethnographic pattern, the choice of methods developed in dialogue with emerging findings. The interviews were complemented with descriptions of critical incidents from Aboshiha's own experience as a practising teacher which had much in common with that of her subjects. This helped her to understand the deeper meanings of what they were saying, and then to pursue conversations with them along these lines, which in turn became extended instances of 'storytelling'. The rigour of the approach does not depend on a modernist pretence of objectivity, but on the researcher's careful accounting of the process, and

> A continued interplay of commentary and exemplification as the story moves from voice to voice ... a kaleidoscope of differing and complementing dialogues which shift from the abstract to the concrete, from ... [the] researcher's voice to the voices of the researched, from the past time of the teacher respondents and the researcher as teacher to the present time of the reader and the researcher as analyst. (Aboshiha, 2008: 79)

In this manner, an unspoken 'native speaker' teacher discourse begins to be revealed; and there is a particular breakthrough when Aboshiha recognizes reference to race in a teacher's understated description to attitudes to a 'non-native speaker' because of her own role in co-constructing it:

> In this exchange with Jane it appears that the learners reject the teacher in question because he is not 'white', although the word is not articulated when explaining why the learners have rejected the teacher. Moreover, Jane and I both refrain from saying 'coloured', although I say 'brown'. However, earlier I have refrained from asking 'So they really want a white teacher?' In fact Jane even talks about this teacher as 'the one', rather than 'the teacher', demarking him as different in her own mind. I also say 'someone who'd been born in London', again avoiding having to say 'a coloured teacher' but we are both aware that this was the issue and yet continue to avoid the reality. (Aboshiha, 2008: 130)

It is significant here that even though the teacher being interviewed does not seem to intend any malice to the teacher she is talking about, there is an element of Othering in the seemingly innocent discourse.

It is also significant that this 'native speaker' research is carried out by a 'native speaker', who is in a position to recognize the hidden elements of the discourse she is investigating. In my own research into native-speakerism, although many of my interviewees have been teachers who perceive themselves to be Periphery, I am concerned with what they can tell me about Centre native-speakerist discourse which they encounter, and my purpose is to understand better how it operates. As part of this process of understanding, I also reconstruct parts of my own professional past, implicated as I have been in the formation of native-speakerism (Holliday, 2005a, 2005b).

Researching cultural contribution

Researching the diverse cultural contribution of teachers, and of students, is an equally difficult task. It requires that teachers who may previously have identified themselves with a 'native speaker' model must now consider that the English which they are teaching, and the way in which it is taught, is open to a far wider range of cultural realities which they and their students may bring from their diverse linguistic and cultural environments. The voices of teachers who have been marginalized by cultural disbelief are paramount. One such account is Wu's (2005) ethnography of Chinese teachers' informal construction of an indigenous curriculum. Other research which must be seen as representing the norm is the one which focuses on the way in which students are able to play with English in their own terms, e.g. Canagarajah's (1999b) accounts of Tamil high school students writing their own secret scripts on the margins of the textbook, Clemente and Higgins' (2008) ethnography of how Mexican students appropriate, modify and redefine their use of English as a series of multilingual social and cultural, postcolonial performances.

New Issues

I have argued in this chapter that to overcome the problems associated with the native – non-native speaker distinction requires a major paradigm shift in the way in which we think of teachers, students and culture. I have accused the established modernist paradigm of imagining that distinctions between 'native speaker' and 'non-native speaker' teachers and students, and the cultures which they represent can be neutral and useful as long as they are properly defined, whereas they are in effect ideological, chauvinistic and divisive. While the modernist paradigm has tried to put right the relationship between Western and other cultures and their practices by means of more precise and fairer definition, the postmodern critique positions the entire enterprise as a Western imposition which hides what the non-West has to offer. At the same time, this Western thinking has encroached on thinking everywhere so that the cultural disbelief of native-speakerism, to greater or lesser degrees, draws the entire profession into its trap.

Cultural belief therefore requires a major re-drawing of how we all think. My description in this chapter of how a postmodern sensibility must recognize the ideologies underpinning the common labelling of teachers and cultures resonates with a broader movement to critique the common boundaries of English and its pedagogy. Examples of this are moves to do away with old boundaries of English use such as ESL, EFL, EAL, ELF and EIL, Kachru's inner, outer and expanding circles, and of differently defined and diversely owned world English (e.g. Kumaravadivelu, 2012; Saraceni, 2010).

The changing and removing of established boundaries will, however, cause difficulties for practising teachers who need professional stability. It is not an easy matter for teachers to change their ideologies, to recognize and get rid of their prejudices. This will require an equally dramatic shift in teacher education and training. There is no space here to go into current discussions concerning the ownership of English, but as a clearly multicultural language it can be enriched only with the other linguistic and cultural experience which students and teachers bring to it, wherever and by whoever it is taught; and all teachers will need to struggle with the real possibility of non-Anglocentric English which young people everywhere are making their own in their own terms. In a world where English swirls around, taking on many cultural forms, with an uncontrolled life-of-its-own in the hands of young people outside classrooms, there will also be the issue of teachers everywhere wishing for a firm body of linguistic knowledge on which to base their professionalism and status. Fielding the diverse contributions which students bring with them has always been difficult for less experienced and less confident teachers.

Part 2

'Native Speaker' Teachers in Workplace Conflict

2 (Dis)Integration of Mother-Tongue Teachers in Italian Universities: Human Rights Abuses and the Quest for Equal Treatment in the European Single Market

David Petrie

Introduction

A citizen's right to take up employment inside the European Union (EU) is one of the fundamental pillars of the European Union as recorded in Article 56 of the Treaty on the Functioning of the European Union (TFEU). Article 18 prohibits discrimination based on nationality. These provisions have for over 50 years been the cornerstone of the attempt to create a European union of peoples and are reaffirmed in Article 45 as follows: 'Freedom of movement for workers shall be secured within the Union' and that 'such freedom of movement shall entail the abolition of any discrimination based on nationality between workers of the Member States as regards employment, remuneration and other conditions of work and employment'.

Member states have an obligation to uphold and implement the TFEU which has direct and binding effect on all European Union territories. Member states which fail to uphold the Treaty can be brought before the European Court of Justice (ECJ) and fined.

On six occasions, between 1989 and 2008, the ECJ ruled that Italy was infringing EU laws prohibiting discrimination based on nationality with regard to non-Italian workers employed in its universities.

This chapter deals with the biggest case of mass discrimination based on nationality in the history of the EU: foreign lecturers working in Italian universities.

In 1980, the Italian government reformed its universities with decree law 382 granting tenure to its existing teaching staff as full professors, associate professors or tenured researchers. Equivalence with tenured researchers was granted to one pre-reform category called assistants; however, assistants teaching in their mother tongue were excluded from this provision. Instead, Article 28 of decree law 382 created a new category of workers, *lettori* (literally 'readers' and *lettore* in the singular). Contracts were annual and could be renewed for a maximum of five times, and salaries could not exceed that of associate professor.

I regard the term 'mother-tongue speaker' as an exact or almost exact synonym of 'native speaker'. None of the terms allows any direct inference as to the person's nationality. Both terms would tend to be used for persons residing in a country other than that of their birth and/or nationality. However, there are exceptions, for example, Italian citizens who are mother-tongue speakers of German (mostly from Alto-Adige, formerly governed by Austria), citizens born of mixed parentage whose mother tongue may not coincide with the official language(s) of that person's nationality or place of residence. Throughout this chapter, I use the term *lettori* as defined by Article 28 of the decree law which specifies that applicants for a post as *lettore* must be 'mother tongue'. Competence for the post had to be judged by individual university faculties. *Lettori* were employed to teach civilization, language, literature, translation and history. One feature which distinguishes *lettori* from other autonomous teaching staff was that they were teaching subjects (only one of which was language) in their mother-tongue languages (mostly English, French, Spanish and German).

It will be shown how the term 'mother tongue' led to occult discrimination based on nationality in breach of EU law.

The (in)effectiveness of the institutions of the European Union will be examined in the context of the Italian state's resistance to the new legal order, first enshrined in the Treaty of Rome in 1957, with subsequent amendments culminating in the TFEU which came into force on 1 December 2009.

Citing the supremacy of European law, hundreds of *lettori* petitioned the European Parliament, ran a vigorous press campaign and raised actions in Italian courts seeking equal and fair treatment in the place of work.

At the outset, it should be noted that EU law does not attempt to harmonize practices among the member states as each state is free to organize its affairs as it deems fit. EU law simply prohibits all forms of discrimination based on nationality including occult discrimination. In effect, direct discrimination based on nationality is rare. The test for discrimination is equal and fair treatment, and the bar is set very high. Illegal discrimination will exist where laws and practices could be capable of an interpretation which might favour citizens of the host state over legally resident migrant workers. In the *lettori* case, the Italian government legislated in a way which made 'mother tongue' a prerequisite for access to a category of teaching jobs in its universities. The term mother tongue, when used in the context of a migrant worker, is likely to coincide with non-citizen.

This point was illustrated succinctly by ECJ Advocate General Fennelly in his opinion on 20 March 1997, in ECJ case (C-90/96):

> Article 28 of the 1980 Decree relies on mother tongue-linguistic competence to define a specific form of private-law employment, thus creating a virtually self-defined discriminatory category and providing the basis for the applicant's complaint. Foreign-language teaching thus has far greater potential for complaints on grounds of discrimination than other branches of learning. (ECJ, 1997)

Indeed, in the case of the *lettori,* the ECJ found that only around 15% held Italian citizenship. One might add that the term is so ill-conceived that it has the potential to create reverse discrimination. An Italian citizen, for example, whose competence in Castilian is equal to that of a Spanish citizen's, might nevertheless be excluded from applying for jobs reserved for 'mother-tongue' speakers.

The Wall Street Journal, 2 December 1998, reported lettori claims as:

> ...a clear cut test of Europe's commitment to labor mobility, which along with a common currency is key to the success of the EU's vaunted single market. If teachers from Scotland can't go to Italy to work, "Europe" won't be much more than a nice idea. (p. A)

The Irish Times, 5 February 1999, noted:

> The persistent refusal of the Italian university authorities to pay foreign lecturers on the same scale as Italian lecturers, to recognise continuity of employment and their refusal to hold fair competitions for full academic posts have been found to be in breach of European law and are, without doubt, the clearest mass systematic breaches of the treaty. (p.11)

Hundreds of law suits were lodged in Italian domestic courts, and four of the six ECJ cases were referrals from these Italian domestic courts, where a local judge could ask the ECJ for guidance on how to decide a case in which there appears to be a contrast between domestic law and EU law. The latter has direct effect and is binding on all EU member states. The ECJ ruled, in each of these cases, in favour of the *lettori*. The European Commission, in its role as guarantor of the Treaty, took two cases to the ECJ which ruled that Italy had failed to uphold its obligations under the TFEU. It should be noted that a citizen has no direct access to the ECJ but does have access to the General Court (formerly called the Court of First Instance) which deals with administrative matters.

Blitz (1999: 44) has carried out a considerable amount of empirical research on the *lettori* question finding that [the] 'fact that non-Italians have been repeatedly victimised by a system closely protected by a bureaucratic state suggests that there are institutional patterns of prejudice working against the goals of integration', Italy's relationship with its universities is compared with 19th-century craft guilds that resisted economic liberalism in order to maintain their institutional traditionalism, while a follow-up essay examines the effects on the individuals suffering the illegal discrimination. Professor Blitz, who conducted interviews with *lettori* throughout Italy between 2005 – 2010, catalogues complaints of *lettori* removed from their teaching jobs, *lettori* told they were part-time workers, *lettori* told they were not allowed to explain grammar rules and *lettori* removed from examination boards. Many of them used the word 'mobbing' to describe their predicament. Several *lettori* attributed their unsatisfactory working environment to their ill health. One French woman attested to 'having been cut out of everything' and of having had a 'violent asthma' attack in the midst of a crisis of humiliation. (Blitz, 2010: 135). Blitz is not alone in recording these abuses; the THES, in an article, 8 May 2008, entitled 'Second-class colleagues,' cites an open letter to the Rector of the University of Trieste from a distressed husband commenting on his German wife's suicide, 'struck down by an illness greatly contributed to by your arrogance and your scorn for other people's rights'. While a colleague commented on her death as follows:

> During the past 25 years, like hundreds of colleagues, I've been sacked, redefined, demoted. I've been told by my direct superior that my category deserves to be 'exterminated' and that I will be 'made to pay' for arguing. I've been threatened with undefined 'measures' for taking time off to attend my father's funeral. I've been promised publications that failed to appear, through incompetence and malice, and had more prestigious

publications outside Italy ignored. I'm strong. I've coped. Sigrid, finally, didn't. (THES, 2008: para. 7)

The Dispute

The first case to reach the ECJ was a referral from a Venice Tribunal. The ECJ, on 30 May 1989, in case (33/88) ruled that employing *lettori* with annual contracts renewable for a maximum of five times was in contravention of EU law prohibiting discrimination based on nationality, since this rule did not apply to Italian teaching staff.

Certain Italian universities noted that although the ECJ had prohibited the 5-year renewability clause, it had not specifically outlawed annual contracts. The case was again referred to the ECJ which had to spell out on 2 August 1993, case (C-259/91), that contracts had to be open-ended since Italian staff enjoyed open-ended contracts (ECJ, 1993). Thus, it was legally established that Italy was breaching EU law with regard to discrimination based on nationality.

It is worth examining some of the claims made against the *lettori*. It was argued that *lettori* would lose the freshness of their language and, above all, that since they had not passed *concorsi* (open competition exams), they could not be compared with tenured teaching staff. Furthermore, it was pointed out that Italian contract professors, who carried out similar duties to *lettori*, were employed on annual renewable contracts. None of these arguments impressed the ECJ. First of all, non-Italian citizens were barred from *concorsi* for research position until 1995, and then the Italian authorities could have recruited *lettori* by *concorsi*, but after choosing not to could not now rely on their own recruitment practices to justify different treatment. Contract professors with short-term contracts, the ECJ noted, were the exception in Italian universities, and *lettori* should benefit from comparison with the norm, not its exception. Finally, the ECJ pointed out that universities were free (at their own expense) to send *lettori* back to their countries of origin for retraining if freshness of their language was a concern.

Blitz's comparison of the *concorsi* system, and the professorial barons who control them, with medieval guilds resisting innovation was echoed by Italian historian Indro Montanelli, in an article entitled 'Clan Mentality Rules in Italian Universities', in the THES, 9 January 1998, as follows:

> It is forbidden to step outside the academic fortress. The very language of our teachers is mafia language ... Servility is the chief quality required to enter the system. The best way to get on is to marry the daughter of a barone. (THES, 1998a: para. 8)

(*Note*: Barone here means a university professor who treats his tenured chair as his personal fiefdom.)

The *concorsi* system has been widely and thoroughly discredited. For a brief examination of the phenomenon, see *The Independent*, 25 September 2010, 'Family fiefdoms blamed for tainting Italian universities' which quotes Professor Roberto Perotti as saying,

In some of Italy's state university departments 30% of the staff have a close family relative present. This is nepotism and corruption, and it's everywhere. (*The Independent*, 2010: para. 5)

However, the last word on how the *concorsi* system operates should be attributed to Professor Cesare Cecioni, former Director of Florence University's language teaching centre, quoted in the THES, 13 February 1998, telling a conference of *lettori* in Bologna in January 1998:

> It seems the lettori have still not understood that tenure has nothing to do with teaching: it rather concerns the privileges that a professor enjoys. If you were to apply for promoted posts you would have no chance of success. As we would be judging you, it would simply be the slaughter of the innocents. (THES, 1998b: para. 12)

Three British *lettori* did apply for promoted posts in 1995 and were barred by their faculty boards. Their subsequent legal challenge went from a domestic court to the ECJ and back to the domestic courts, where after 15 years, in 2010, they were each awarded 5000 euros in damages.

The Challenge from the European Parliament and European Commission

The *lettori* ran a very public campaign that focused on the European Parliament, busloads of *lettori* and students arrived in Brussels and Strasbourg with petitions cataloguing abuses. One petition, addressed to former President of the European Parliament, Simone Veil, dated 24 June 1996, contained a statement from KB, who wrote:

> I have worked at the Istituto Universitario Orientale di Napoli for seven years as a mother-tongue English language lecturer. On eighteenth September 1990 I gave birth to twins. I had no maternity leave neither before nor after the birth even though I suffered serious health problems particular to a multiple pregnancy. I was required to return to work two weeks after the birth with a full timetable, including invigilation of

5-hour written examinations and full-day exam commissions. As a result of physical and psychological stress I lost my milk and was unable to breast feed my two-week old twins. I could not insist on having my legal rights to maternity leave because the renewal of my contract was subject to the head of department's approval. (Petition to European Commission High Level Panel, 1996: 3)

There were a total of 223 mass sackings at the universities of Bologna, Naples, Salerno and Verona. *Lettori* who had previously taught literature, history and other subjects were excluded from teaching those subjects, their names were removed from internal phone books and they were removed from examination boards. This mobbing was the subject of the first of four resolutions in the European Parliament, B4-0968/95, of 13 July 1995 which noted:

... whereas the basic human rights and democratic freedoms of fourteen [University of Verona] foreign language teachers are being violated following eviction from their offices to a basement measuring six metres by four and through other forms of intimidations and legal filibustering. (European Parliament, 1995: para. C)

Under pressure from the Parliament, the European Commission had launched infringement proceedings against Italy which in turn enacted a new law, 236, in 1995. Law 236, instead of converting existing fixed-term *lettori* contracts into open-ended contracts, merely offered the *lettori* priority in the selection process for new contracts as *collaboratori ed esperti linguistic* (collaborators and linguistic experts).

This law, however, had a sting in its tail, the *lettori* discovered that CELs were no longer part of the teaching staff and therefore could be paid less.

In a programme broadcast on BBC File on Four, 3 June 1997 (cited in ALLSI, n.d.), Mark Whitaker, interviewing First Secretary Fernando Gentilini at Italy's permanent mission to the European Union in Brussels, asked:

How would you feel if you had been doing your job for several years and then your bosses suddenly say actually your job isn't that, we are now going to call it something else and we're going to pay you 50% less?

In an attempt to consolidate the 1995 law, collective contracts were signed between Italy's leftist leaning *Confederazione Generale Italiana del Lavoro* (CGIL) as well as other trade unions and the government, in what one Italian Member of the European Parliament, MEP, saw as an underhand exchange of favours. Gianni Tamino, himself a university researcher, told the THES, 13 February 1998, that his government's response was 'totally unacceptable, disrespectful and at times even ridiculous' while adding that the CGIL ' [in] Sacrificing the legal rights of a minority, in this case those of the *lettori*, for wider interests is no way for a trade union to conduct its business and will not wash in Europe' (THES, 1998: para. 3).

Unconvinced by the measures taken by the Italian authorities, the Commission, acting upon information provided by the *lettori*'s independent trade union ALLSI, the Association of Foreign Lecturers in Italy (www.allsi.org), continued with its infringement proceedings. Italy, however, resisted. The infringement proceedings continued, but far from smoothly.

Citizens who believe their rights are being denied can complain to the Commission in its role as guardian of the TFEU. The author of this chapter targeted the University of Verona, where he was first employed in 1984.

The Commission replied that it could not proceed on the basis of one university's alleged infringement. ALLSI put together files from over 20 universities. From these, the Commission cited as examples six universities, Basilicata, Milan, the Eastern University Institute of Naples, Palermo, Pisa and Rome's La Sapienza, and sent a reasoned opinion to the Italian government on 16 May 1997, laying out its legal position and inviting the Italian government to rectify its law and its practices under threat of being hauled before the ECJ.

ALLSI requested copies of the correspondence between the Commission and the Italian government, which the Commission rejected on the grounds that documents in infringement proceedings were covered by rules of secrecy.

Unknown to ALLSI, the complainant, the Commission altered its claims in law as set out in its reasoned opinion of 16 May 1997 and wrote another letter to Italian Minister Lambero Dini on 19 July 1998. This revealed that the Commission had abandoned its pursuit of the question of status. In other words, the question of whether the new posts offered as CEL would downgrade the *lettori* to that of non-teaching staff was dropped.

The Commission's case now rested on the alleged failure of the Italian Republic to guarantee the acquired rights of the former *lettori*; that is to say, to compensate them for unpaid arrears in wages, pensions and increments for years of service dating back to the first day of their contracts in line with treatment enjoyed by Italian teaching staff.

ALLSI came into possession of these and other documents and made them public, through the European Parliament. On 6 July 2000, 446 *lettori* signed a petition addressed to the President of the European Commission,

Romano Prodi, alleging that the Commission was receiving false and allegedly criminally false information from the Italian authorities. The documents showed that 38 *lettori*, who had refused to sign new contracts as technicians, were not listed in data sent to the Commission. ALLSI's lawyer Professor Lorenzo Picotti examined these documents and wrote:

> ...the Commission accepted the deliberately instrumental, unfounded and unproved justifications which have been presented as facts in defence arguments by the Italian Government on the basis of partial information, obvious omissions and at times complete and utter falsehoods [and] has taken a position which is from a legal perspective incomplete, imprecise, unclear and also contradictory. (Petition to President of the European Parliament, Romano Prodi, 2000)

Law Professor Sir Neil MacCormick MEP, Q.C. (cited in ALLSI, 2007) commented:

> There must be strong suspicion that the information in question is actually false and may even have been supplied in the knowledge either that it was false or that it amounted to deliberate suppression of a material truth. If such knowledge existed, the act of supplying the information would have been plain fraud. At this very time, the question of whether there was such an act of official fraud is being investigated through criminal proceedings in Rome.

This is by no means the only example of authorities attempting to thwart the work of the ECJ. In Commission vs. Italy case (C-371/04), the Advocate General (AG) whose duty is to advise the ECJ on how a case should be decided complained that the Italian authorities repeatedly failed to reply to letters and when they did the AG described the reply as (a)

> flurry of legislative references ...[which] were not supported by any annexed legislative texts or explanatory memoranda ... a bundle of over 100 pages of assorted documents ... No explanation has been given of how those texts are relevant. [Adding that] It is unusual that in infringement actions for the Member State concerned to provide the Court with comprehensible information about its relevant law. In the present case, the situation in Italy was not entirely clear even after the hearing. [And] It is manifestly unsatisfactory for the Court to be left so ill-informed at this stage in the procedure. (ECJ, 2006a: para. 16/21)

This is tantamount to contempt of court, aggravated by the fact that the Court is impotent to sanction the contempt.

This damning comment, coming from an Advocate General of the ECJ, illustrates the inherent weakness in the entire legal procedure. Member states sign up to upholding the EFTU but little can be done to ensure that cooperation is efficient and carried out in good faith.

ALLSI took a complaint of maladministration to the European Ombudsman, who criticized the Commission for 'fundamentally alter[ing] the basis on which it was dealing with the complainant's case, in a way which the complainant considered highly damaging to his interests' (Decision of the European Ombudsman on complaint 161/99/IJH against the European Commission, 2000: para. 4).

In addition, ALLSI took the Commission before the General Court (formerly the European Court of First Instance), requesting that 16 documents pertaining to the Commission case be disclosed. The Court rejected the application on the grounds that 'such disclosure may adversely affect the public interest' (ECJ, 2001b: para. 80).

In this specific case, it is difficult to imagine what public interest was being protected. The lettori merely wanted to ascertain whether or not documents potentially usable in the infringement proceedings contained false information which if put before the ECJ would skew its judgment to their detriment. The ECJ ruled on 26 June 2001

> that, by not guaranteeing recognition of the rights acquired by former foreign-language assistants who have become associates and mother-tongue linguistic experts, even though such recognition is guaranteed to all national workers, the Italian Republic has failed to fulfil its obligations under Article 48 of the EC Treaty (now, after amendment Article 39 EC). (ECJ, 2001a: para. 37)

Thus, law 236 of 1995 did not conform to EU law.

Any Italian worker with a plurality of contracts is entitled to have their acquired rights maintained from the first day of the first contract. It will be recalled that law 236 merely offered *lettori* priority in a selection process to become CELs, thus creating three categories of workers, *lettori* who refused to sign contracts as CELs, ex-*lettori* who signed as CELs but insisted on their acquired rights and CELs employed for the first time under law 236. Subsequently and unsurprisingly, Italian university authorities cavilled and equivocated on which rights were acquired and from which dates and to whom.

Not satisfied by law 236, the Commission continued to pursue Italy for failure to implement previous judgments of the ECJ.

Italy changed its legislation with law 63 of 2004, which set a minimum wage pegging *lettori* to tenured researchers, which the Commission regarded as inadequate. Italy was brought back to the ECJ and the AG, a full member of the Court whose opinion is persuasive though not binding on the Court, recommended fining Italy 265,000 per day until its law and its practices conformed to previous judgments of the ECJ.

On 15 November 2005, scores of *lettori* attended the hearing of the Grand Chamber of 13 judges in the ECJ in Luxembourg. The Italian State Advocate submitted evidence suggesting that Italy's latest law, law 63 of 2004, conformed to EU law and that the universities had, by and large, put this law into practice. Were this the case the *lettori* monthly pay slips would show minimum salary as equivalent to tenured researchers. The *lettori* had for months sent their pay slips to the Commission showing that this was not the case.

The judgment, ECJ case (C-119/04), delivered on 18 July 2006 found Italy yet again to have breached its Treaty obligations but declined to impose fines, stating at paragraphs 45 and 46:

...the Court does not have sufficient information to permit it to find that, on the date of the Court's examination of the facts, the breach of obligations persisted. The imposition of a penalty payment is not, therefore, justified. (ECJ, 2006b)

Professor Sir Neil MacCormick MEP, Q.C. issued the following statement:

It is a scandal that Italy has been yet again found in breach of its Community obligations to a group of European citizens, but yet again suffers no sanction. What trust can we citizens place in our rights under the treaties if a cosy club of Commission, Court and member state can agree that wrong has been done yet fail to ensure the wrong is righted. The Commission in this case failed to put forward a sufficient case to show that Italy's default continued up to the time of the hearing. Did the Commission really try to win its case? If the Court needed further evidence from the Commission, why did it not direct the Commission to adduce such evidence before proceeding to final judgment? (cited in ALLSI, 2007)

At a law seminar held at the University of Trento on 13 February 2007, now retired ECJ judge Ninon Colneric, one of the 13 judges adjudicating the case, said:

The problem of that case in the end was the enforcement proceedings, linked to procedural rules [...] that the Court has to apply...a French tradition, I often thought it highly difficult to accept.

So the Court is linked to what is put forward by the parties. It cannot do its own research on what happened even if you see that something has gone seriously wrong. You are stuck, you are confined to the pattern of arguments put forward by the parties ... the Commission had not challenged that material in detail. That's why we had to proceed from the basis of what the Italian state had said. Our hands were ... bound by these procedural rules.

The Court has to have the courage to change its procedural rules and if you compare it with the rules of French administrative law, you see that in French administrative law things have developed. The Court in that sense are like immigrants: it's very, very hard to change the basic procedure of the Court. The litigants must have been very, very disappointed. (Cited in ALLSI, 2007)

A Supreme Court composed of 'immigrant' judges who feel themselves bound by archaic principles of French administrative law hardly inspires confidence.

Had the lawyers representing the *lettori* been allowed to intervene, they would certainly have filled the gap left by the Commission and rebutted the evidence presented to the Court by the Italian State Advocate. But it is the Commission which takes the case to the ECJ, and the complainant, technically a third party, is deprived of the fundamental right to choose a lawyer and be represented in court by that lawyer.

Questioned on this point at a law conference (the University of Edinburgh, 2007) on 1 March 2007, ECJ judge David Edward said that allowing citizens direct access to the ECJ would lead to too much vexatious litigation.

Citizens might prefer the risk of vexatious litigation to that of litigation based on false or partial evidence. In any event, there is no reason why lawyers representing complainants should not be granted access to the Court as an interested party.

On 23 December 2010, the Italian government altered its law yet again, this time to 'extinguish' law suits concerning *lettori*. This new legislation has given rise to further litigation in the Italian domestic courts, with judges in Padova, Pavia, Naples and Milan refusing to implement the legislation. A magistrate in Turin has asked the Italian constitutional court to rule on whether or not the clause extinguishing *lettori* rights is in conflict with the Italian Constitution. The author of this chapter addressed the European Parliament on 25 January 2011, saying that the 'extinguishing' of non-citizens' right to have claims adjudicated in a court of law is unprecedented in Europe after the Second World War (Petrie, 2011). In a letter to this author dated 11 May 2011, the European Commission said that its 'investigations' into this law are 'on-going'.

To date, approximately 20% of the *lettori* have received a remedy, a number have died, while many, now approaching retirement, fear they too will die without having enjoyed the equal rights enshrined in the TFEU which their governments have all been signatory to.

Conclusions

Descriptors such as 'mother tongue' and 'native speaker' are to be avoided in recruitment procedures for access to employment; these terms cannot reasonably be added to a *curriculum vitae* as a 'qualification'. Legislation or norms using these terms have more potential to fall foul of prohibitions on discrimination based on nationality, since they are more likely to attract applicants who are not citizens of the host state, and indeed may even be reserved for guest workers. The entire infringement proceedings are woefully flawed, on two points. First, the complainant has no direct access to the Court, without which there can be no justice. Second, the TFEU relies on the member states' cooperation for its implementation; however, this cooperation has been shown to be wanting and enforcement procedures are lengthy and weak.

Recalcitrant and recidivist governments have little to fear from Brussels. As one thinker, Domenico Pacitti, put it (http://www.pacitti.org/interviews_26082003.htm), 'Italy's major contribution to the EU will be to teach other member states the twin related arts of evading laws and legislating in order to evade them at a later date.' (Just Response, 2003)

The Italian government's legislation of 1980 was found to infringe EU single-market rules, the 1995 reform failed to satisfy the ECJ, its 2004 legislation was deemed to conform at least in theory, if not in practice. The 2010 legislation 'extinguishes' court cases where *lettori* are seeking to have these theoretical rights implemented as interpreted by the ECJ.

3 Kumamoto General Union vs. the Prefectural University of Kumamoto: Reviewing the Decision Rendered by the Kumamoto District Court

Kirk Masden

Introduction

In July 1997, a group of teachers at the Prefectural University of Kumamoto (PUK) formed the Kumamoto General Union to force the university management to negotiate. The union claimed that they were being discriminated against because they were foreigners and demanded full-time status commensurate with the full-time work they were doing. In June 1998, after attempts to negotiate failed, three of the teachers held a half-day strike and by the fall of the same year PUK's President had announced the termination of the one-year positions that were in dispute. Of the six teachers who were employed on one-year contracts, one left to take a position elsewhere and five applied for three new slots. Inevitably, two were not selected: Union President Cynthia Worthington and Sandra Mitchell. With the full support of the union and others, Worthington and Mitchell fought tenaciously to challenge their termination by the university. They succeeded in forcing the university to back down and keep them on for the 1999 – 2000 academic year but then lost their jobs in March 2000. They took PUK and the Prefecture of Kumamoto to court over the issue but lost in Kumamoto District Court (October 2002) and then in Fukuoka High Court on appeal (November 2003).

Though the efforts to prevent PUK from firing Worthington and Mitchell failed, the court case and the media attention garnered by the union and their supporters produced a remarkably rich public record of PUK's egregious employment practices. This chapter draws upon this public record to present an account of the primary dimensions of the court case. Among these, the following dimensions of the conflict are particularly relevant to the topic of this book, native-speakerism:

(1) PUK designated native speaker status as a requirement for the posts that became the focus of the dispute.
(2) Native speaker status and foreign status were conflated and linked from the outset. A 'native speaker' was assumed to be a 'foreigner' and, therefore, the decision to employ 'native speakers' resulted in a series of decisions about how to employ foreigners.
(3) Focus on native speaker status and its conflation with foreign status were factors that contributed to the development of a divisive, unequal work environment.
(4) PUK associated native speaker status with special competence in the teaching of oral/aural English when the native speakers were first hired but, conversely, pointed to an assumed incompetence to teach the reading and writing of English to Japanese students in justifying a curriculum change that resulted in the dismissal of the two teachers.
(5) While their status as native speakers of English imbued the teachers with a certain level of authority in the classroom (at least in regard to oral/aural English), outside of the classroom PUK employed a strategy of what might be called 'reverse native-speakerism' in which it attempted to dismiss claims made by the teachers as misunderstanding of Japanese documents, terminology and culture.

The Court Case: Putting the Pieces Together

Most of the fundamental issues at stake in the labor dispute between the Kumamoto General Union and the PUK can be identified in the decision that was issued by the Kumamoto District Court (Kumamoto District Court, 2002). Though only two individuals, Worthington and Mitchell, were dismissed by PUK and were thus in a position to sue the university and Kumamoto Prefecture for reinstatement, the claims they were making represented the claims of the Kumamoto General Union as a whole. The union was, in turn, representative of a still larger group of supporters.

In order to understand the larger group of individuals and interests that the case represented, it is first necessary to describe the Kumamoto General Union and the support it received. When the union was formed in 1997, there were eight non-Japanese teachers, all native speakers of English, who were employed on one-year contracts: Worthington, Mitchell and six others. Seven of the eight chose to join the union as founding members. Ironically, a primary grievance of the union, that is, their official 'part-time' (*hijoukin*) status, made its formation possible. Because PUK was a public university, full-time employees were considered to be public servants and therefore were subject to the Regional Public Servants Law (*chihou koumuin hou*), which exempted them from the Labor Union Law (*roudou kumiai hou*). Under the Regional Public Servants Law, public servants could apply to form 'employee groups' (*shokuin dantai*), but these groups did not have the right to enter into formal agreements with their employers and were prohibited from engaging in actions such as strikes or slowdowns. The 'part-time' positions were classified as 'special' (*tokubetsushoku*) and therefore exempted from the restrictive provisions of the Regional Public Servants Law. This exemption meant that the holders of the 'part-time' positions were entitled to the protection of Labor Union Law. Persons in full-time positions, however, did not enjoy this exemption and therefore were not able to participate fully in all union activities, notably the strike. Nonetheless, four of the five 'full-time' (*joukin*) non-Japanese faculty members who were employed by PUK on three-year contracts stood in solidarity with the seven formal members at the union's first press conference. The union subsequently received the support of a much larger group of Japanese and non-Japanese who coalesced around Masanori Hanada of Kumamoto Gakuen University to form the 'Coalition Against Discrimination by the Prefectural University of Kumamoto'. This group collected over 10,000 signatures in support of the union (KNS, 2002).

Thus, the court case represented the grievances of a substantial group of individuals, not just those of Worthington and Mitchell. Worthington's case is particularly instructive because it contains some elements of the dispute not represented in Mitchell's case. Mitchell came to PUK in 1995, one year after the establishment of the new Administration Studies Faculty in 1994. For this reason, she was not involved in PUK's submission of documents to the Ministry of Education in 1993 in order to win approval for the creation of the new faculty. In addition, Worthington was President of the union and thus the claim, adjudicated by the court, that PUK's dismissal of the two constituted union busting is particularly relevant to her case. Accordingly, in this chapter, I shall focus on Worthington's case against PUK in order to simplify the discussion and to present in microcosm the array of issues faced, to varying degrees, by a much larger group of employees.

The District Court's decision rejecting Worthington's claims was organized under the following hierarchical headings:

(1) Plaintiffs' demand: Confirmation of status as foreign language instructors
(2) Case overview
   (1) Points not in dispute
   (2) Points in dispute:
      (a) Was there a private contract?
      (b) Do legal principles regarding unfair dismissal apply in this case?
      (c) Do PUK's actions constitute unfair dismissal?
(3) Decision of this court
(4) Conclusion

PUK's position was that Worthington was appointed, not given a private contract, and that therefore she was not entitled to the protections that might apply to her under private contractual law. In order to make a case for unfair dismissal, Worthington's lawyers had to begin by arguing that the arrangement was indeed equivalent to a private contract (*keiyaku*) and that therefore the legal principles of 'unreasonable refusal to renew a contract' (*koushin kyozetsuken no ran'you*) and unfair dismissal (*kaikoken ran'you houri*) were applicable by analogy in the case (Kumamoto District Court, 2002: 5 – 7). It was necessary to call for the application of these principles by analogy because they were not part of the body of laws governing government appointments. The issue of discrimination was not the primary focus of the legal argument but rather was brought up in connection with the claim of unfair dismissal. Although the court sided with PUK in its technical claim that the document it presented to Worthington and others was not a 'contract' but rather one stipulating the terms of an 'appointment', I shall follow arguments made by Worthington's lawyers and refer to the arrangement as a 'contract' in this chapter because the terms of employment were stipulated in documents that employees were asked to sign.

In the third section ('Decision of this court'), the arguments pertaining to each of the three main issues in dispute (a – c) were considered and, in each case, the plaintiff's arguments were rejected. In the process, the court summarized and then dismissed as irrelevant or erroneous a large number of claims against the university. In this chapter, I shall examine those claims, and how the court dismissed them, through the following four questions:

(1) Was the position in question full-time or part-time?
(2) Was it a *sennin* or *hijoukin* position?
(3) Were the positions eliminated to break the union or reform the curriculum?

(4) Were substandard terms of employment assigned to Worthington and her non-Japanese colleagues because they were foreigners, or was it merely a coincidence that they happened to be foreigners and in these positions?

Full-Time or Part-Time?

As documented in the court's decision, Worthington saw a notice in 1992 that the Foreign Language Center of Kumamoto Women's University (the precursor to the PUK) was seeking 'a teacher of English (a native English speaker) on a full-time basis' to begin work in April 1993. Upon arriving in Kumamoto to begin work, Worthington was asked to sign a Confirmation of Terms of Appointment document (*nin'you jouken kakuninsho*) that said she was to work not more than 30 hours per week and a maximum of 20 days per month. Worthington told PUK staff that she could not sign a document in which she formally recognized (and thereby be seemed to accept) a part-time position after being promised a full-time one. She was told, however, that the document was merely a formality and that in fact her position was full-time (*joukin*) and that she would be able to renew her contract indefinitely (Kumamoto District Court, 2002: 8). Indeed, the following observation in the court's decision obliquely indicates that Worthington actually worked full-time, beyond the maximum stipulated in the Confirmation of Terms of Appointment document: 'Beginning in 1998 at the latest, the plaintiff was informed that when her working schedule would lead her to exceed 20 days per month, she was to adjust it so as to remain within the limit and, similarly, to limit her working days to seven hours, including a one hour break, so that she would not exceed 30 hours per week' (Kumamoto District Court Decision, 2002: 25 – 26). The phrase 'beginning in 1998 at the latest' tells us that until 1998, Worthington was not told to limit her working routine.

Moreover, despite any directives given to her by the university to complete her tasks without going beyond the limits of her contract, the workload she was assigned was, in fact, commensurate with that of her full-time Japanese colleagues. In addition to teaching courses, she was to conduct research (using her private office and research budget) and to contribute to the administration of the university by 'advising the university in regard to language education' (Kumamoto District Court Decision, 2002: 15). The court accepted PUK's argument that Worthington's advisory work was not equivalent to that of staff who had been officially accorded full-time status because Worthington was allowed to attend faculty meetings only as an observer and was not given normal committee assignments. One point, however, that was not mentioned by the court was that the class load assigned to Worthington and her colleagues on one-year contracts was actually heavier than that of the full-time faculty at PUK. This increase in teaching responsibilities seems to have been conceived of as offsetting the lack of committee and administrative work (Cleary, 2010).

Another point not addressed by the court is how Worthington's 'part-time' status enabled PUK to pay her substantially less than *gaikokujin kyoushi* (foreign teachers) employed at national universities. Traditionally, such *gaikokujin kyoushi* have been paid more handsomely than their Japanese colleagues. This elevated pay scale was necessary during the early years of Japan's modernization because standard Japanese salaries would have been inadequate to entice leading professionals from abroad to move to Japan (see Uemura, 2008). In more recent years, the higher salaries of *gaikokujin kyoushi* may also be viewed as compensation for the lack of job security. Worthington's official job title was also *gaikokujin kyoushi* but her 'part-time' status enabled PUK to calculate a salary that was roughly three fourths of what she would have received as a *gaikokujin kyoushi* at a national university. Because the *gaikokujin kyoushi* salary was somewhat inflated vis-a-vis standard full-time salaries, it is difficult to say how her compensation compared with what she might have received if she had been employed on the same basis as her Japanese colleagues. In comparison with *gaikokujin kyoushi* employed with similarly compromised job security, however, PUK gave itself a substantial discount by paying its *gaikokujin kyoushi* on a notional part-time basis (Worthington, 1999).

Even if one were to argue that the salary Worthington received was ultimately not very different from what the Japanese staff received, it must be noted that the nominal 'part-time' status enabled PUK to avoid compensating Worthington and others for the insecurity associated with the one-year contracts. Moreover, persons who later took other positions in Japan after working under PUK's 'part-time' designation would suffer the economic impact of their years of part-time status for the rest of their careers. Salaries at Japanese universities are not negotiated but, rather, the employee's position on a predetermined pay scale is determined according to, among other things, the number of years of full-time work experience. A year of work in a 'part-time' position would be counted as less than a year of full-time work by a subsequent employer and thus would lead to a lower salary.

Worthington's suit claimed that she was brought to Kumamoto under false pretenses and was thus deceived; the job notice said 'full-time' and PUK officials did not inform her of the part-time nature of the position before her arrival in Kumamoto. In its ruling in favor of PUK, however, the court dismissed this claim as one that 'cannot be accepted easily'. In doing so, it cited the university's explanation regarding the meaning it attributed to the English phrase 'full-time'. As quoted in the decision, the university claimed that '"full-time" means working exclusively for our university' (Kumamoto District Court, 2002: 28). In other words, the court took no exception to PUK's claim that it used the term 'full-time' to indicate that Worthington and others would be unable to augment their income by taking on additional work elsewhere but, at the same time, would be compelled to accept 'part-time' status and remuneration at PUK. This portion of the court's decision makes one wonder if this court might not have sided with Humpty Dumpty against Alice: 'When *I* use a word . . . it means just what I choose it to mean – neither more nor less' (Carroll, 1871). The court is silent on how Worthington and others were to have divined the extremely idiosyncratic definition PUK ascribed to the English 'full-time' without any explanation. If the court viewed PUK's usage of the word 'full-time' in the job advertisement as an innocent error, why did it assume that Worthington must accept the consequences of PUK's error without compensation? Still more disturbing is the court's pronouncement at the very end of its decision that Worthington was employed 'after having accepted the working conditions in advance' (Kumamoto District Court, 2002: 31). 'In advance' in this case must mean 'in advance of putting pen to paper' because it could not possibly mean 'in advance of her arrival in Kumamoto'.

The Japanese phrase that PUK used to explain the meaning it ascribed to the English 'full-time' is *'moppara hongaku ni kimmu suru'* ('working exclusively for our university'). This definition is virtually identical to that of another term at the heart of this dispute: *sennin*. The *Koujien*, Japan's best-known Japanese – Japanese dictionary, defines *sennin* as *'moppara sono nin ni ataru koto'* ('to devote oneself exclusively to a duty'). The *Koujien* definition of *sennin* and PUK's definition of 'full-time' both begin with the word *moppara*, which means 'exclusively' and is another reading of the first character in the two-character compound *sennin*. The second character in the *sennin* compound, *nin*, means 'work' or 'duty'. In its definition of the English 'full-time', PUK merely adjusted the typical definition of *sennin* so that the specific duty in question (i.e. working for PUK) was made explicit. This attempt to wriggle out of the misuse of the English 'full-time' by claiming that it means *sennin* and the court's unquestioning acceptance of this claim are truly astounding because *sennin* is the very status that Worthington and her colleagues were demanding but that PUK refused to grant them.

Sennin or *hijoukin*?

The court's decision states that on 16 July 1993 Worthington signed a second document, called the Acceptance of Appointment (*shuunin shoudakusho*), that described her position as *sennin* in Japanese and 'as a full-time faculty' in English. This came a few months after Worthington had complained about the discrepancy between the job advertisement she responded to and the terms of employment she had been confronted with upon arrival in the first document, the Confirmation of Terms of Employment (*nin'you jouken kakuninsho*). Naturally, she saw this new Acceptance of Appointment document as a welcome correction of her status:

> We fully expected that upon signing the Acceptance of Appointment documents, which stated that our status was *sennin*, we would have permanent status and be full-time, regular faculty members, just like our Japanese colleagues who signed those documents. Japanese full-time regular teachers had confirmed to us that *sennin kyouin* meant full-time teacher, and administrators had assured us prior to signing that we would be full-time regular faculty members in fact as well as in name. (Worthington, 1999)

Sennin is indeed close in meaning to the English term 'full-time'. However, while it might be possible for one to work 'full-time' (e.g. 40 hours per week) for an employer who offers little or no job security, the term *sennin* also meant one would enjoy the security associated with Japan's lifetime employment system. *Sennin* positions are in sharp contrast to *hijoukin*, or irregular, positions which offer little or no job security beyond the contracted period of employment. As Worthington was dissatisfied with the *hijoukin* status that had been foisted upon her, the *sennin* designation was particularly important.

> At a special meeting late in 1993, however, the university informed us that we would be continued in our part-time, irregular status. When we asked how official documents stating we were *sennin kyouin* affiliated to the Faculty of Administrative Studies could be reconciled with part-time employment conditions, the official university line was that *sennin kyouin* merely meant someone 'based' at the university. In a linguistic contortionist's act, they added that *sennin* was compatible with part-time, special, irregular employment status. (Worthington, 1999)

PUK never had any intention of improving or altering the *hijoukin* status of Worthington and her cohorts. Rather, the Acceptance of Appointment documents had been prepared for submission to the Ministry of Education in order to win approval for the new Faculty of Administrative Studies. Under the Japanese system, a university must obtain approval of the Ministry of

Education of the curriculum and staff before a new faculty can be set up. PUK had an incentive to present the foreign staff as *sennin* because doing so would bolster the number of *sennin* in the faculty as a whole and thus ensure approval of the new faculty. At the same time, PUK must have assumed that the foreigners signing the documents either would not understand their significance or would simply forget about any enticing words that might be contained in the documents and docilely continue to work as *hijoukin* instructors.

Worthington, however, was a lawyer, trained and qualified to practice law in the United States. Her legal background and the eye-opening experiences she had already had with PUK made it unlikely that she would dismiss the documents she had signed as a mere formality. After signing the Acceptance of Appointment documents in 1993, Worthington and colleagues consistently demanded that the university grant them the *sennin* status which they believed that had been accepted by signing (Worthington, 1999).

In 1997, Worthington and colleagues formed the Kumamoto General Union in order to force PUK to come to the bargaining table and address their demands. A breakthrough came in 1998 after the one-year-old union used Kumamoto's newly established Freedom of Information Law (*jouhou koukai jourei*) to obtain copies of the documents that had been submitted to the Ministry of Education by PUK (Worthingon, 1999). The documents showed that the university had falsely represented *hijoukin* employees as *sennin*. When this was made known to the Ministry in February of 1999, it resulted in a significant public scandal. On 19 February, the day after a delegation made up of union members and various supporters visited the Ministry of Education to discuss the documents, Kumamoto's most widely read newspaper, the *Kumamoto Nichinichi Shimbun* (commonly referred to as the *Kumanichi*) published an article with the following headline: 'Ministry to Question PUK' (KNS, 1999a). The Ministry also told PUK that the term *sennin* could not be applied to the *hijoukin* foreigners and required them to resubmit their documents and be evaluated once more to determine whether or not they were adequately staffed (KNS, 1999b).

In the court's decision, PUK's use of the term *sennin* is presented in an exceedingly charitable light. It says, first, that the responsible official (*tantousha*) believed *sennin* to mean 'working 30 hours a week exclusively for our university'. The reference to 'responsible official' implies that it was a matter of individual error, rather than a decision that was confirmed systematically at various levels within PUK – a dubious claim considering the importance of having a sufficient number of *sennin* in order to win approval. The court goes on to explain, 'The defendant noticed the error and, on March 25th, 1999, submitted corrected documents along with a letter from the

Governor explaining how the error occurred' (Kumamoto District Court, 2002: 16). However, the impression that the defendant 'noticed' the error and then promptly corrected it does not fit the facts of the case. The union informed the President of the false representation to the Ministry on 15 October 1998 (Worthington, 1998). It was not until 25 March the following year, after the Ministry had been informed directly by the union, after the issue had become public in the local newspaper and after PUK had been investigated by the Ministry, that PUK finally got around to correcting the 'error' (Kumamoto District Court, 2002: 16).

It should also be noted that PUK's prevarication was not limited to the inappropriate use of the term *sennin*. In order to claim the *hijoukin* as *sennin*, PUK needed to represent them as having the rank of lecturer (*koushi*). As *hijoukin*, however, they were formally denied this rank and the possibility of promotion to higher positions. Another matter that was tangentially related to *sennin* status also came to light in February 1999. On 26 February, only a day after a *Kumanichi* article reported that PUK would be required to resubmit its documents to the Ministry of Education, the *Kumanichi* published another article reporting that PUK had failed to enroll the *hijoukin* teachers in employment insurance as required by law (KNS, 1999d). This would not have been required if the teachers had indeed been *sennin* but, because they were *hijoukin tokubetsushoku*, enrollment was required.

An examination of the record reveals a pattern of PUK choosing to use terms like 'full-time' and *sennin* when it seemed to be convenient or advantageous. In recruiting new staff, for example, the use of the word 'full-time' made the position seem more desirable. When submitting documents to the Ministry of Education, the use of the term *sennin* made the staff appear to be more stable and supported than was actually the case. Imagining that the teachers were, or assuming that they could be passed off as being *sennin* eliminated the need to enroll them in employment insurance. One more area in which PUK might have had an incentive to represent the teachers as *sennin* or full-time was student recruitment. On 30 December 1993, a few months before the new faculty was to admit its first students, an article appeared in the *Kumanichi* explaining that 'in regard to foreign language instruction, foreigners and persons who have lived in English-speaking countries for extended periods of time will be employed as English *kyoukan* in order to place greater emphasis on spoken English' (KNS, 1993). The term *kyoukan* (literally, 'teaching official') is similar to *sennin* in that it implies that the position is full-time and secure. It is possible that the *Kumanichi* reporter came up with the neologism 'English *kyoukan*' (*eigo kyoukan*) independently, but I think it is more likely that the term came from a PUK official who was eager to represent the new faculty as positively as possible. The phrase 'and persons who have lived in English-speaking countries for extended periods of time' is also worth noting because it implies that non-Japanese native speakers and Japanese persons with native levels of skill would be working side-by-side as equals – something which did not occur and was not in the works at the time.

A promotional video put out by PUK in 1996 featured the non-Japanese teaching staff prominently and stressed the high-quality, practical English instruction that the native speakers would provide (Prefectural University of Kumamoto, 1996). Of particular interest are the references to native speakers in the Japanese narration. In regard to the Department of English Language and Literature and the Foreign Language Education Center, for example, viewers are told that roughly half the 20 *kyouin* (faculty) are native speakers. This representation of the teaching staff as a group of 20 that is composed of both Japanese staff and native speakers of English gives the false impression that all are members of the same team and working with similar full-time status. Moreover, the use of the word *kyouin* is significant because it, like the word *kyoukan* used in the *Kumanichi* article, gives the impression of *sennin* status. The official title of all the native speakers of English employed on one-year contracts was *gaikokujin kyoushi* ('foreign teachers'). Unlike *kyoushi* (teacher), the term *kyouin* is strongly associated with *sennin* status. *Kyoushi*, for example, do not have ranks such as associate professor or professor while *kyouin* do. Indeed, in the decision published by the court, the term *kyoushi* is consistently used to refer to *hijoukin* positions, while the term *kyouin* is used only in reference to *sennin* positions. Frequent images of the Caucasian native speakers that are interspersed throughout the 30-minute video in combination with several passages in the narration stressing the new and important role the native speakers are playing in the curriculum gives viewers of the video the impression that the native speakers are making a highly significant contribution to the improvement of language education at the university. At the same time, nothing in the language or visual presentation gives viewers any reason to suspect that the native speakers are merely 'part-time' teachers.

Union Busting or Curriculum Reform?

Increasingly willing to air its grievances in public, the Kumamoto General Union, led by Worthington, was becoming a thorn in the side of the PUK administration. On 22 October 1997, the *Kumanichi* published an article with the heading '"No" to Discrimination Against Foreigners' (KNS, 1997). The article reported on a press conference held by the newly formed union in which the union presented its grievances against the university and demanded to be employed as Japanese nationals were – without limited-term contracts. The following year, a *Kumanichi* article published on 18 June reported that the union was planning to hold a half-day strike against the university on 24 June 1998 (KNS, 1998). The article explained that the university had met five times with the union since October 1997 but that the two parties had not been able to reach an agreement. This was followed on 25 June, the day after the implementation of the strike, with a *Kumanichi* article in which the event and the union's complaints against PUK were described (KNS, 1998). Finally, on 1 October 1998, a *Kumanichi* article presented PUK President Teshima's announcement that the one-year contracts would not be renewed but that three new *sennin* positions would be established (KNS, 1998). The article included the following quote from Teshima:

> The strike disrupted the university. Our objective is the stabilization of university governance, not union busting. The six teachers on one-year contracts may apply for the new positions.

Efforts by the university administration to 'stabilize university governance' (i.e. counter the union) did not begin with Teshima's October surprise. In an article published in December that year, Worthington wrote as follows:

> The university applied illegal pressure on the legitimate activity of the union to strike by (1) distributing leaflets to faculty telling them that a strike on campus would cause undue disturbance; (2) warning them that as regular public employees it is illegal to participate or help out in strike activity under the Local Government Employees' Act, Art. 37, Sec. 1; (3) on the day of the strike deploying personnel to take notes on who showed up at the strike activities. After the strike the university delivered a warning to the union to avoid a repeat strike performance. The union asserts the university's actions clearly show it intended to interfere with a protected union activity – a strike. (Worthington, 1998)

The warning regarding Article 37 of the Regional Public Servants Law (rendered Local Government Employees' Act by Worthington), which does indeed prohibit striking work by public servants, is disingenuous because Article 4, Section 2 of the same law clearly exempts all 'special' status (*tokubetsushoku*) employees from its provisions. The university must have been well aware of this because this very exemption is what allowed the teachers to form a union and force the management of PUK to meet with them to negotiate in the first place.

In its decision, the court exonerated PUK of the charge of union busting without mentioning Teshima's statement about 'stabilizing governance' or the anti-union activities Worthington had described. This exoneration was based solely on PUK's claim that the decision not to renew the six one-year contracts and instead to create three *sennin* positions was a matter of curricular reform.

According to the summary of events presented in the court's decision, President Teshima proposed the re-evaluation of language instruction at PUK in a meeting of the university's executive council that was held in April 1998. Following discussions in the various faculties, a committee to re-evaluate language education at the university was established in May by the executive council and another working group was established in June. After several meetings in which language education throughout the university was discussed, the committee reached the following conclusions:

(1) Language education should not be limited to English. It is necessary to provide more opportunities to study other languages.
(2) It is necessary to re-evaluate the emphasis on conversation in the English-language curriculum.
(3) Measures should be taken to remedy the decline in reading ability that has been observed as students move through the curriculum.

As a result, the minimum number of English credits required for graduation was reduced from eight to six and students were required to earn two more credits studying a language of their choice. Moreover, the committee recommended that the focus of the English language curriculum be moved from conversation to 'expression' (writing) and reading comprehension. The court observed that, while the eight English credits in the curriculum up to that time all focused on conversation and were all taught by native speakers, 'the re-evaluation of the curriculum reduced the number of native speakers required by the university' (Kumamoto District Court, 2002: 22).

One point not mentioned in the court's decision is that class sizes were to be increased from 25 to 40 – 50 (Worthington, 1999). The increase in the class size may have been omitted by the court because it is virtually impossible to justify it as a reform leading to higher quality language instruction. The court cites what might seem to be a more plausible argument: Emphasis on 'conversation' had been excessive and correction of that excess was necessary.

The court's decision accepted PUK's denigration of an emphasis on developing communicative competencies as mere 'conversation'. In fact, however, PUK's hiring of significant numbers of non-Japanese and the heavy promotion of their presence was in keeping with a national movement to foster the development of the full range of communicative competencies in English. In 1988, the Ministry of Education first made 'communication' the central concept in its 'Course of Study' pronouncements about language education in Japan's secondary schools. Wide recognition of the importance of communicative skill made PUK's emphasis on classes designed to help students develop communicative competence a logical selling point to emphasize in its 1996 promotional video. In July 1996, the Ministry's Central Educational Advisory Committee called for stronger efforts to improve communicative competencies in secondary school education, particularly listening and speaking (Ministry of Education, 1996).

While PUK downplayed communicative skills as mere 'conversation', it also called for greater emphasis on 'expression' (*hyougen*) and 'reading' (*dokkairyoku*). The assertion that such a shift in emphasis would mean a reduction in 'the numbers of native speakers required' by the university is based on the idea that the study of written English means a reversion to the old grammar translation method because, presumably, the Japanese skills of the native speakers of English were not adequate to allow them to employ this method. Dan Kirk, employed at PUK on a three-year contract at the time, has reported that when he inquired about the practical meaning of 'expression' and 'reading', his Japanese colleagues told him that they meant 'translation' (Kirk, 2001). The call from the Ministry of Education and others for greater emphasis on communication was in part a reaction to the proven inadequacies of the grammar-translation method. Thus, the shift from communication-centred instruction back to the grammar-translation method not only constituted a reversal of PUK's stance but also constituted a repudiation of contemporary thought regarding foreign language education. Of course, scholars are free to repudiate or ignore national trends and innovate on their own. It is hard to imagine, however, that the consensus to embark on a 180-degree reversal in this educational policy could have taken place in a matter of months without some sort of pressure from the leadership of the university. Indeed, the review of the language curriculum was initiated after the formation of the union and, as Worthington has observed, deliberations were accelerated after the strike. Despite the court's pronouncements about curriculum reform and staffing requirements of that reform, it is hard to argue with the union's view that the curriculum review process was 'a thinly-veiled attempt to get rid of the union members' (Worthington, 1998).

Foreign Identity: Essential or Coincidental?

Perhaps the most disappointing aspect of the court's decision was the manner in which it dismissed the claim of discrimination on the basis of nationality. The court reasoned that since the part-time, one-year contract status (*hijoukin tokubetsushoku*) was also used to employ Japanese persons 'in support roles' it did not constitute discrimination to employ the non-Japanese language teachers under this status (Kumamoto District Court, 2002: 32). The court admitted that no Japanese were employed to teach a foreign language as *hijoukin tokubetsushoku* but neglected to add that no Japanese nationals were hired to teach *any* subject with that status. The *hijoukin tokubetsushoku* status seems to have been given to library support staff and persons in other technical positions – but not to teaching staff.

A brief review of the history of the employment of foreigners as *hijoukin tokubetsushoku* quickly reveals the absurdity of suggesting that it had nothing to do with foreign identity. To begin with, as documented in the court's decision, foreign identity was actually part of the job title: *'gaikokujin kyoushi'* (literally, 'a teacher who is a foreigner'). In 1998, in response to criticisms from the union, this was changed to *'gaikokugo kyoushi'* (foreign language teacher). On 25 June that year, the *Kumanichi* reported that foreign status had actually been a condition of employment as *'gaikokujin kyoushi'* but now that the title had been changed to *'gaikokugo kyoushi'* Japanese nationals who were native speakers of English could also be employed under the rubric (KNS, 1998). But as Farrell Cleary, then Vice-President of the union, wryly observed, 'The university failed to explain why the ability to speak English well should be the basis for a Japanese teacher working under inferior conditions to those of less linguistically endowed colleagues' (Cleary, 1998).

The connection between foreign or native-speaker identity and the substandard terms of employment was also confirmed early in the formal negotiations between the union and the university:

> When asked why only foreign teachers are given worse conditions, separated out, called part-time, special, irregular, temporary when in fact they work full-time, officials only repeated that the employment practices were 'appropriate' (*tekitou*) for teachers who were native speakers of English. They explained that since there was a qualitative difference between the English spoken by Japanese teachers of English and that spoken by native teachers, it was natural to employ us differently. When asked how the university officials could tell the nationality of a native English teacher, one administrator replied, 'We know by looking at you that you are not Japanese'. (Worthington, 1999)

When questioned about the connection between appearance and citizenship, Worthington reported that one PUK negotiator explained that naturalized Japanese citizens are not racially Japanese. It seems, however, that PUK officials later realized that openly connecting race with employment status might not be a winning strategy.

Shortly after this exchange, PUK 'repeatedly denied that nationality was a factor in the hiring of foreign teachers as irregulars' (Worthington, 1999), a position that, despite all of the evidence to the contrary, was supported by the court.

Before taking her case to court, Worthington had been warned by her lawyers, 'district courts in particular do not like to interpret the law and will use any shred of evidence to make a factual finding denying coverage of protection' (Worthington, 1999). Indeed, after reviewing this decision, 'any shred of evidence' strikes me as a very apt expression.

Conclusion: PUK as Native Speaker

In May 1999, the *Kumanichi* published its first and, to my knowledge, only extensive interview with President Teshima (KNS, 1999e). In response to the claim that PUK's practices constituted discrimination on the basis of nationality, Teshima declined to go into the details of the case but said that 'differences in cultural background between Japanese people and people from English-speaking countries were the fundamental source of the problem.' Putting culture at the centre is both self-serving and inaccurate. It is self-serving in that reducing the conflict to a matter of cultural difference implies that the non-Japanese should have made accommodations to Japanese 'culture'. Reduction of the issue to 'cultural misunderstanding' implies that the non-Japanese were unable or unwilling to adjust to the host culture.

The idea that the conflict between the foreign teachers and the PUK management was a conflict between 'English-speaking culture' and 'Japanese culture' is belied by various domestic responses to the PUK's employment practices. Union members and their supporters (many of whom were Japanese) managed to collect more than 10,000 signatures, mostly from residents of the Kumamoto area, urging PUK to abandon its discriminatory practices. The Ministry of Education did not approve of PUK's use of the term *sennin*. PUK was forced to extend the contracts of Worthington and Mitchell in part because of the intervention of Kumamoto's Regional Labor Commission. Local press coverage, particularly by the *Kumanichi* newspaper and by RKK television, tended to be favourable to the foreign unionists. In fact, Teshima's interview in the *Kumanichi* was published along side of a scathing editorial that compared the firing of Lafcadio Hearn, also a *gaikokujin kyoushi* and employed on one-year contracts, by Tokyo University in 1903 with PUK's treatment of Worthington and Mitchell (KNS, 1999f). Japanese individuals were by no means uniformly in favour of what PUK had been doing. And, for the record, it should also be pointed out that the union and its supporters encountered more than a few people from English-speaking counties who expressed scorn and hostility toward the union's efforts to engage PUK in a political struggle.

I believe the account of the conflict I have presented in this chapter demonstrates that the conflict between the Kumamoto General Union and the PUK was first and foremost a labor struggle caused, not by mere misunderstandings, but by duplicity and incompetence on the part of PUK. Depicting the struggle as primarily one of differing cultures only serves to obfuscate the ways in which PUK tried to have its cake and eat it too: full-time, yet part-time; *sennin* yet *hijoukin*. Nonetheless, there were undoubtedly assumptions, perhaps cultural in nature, that exacerbated the conflict. Some in the union may have been overly sanguine about the possibility that the strike and other union measures would cause PUK to soften. PUK, for its part, clearly did not anticipate the fiasco that its machinations would lead to and paid dearly for this failure. Though it is true that PUK ultimately prevailed in court, it suffered significant blows to its prestige. In addition to domestic publicity about the strike at PUK, *The New York Times* and the *Chronicle of Higher Education* also ran articles about the labor conflict (French, 1999; Brender, 2001). Coverage by *The New York Times* was itself a major news story in Kumamoto (KNS, 1999g). As a result of the conflict at PUK, several competent non-Japanese teachers left for other universities or simply resigned (Kirk, 2001). In the spring of 1999, the people of Kumamoto read in their local newspaper about how Kumamoto's Regional Labor Commission had forced PUK to employ Worthington and Mitchell for one more year. Shortly thereafter, the *Kumanichi* published an article reporting that English classes at PUK would have to be cancelled because they could not find enough teachers (KNS, 1999b).

The seeds of the disaster were all sown by PUK from the fall of 1992 through the fall of 1993. PUK began by advertising their position as 'full-time', then when the successful applicant, a American lawyer, arrived in Kumamoto, they asked her to sign a document acknowledging her 'part-time' status. This she was asked to accept despite the presence of other foreign staff at PUK who had been accorded full-time status, albeit with three-year term limits. Then, as if to add insult to injury, PUK presented another document for her signature a few months later that contained the word *sennin* in the Japanese and 'full-time' in an English translation. This document, she was later told, was for the Ministry of Education – her job was indeed 'part-time' after all. This amazing series of events is documented as a matter of public record in the court's decision. Unfortunately, the court does not attempt to explain what thought process was behind PUK's decisions. What made them think they could get away with it?

One possible explanation is that PUK officials simply failed to imagine that a small group of foreigners, some of whom did not speak Japanese at all, could figure out what the university was doing and then force it to take notice of their demands. Notions of foreign befuddlement in the face of Japanese language and culture may have led managers at PUK to assume that they could get the foreigners to go along with their plans or, if not, that the foreigners would be powerless to oppose them. In the classroom, the non-Japanese teachers were the native speakers of English. Outside of the classroom, however, I suspect that PUK officials believed they had insurmountable advantages as native speakers of Japanese.

Acknowledgements

Comments and criticisms provided by Cynthia Worthington, Farrell Cleary, Paul Beaufait, Joseph Tomei and Allan Sutherland contributed significantly to the development of this chapter. As editor of the *PALE Journal*, Arudo Debito facilitated the documentation of events as they unfolded – documentation that proved invaluable in the preparation of this chapter.

4 The Overthrow of the Foreign Lecturer Position and its Aftermath

Stephanie Ann Houghton

Introduction

The purpose of this chapter is to document and critically reflect upon my transition in employment status, over a decade of working at a university in southern Japan (hereafter referred to as University X), from a foreign lecturer as a *gaikokujin kyoushi* (外国人教師) to a language lecturer as a *gogaku kyoushi* (語学教師) and finally to a teacher of different languages and cultures as an *ibunka gengo kyouiku tantou kyouin* (異文化言語教育担当教員). This last Japanese term was coined by University X to describe a newly created employment category, the nature and importance of which will become apparent over the course of this chapter.

But before proceeding, some legal background is needed to put this transition into context. Before the incorporation of national universities in Japan began in 2004, university employees were legally classed as civil servants, positions that were exclusively reserved for Japanese citizens. While a special law was passed in 1982 to permit Japanese universities to employ foreign faculty members, or *gaikokujin kyouin* (外国人教員), on the same terms as Japanese faculty members (Worthington, 1999), term limits could be imposed upon *gaikokujin kyouin* at the university's discretion although Japanese faculty members were assured of permanent employment.

The employment category of *gaikokujin kyoushi*, or foreign teacher, predated the *gaikokujin kyouin* category by almost a century and was originally defined by nationality (Worthington, 1999). The *gaikokujin kyoushi* were given full-time teaching duties, but were hardly involved in university administration, and were not treated as faculty. While their employment on one-year (renewable) term limits rendered them ineligible for promotion, they were paid more than their Japanese counterparts because they were foreigners. In 1992, the Japanese Ministry of Education issued a verbal directive to all national universities in Japan advising them not to retain *gaikokujin kyoushi* in the senior pay brackets to save money, which had a serious impact upon the older *gaikokujin kyoushi* in particular (Hall, 1998; JPRI, 1996), many of whom lost their jobs sometimes failing to qualify for their pensions.

The Employment of Foreigners and/or Native Speakers

The employment status of *gaikokujin kyoushi* at University X

In 2002, with the support of other *gaikokujin kyoushi* and the university labour union, collective effort was made to gather detailed and accurate information about employment conditions at University X (Houghton, 2002), considering the long-term social security of *gaikokujin kyoushi* in Japan more generally (Houghton & van Dresser, 2002). Analysis of the legal status of *gaikokujin kyoushi* broadly supported Worthington's (1999) analysis, except that at University X, the word *gaikokujin* meant 'foreign' when it was used in the term *gaikokujin kyouin* and 'native speaker' of the language being taught when it was used in the term *gaikokujin kyoushi*. Technically, then, both 'Japanese' and 'non-Japanese' citizens who were native speakers of the language to be taught could become 'foreign' teachers. Petrie (Chapter 2) addresses this in the Italian context.

However, University X did *not* have a working definition of native speaker, leaving its definition in practice to those in charge of recruitment. A *gaikokujin kyoushi* job advertisement written in English in the year 2000 (Arudou, 2009) did *not* make it clear to potential applicants that the word 'foreign' did not mean 'foreign' but 'native speaker', or that Japanese citizens who were also 'native speakers' of English could apply, and no standards were set for such applicants. No applications had ever been submitted by Japanese citizens who were also 'native speakers' of English, so none had ever been employed. Eligibility criteria for *gaikokujin kyoushi* positions included being a 'native speaker' of the language concerned, having some Japanese communication ability and being educated to Master's degree level (having been awarded the degree within the previous eight years, which effectively kept the *gaikokujin kyoushi* in the lower salary brackets by keeping them lower down on the pay scale). At University X, they were employed to teach either English or Korean on one-year contracts, renewable up to four times, and then they had to leave.

The *gaikokujin kyoushi* struggle for continued employment at University X

In July 2004, the *gaikokujin kyoushi* used the Japanese Trade Union law (*roudou kumiai hou*) to initiate collective bargaining through Fukuoka General Union (supported by the labour union of University X) to negotiate for continued employment invoking not only domestic labour law but also two international human rights treaties:

(1) Article 1 (1) of the International Convention on the Elimination of All Forms of Racial Discrimination ratified by Japan in 1995 (ICERD, 1969), which defines racial discrimination as distinctions 'based on race, colour, descent, or national or ethnic origin which have the purpose or *effect* [emphasis mine] of nullifying or impairing the recognition, enjoyment or exercise, on an equal footing, of human rights and fundamental freedoms in the political, economic, social, cultural or any other field of public life'.

(2) Article 2 (2) of the International Covenant on Social, Economic and Cultural Rights ratified by Japan in 1979 (CESCR, 1976), which guarantees social, economic and cultural rights without discrimination 'based on race, colour, sex, language, religion, political or other opinion, national or social origin, property, birth or other status'.

In practice, at University X, the national origins of the *gaikokujin kyoushi* employed to teach English were *always* English-speaking countries (including the United Kingdom, Australia, Canada, the United States of America and New Zealand) and the national origin of the *gaikokujin kyoushi* employed to teach Korean was *always* South Korea. The terms and conditions of employment of the *gaikokujin kyoushi* were *always* inferior to Japanese citizens, and so we argued that the university employment policy had the *effect* of impairing the exercise of our human rights and fundamental freedoms, in breach of ICERD. In addition, we claimed social, economic and cultural rights under CESCR without discrimination based on language, national or social origin, birth or native speaker status.

Collective bargaining took place in the months leading up to university incorporation in April 2005, a consequence of which was that employees of national universities in Japan lost their status as civil servants, which in turn allowed them to employ foreigners freely. And generally persuaded by union argumentation, University X officially abolished the *gaikokujin kyoushi* position and replaced it with a new yet peripheral non-tenured *ibunka kyouin* employment category open to native speakers of English or Korean, ostensibly regardless of nationality. Post-holders, employed by University X on five-year renewable contracts, are based in a peripheral centre for foundation studies (hereafter referred to as Centre Y). An unlimited number of contract renewals are awarded upon promotion to professor, which must be achieved within 15 years (although this has not happened to date to the best of my knowledge). Sufficient Japanese language ability (in all four language skills) is required for daily administrative duties for non-Japanese nationals. Tenured positions are also open to non-Japanese nationals who have passed the level 1 Japanese language proficiency examination (Arudou, 2009), but all new positions have been occupied by Japanese nationals to date to the best of this author's knowledge. Thus, as legal barriers to the employment of non-Japanese nationals in Japanese universities were removed, 'native speaker' status and Japanese language ability gradually became the only remaining *de facto* grounds for employment distinction at University X.

Educational Roles and 'Native Speaker' Status

Curriculum reform and 'native speaker' status

While the difference between 'native speaker' and 'non-native speaker' foreign language teachers has long been an issue worldwide, University X did *not* have a working definition of 'native speaker', although this is not surprising given that 'the criteria for determining "native-speakerness" are fuzzy and controversial' (Medgyes, 2004: 436). Nonetheless, ascribed 'native speaker' status influenced English language curriculum reform in Centre Y (Houghton, 2008) through analysis of the old curriculum, which led to the development of the new curriculum, in 2006 – 2007.

Medgyes (2004: 436) claims that 'native-speakers of foreign languages can serve as models for language learners only if their distinguishing features have been identified' and to explore whether any such features existed, I analysed syllabuses submitted by English teachers in either Japanese or English prior to the start of the 2005 academic year once classes had been assigned to teachers. Teachers were left free to write their syllabus in English or Japanese, but regardless of their actual native languages, teachers who had submitted their syllabuses in Japanese were classified as NSJ and those who had submitted their syllabuses in English were treated as NSE. Insofar as the 'native speaker' status of the teachers was ascribed solely on the basis of their syllabus submissions, the resulting curriculum was probably based upon false assumptions.

The English language teacher group was taken to comprise 26 NSJs and 13 NSEs. Of the 191 classes considered, 123 were taught by NSJs and 68 were taught by NSEs. The curriculum was then subjected to qualitative data analysis and analysed in terms of teaching approach, teaching materials and other factors to highlight any patterns. For example, NSJs seemed to prefer to train students to pass the TOEIC, to focus on the development of receptive rather than productive skills, and to rely mainly on published textbooks. By contrast, all NSEs exhibited a clear preference for teacher-generated materials over textbooks, and few focused exclusively on TOEIC training and receptive skill development. Consequently, English classes were split equally between NSJs and NSEs, with the former being assigned TOEIC and reading classes and the latter being assigned communication-oriented classes.

Curriculum reform and cultural tension?

While the language background of a given teacher neither qualifies nor disqualifies any teacher to teach either receptive or productive skills, the concept of the four skills served as 'the natural, default mechanism for solving curriculum problems' (Holliday, 2005a: 43), insofar as it was the pivotal concept around which curriculum-related decisions were made.

Holliday (2005a: 44 – 45) argues that like 'the four skills', the terms 'learner-centredness' and "learner autonomy" are iconic concepts in English language teaching rooted in 'native-speakerism', defined as 'an established belief that "native-speaker" teachers represent a western culture from which spring the ideals both of the English language and of English language teaching methodology' (Holliday, 2005a: 6). The development of such iconic concepts as guides for teaching practice may be rooted in the socialization of 'Western' native speaker teachers, and in preferences for small group interaction that both characterize the 'Western' ELT classroom and imply certain attitudes towards relationship and status (Holliday, 2005a: 44 – 45). Insofar as teacher authority over students in the classroom context is valued more than learner autonomy in some non-Western countries (Hofstede, 1991), including Japan, the development of the four skills, learner-centredness and learner autonomy *may* be problematic for *some* Japanese teachers of English. Splitting the curriculum equally between NSJs and NSEs, with the latter taking charge of communication and productive language skills, *may* thus have been diffusing underlying cultural tension towards classroom activity reflected in apparent syllabus preferences. But like the old curriculum, the new curriculum teaches that 'Japanese' and 'native speaker' English teachers are to be categorized differently and that Japanese people do *not* speak English, not even Japanese teachers of English.

It is as if the ineptitude of foreign language instruction and learning is maintained (though, needless to say, unconsciously) for the very purpose of convincing millions of Japanese of their separateness from foreigners. (McVeigh, 2002: 148)

The presence of 'otherness' in Japanese universities, through English and foreigners, may ironically build national identity among students since 'Japaneseness, as a powerful ideology embedded in an array of institutions, converts English and non-Japanese instructors into practices and people that reinforce Japanese identity' (McVeigh, 2002: 148), and such an argument relies upon stereotypes. Curriculum reform in Centre Y relied partly upon perceived NSJ and NSE tendencies extrapolated from data based solely upon the teacher's choice of language in the syllabuses submitted to the administration office, despite the fact that cases were also identified that ran counter to the pattern. Since curriculum reform relied upon over-generalization about teacher groups defined by ascribed 'native speaker' status, it was stereotypical. Stereotypes are considered in Holliday's (2005a: 19) discussion of 'the generalized Other' in ELT, which shows how teachers and students from the Far East, including Japan, are often characterized as 'dependent, hierarchical, collectivist, reticent, indirect, passive, docile, lacking in self esteem' in contrast to 'native speaker' teachers and students who are 'independent, autonomous, creative, original, individualist'.

Stereotypes are also addressed by researchers from the Far East such as Nakane (2007), who investigated the silence of Japanese students in Australian classrooms, proposing an analytical model for interpreting silence in intercultural communication rather than rejecting the stereotype outright.

Stereotypes form as we categorize other people in our minds and project characteristics attached to a particular category onto people we encounter (Hamilton & Neville Uhles, 2000; Lippmann, 1922). Stereotypes create and maintain the group boundaries underpinning ethnocentrism and prejudice as individual differences between group members are ignored (Levine & Campbell, 1972). While they can provide reasonably accurate sources of information about others, they can lead to inaccurate predictions about behaviour (Gudykunst & Hammer, 1988), even *constraining* behaviour as people seek confirmation of stereotypes during interaction creating a self-fulfilling prophecy.

Insofar as distinctions between NSEs and NSJs were sought in curriculum analysis, the division of English teachers by native speaker status in the new curriculum became a self-fulfilling prophecy. While the exposure of the native speaker concept ultimately opened it up to public scrutiny in this chapter and elsewhere, it also perpetuated the concept in practice. I, then, was 'hosting the oppressor' (Freire, 1970: 27 – 29) because I was actively perpetuating the very native-speakerist ideology oppressing me. See Rivers (Chapter 5) for another example of this phenomenon.

Native-speakerism and linguicism

Holliday (2006) argues that the undoing of native-speakerism requires the promotion of new relationships as prejudices embedded in everyday practice are addressed by setting aside dominant professional discourses to understand students and colleagues from outside the English-speaking West.

Teachers outside the English-speaking West need themselves to deal with the 'non-native speaker' label and assert identity, professional status and employability. Teachers from the English speaking West need to fight their own prejudices. (Holliday, 2008: 125)

Writing as 'a Centre academic' (Holliday, 2008: 125), Holliday argues for the equalization of power relations between 'native' and 'non-native' speakers in ELT through the empowerment of *the latter*, a view echoed by Clark and Paran (2007), who found that as a pre-interview criterion, the 'native English speaker' criterion served to exclude competent English language teachers from consideration in the recruitment process in the United Kingdom, and by Tsuda (1997), who claims that non-English-speaking people in general are victims of discrimination.

The surface and hidden senses of the ideology of native-speakerism are 'trajectories of the ideology, in that they can take us to particular places in our everyday practice' (Holliday, 2008: 120). Despite the rather neutral and safe surface appearances of the terms 'native speaker' and 'non-native speaker' in popular discourse, there is a 'hidden and dangerous' (Holliday, 2008: 121) level at which 'non-native speaker' teachers of English are being actively *discriminated* against in the workplace, but native-speakerism can cause employment discrimination against *both* 'native speakers' and 'non-native speakers'.

While linguicism specifically involves the 'representation of the dominant language, to which desirable characteristics are attributed, for purposes of inclusion and the opposite for dominated languages, for the purposes of exclusion' (Phillipson, 1992: 55), Holliday's othering of modernism (Chapter 1) necessitates a rejection of nationalism itself, and the existence of prejudice in the human psyche is clearly not limited to any particular group of people. Being characterized by linguistic prejudice makes native-speakerism *linguicist* in nature, and by extension, it can be connected in psychological terms to other generally applicable forms of prejudice, such as racism (Holliday, 2008; Phillipson, 1992).

While echoing the concerns raised above for the positions of non-native speaker teachers, this chapter casts native speaker language teachers as the targets of native-speakerism. Undoing native-speakerism, then, cannot be a *one-way* process whereby the onus is on 'native speakers of English' to understand and respect 'non-native speakers' of English. It must be a *two-way* process through which mutual understanding and respect are developed.

Language as the New Battleground

Japanese versus English in the workplace

When the *gaikokujin kyoushi* were interviewed for the newly created, non-tenured *ibunka kyouin* positions, Japanese language ability (in all four language skills) sufficient for daily administrative duties was required and tested in a 30-minute interview. While all those ultimately employed as *ibunka kyouin* passed the test, there was in fact considerable variation in their actual Japanese language ability (ranging from high levels of fluency in all four skills to intermediate speaking and listening skills combined with beginner reading and writing skills). Meanwhile, tenured positions were also open to Japanese and non-Japanese nationals who had passed the level 1 of the Japanese language proficiency test (Arudou, 2009), but none of the latter have been employed to the best of my knowledge.

The relative status of the Japanese and English languages changed considerably in the English language section of Centre Y (Houghton, 2008) between the period of curriculum design (April – August 2006), when flexible bilingualism was initially used in communication between the four English teachers involved, and later. As a gesture of goodwill, the *ibunka kyouin* (two English and one Korean) informally agreed to teach two extra courses to compensate for their perceived lack of Japanese language ability (despite the fact that the Korean *ibunka kyouin* was highly fluent in all four skills).

Later, a new system was introduced in the university by which tenured faculty members would be paid an extra allowance for any courses they taught over the basic number. The Korean *ibunka kyouin* and I complained that we, as a group, should also be awarded the extra allowance, and a dispute ensued that resulted in our favour. Hitting back, as more tenured NSJs joined the English section, the head of the English section who was also the chief of Centre Y personally banned the use of the English language in the English section. And the teaching of two extra courses per week, initially agreed to by *ibunka kyouin* as personal gestures of goodwill, was then effectively given contractual force on the grounds of precedent, despite the fact that *ibunka kyouin* had no contractual obligation to take any extra classes at all. Insofar as *ibunka kyouin* who were highly competent in Japanese in all four skills were categorized for the purposes of class allocation as if they had only intermediate ability, a sweeping generalization was ultimately made about the group as a whole that ignored individual difference between members of the group, which is 'one of the hallmarks of stereotyping' (Hamilton & Neville Uhles, 2000: 469).

English was never used in the English section of Centre Y during the time frame under consideration, even when discussing English language education itself. In my case, official documents submitted in Japanese were in principle not accepted when accompanied by short email memos written in English, and the expression of opinions and ideas in English by email was ignored. The refusal of tenured NSJs to use English (formally and sometimes informally) with non-tenured NSEs resulted in the systematic and almost complete silencing of all *ibunka kyouin*, which also affected curriculum development. NSJs taught very few communication-oriented courses, and they themselves were not allowed to communicate in English, so the development of communication-oriented courses was consistently ignored in official English section meetings, while TOEIC and reading skill-oriented courses were emphasized and consistently developed over time. Both curriculum development and control of the meeting agendas lay effectively (and almost exclusively) in the hands of tenured NSJs.

Ironically, then, tenured NSJs who taught TOEIC (i.e. Business English) courses were being paid to train students to use English in the workplace, while themselves not only refusing to use English in their own workplace but also refusing to practise the very language skills they claimed to be teaching students. Concerns about the status of English and its speakers may have underpinned the problems associated with the *gaikokujin kyoushi* position at University X from the start (Houghton, 2002), and as many of the legal barriers to the employment of foreigners were lifted over time, the main battleground at University X, at least in Centre Y, did indeed seem to be language itself.

Japanese linguistic imperialism versus English linguistic imperialism?

Linguistic imperialism can be defined as follows:

> The phenomenon in which the minds and lives of the speakers of a language are dominated by another language to the point where they believe that they can and should use only that foreign language when it comes to transactions dealing with the more advanced aspects of life such

as education, philosophy, literature, governments, the administration of justice, etc. (Phillipson, 1992: 56, citing Ansre, 1979)

Through the concept of English linguistic imperialism, Phillipson linked ELT to the forces of British imperialism defining it in terms of the dominance of English, 'asserted and maintained by the establishment and continuous reconstruction of structural and cultural inequalities between English and other languages' (Phillipson, 1992: 47), also highlighting the hegemony of Western culture in English language education worldwide. And using emotive, metaphorical argumentation, Tsuda describes the impact of English upon 'non-native speakers' in terms of 'suffering' (Tsuda, 1997: 22), 'disability' (Tsuda, 1997: 23), 'epidemic' (Tsuda, 1997: 25) and 'death' (Tsuda, 1997: 25) to express concern about the unconscious psychological processes at work in English linguistic imperialism:

As you get colonized and dissolved into the hegemony of English, you are not even aware of your identity being engulfed into the Anglo-American cultural frame of reference and not even understand you are supporting the hegemony of English. (Tsuda, 1997: 25)

Defined as 'dominant ideas we take for granted' (Phillipson, 1992: 72), hegemony is 'primarily a strategy for the gaining of the active consent of the masses', and that by 'universalising ideological assumptions it also generalises predispositions, interest and needs' (Guilherme, 2002: 87). Highlighting Gramsci's (1975) view that domination may rely upon persuasion and consent through ideological hegemony, Guilherme (2002) suggests that as English spreads, many people fear being changed and controlled unconsciously by the language and its agents.

Tsuneyoshi (Chapter 8) reflects upon Japan's imperialist past, but linguistic imperialism is not limited to situations in which one *nation* colonizes another. The term 'imperialism', as used in the phrase 'English linguistic imperialism', has thus been somewhat detached from its original colonial roots in the British Empire, and the concept can now be applied more generally to English language teaching and learning contexts worldwide, even though the demand for English itself remains rooted in Britain's colonial past. And notably, the underlying prejudices associated with linguicism can also constitute linguistic imperialism if 'the actors in question are supported by an imperialism structure of exploitation of one *society or collectivity* [emphasis mine] by another' (Phillipson, 1992: 55). Thus, the speakers of *any* language can be guilty of linguistic imperialism, not just English speakers.

University X was characterized above as a collectivity in which linguicist forms of prejudice translated directly into discriminatory employment practices, which then influenced the curriculum. English linguistic imperialism may be at work because the study of English language is imposed by the university upon students, sometimes against their will. But, in Centre Y, English language teachers are colleagues in a micro-collectivity, which itself consists of two sub-micro-collectivities distinguished primarily on the basis of ascribed 'native speaker' status, which potentially brings situation within the remit of Phillipson's definition of linguistic imperialism.

In practice, in Centre Y, all full-time NSJs were tenured and all NSEs were not. They were employed by University X on the basis of their native language on a limited yet renewable five-year contract, which automatically and consistently placed *ibunka kyouin* in a position of psychological disadvantage within their group, since they were always forced to consider issues in relation to their own contract renewal and job security, while their tenured NSJ colleagues were not.

This psychological disadvantage was played upon as NSEs of English or Korean, regardless of their actual Japanese language ability, were categorized as if they had intermediate levels to justify the effectively obligatory allocation of extra courses. The *de facto* banning of English in the English section in particular took place only after it was decided that *ibunka kyouin* would be awarded the standard allowance for teaching extra courses. The banning of English in the English section effectively silenced all the *ibunka kyouin*, gradually redirecting the curriculum as a whole away from the development of communication skills towards the development of classes that focus on the development of TOEIC skills for business purposes, despite the fact that NSJ teachers themselves *never* used English in their own workplace in English section meetings.

Yet NSJ teachers seemed to recognize the need for English in the workplace and to accept English linguistic imperialism as they supported the University X policy of *forcing* students to study English, and it protected their positions to do so. However, in the English section of Centre Y, this resulted in the erection of linguistic barriers through language banning to mitigate the perceived threat posed by English and its speakers, so backlash dynamics were in play. The English language ability of *ibunka kyouin* was selected and then rejected because of a lack of corresponding fluency in the Japanese language, which resulted in a compensatory system through which, despite already being subject to inferior terms and conditions of employment, *ibunka kyouin* were expected to compensate *even further* for their supposed lack of fluency in the Japanese language by taking extra classes against their will, even if they did *in fact* have advanced Japanese language skills.

Heimlich (Chapter 12) explores backlash dynamics in the Japanese context, and Hatori (2005) warns that there is historical precedent for it in

Japan at the national level. Japanese language policy was discussed by the Council on the National Language, an advisory body of the government, which recommended the promotion of the Japanese language in 2000 to promote 'ecological diversity to *counter the English-dominant trend* [emphasis mine]' (Hatori, 2005: 51 – 52). But Hatori (2005) warns that the report fails to justify the promotion of Japanese to others suggesting that such logic is analogous to the way that the Japanese imperialism of the past was used as a *countermeasure* (i.e. as a form of backlash) against European and American imperialism, the consequences of which were the suppression of human and linguistic rights of the colonized peoples of Japan.

Backlash is not a sustainable problem-solving mechanism. An informed understanding of the underlying psychological processes is needed if the problems posed by the so-called 'English linguistic imperialism' are ever to be addressed. Without that, it is all too easy to fall back upon the kind of slippery-slope argument used in Tsuda's analysis whereby, for example, the mere purchase of a single McDonald's hamburger threatens to convert the buyer almost automatically into *'an ardent believer* [emphasis mine] of American culture and consumption-centred way of life' (Tsuda, 1997: 24), or to give in to crude, dichotomous thinking that leads one to feel forced to choose between either one's own language and culture or English language culture.

> ... faced with the hegemony of English, you become willing to use English and tend to keep yourself away from your own language. In other words, you tend to identify with English and dissociate from your own language. You glorify English and its culture while stigmatizing and devaluing your own language and culture. (Tsuda, 1997: 24 – 25)

If people *can* fall victim to their own unconscious processes as they are (increasingly) exposed to English language and find their very identities shaped by it over time, who are the perpetrators? While native-speakerism and linguicism are rooted in prejudice, even perpetrators of linguistic prejudice may themselves be falling victim to their own unconscious processes. '(L)ike racism, linguicism may be conscious or unconscious on the part of the actors, and overt or covert' (Phillipson, 1992: 55). In addition to the general problem of conscious, overt and deliberate forms of prejudice, the existence of which cannot be blamed on any particular group, a problem that clearly needs to be addressed in English language education, and in intercultural communication more generally, is the nature and depth of control the human unconscious can exert upon its holder.

The nub of the problem, according to Freire (1970: 27 – 29) and supported by Wallis and Poulton (2001), is that the oppressed 'host the oppressor' by internalizing the ideals of the oppressor models through prescription, which involves the imposition of the choices of the oppressor upon the oppressed, and is compounded by fear. The fact that the oppressed are predisposed to become oppressors themselves when power is placed in their hands explains why those who feel oppressed by (linguistic) imperialism can themselves become perpetrators of (linguistic) imperialism.

Conclusions

Tsuda (1997: 28) asks 'how in the world the English Language Teaching can contribute to the betterment, the moral uplifting of human beings, and the establishment of a more equal communication', but despite promoting the development of 'critical knowledge' (Tsuda, 1997: 21) in analysis of the issues surrounding the hegemony of English, and despite recognizing the need for Japanese people to take a critical view of their identification with English and its culture, Tsuda (1997) does *not* suggest that the development of criticality should *itself* be introduced as a goal of English language education to counter the hegemony of English. And Tsuda does not suggest that Japanese students should be encouraged to take a critical view of their own language and culture either, which can sometimes be the explicit goal of intercultural education and sometimes result naturally from unplanned intercultural interaction (Tsai & Houghton, 2010).

To resist English linguistic imperialism, and ideological, hegemonic forces more generally, however, the implementation of critical approaches to foreign language education is often encouraged (Byram, 2008; Canagarajah, 1999b; Guilherme, 2002; Hatori, 2005; Phillipson, 1992; Houghton, 2012; Houghton & Yamada, 2012; Tsai & Houghton, 2010), and Freire (1970) in particular recommends the ejection of the oppressor image and its replacement with autonomy and responsibility through the 'pedagogy of the oppressed'. Highlighting the problem of students being authored by others, recognizing that student utterances naturally conflict since their language is populated by the intentions of others that they cannot easily differentiate from their own meaning, Kramsch (1993) suggests that students need to learn to become authors of their own words.

Foreign language education should aim to develop intercultural communicative competence (Byram, 2008), but this needs to be reconciled with the *de facto* dominance of English. The protection of democratic participation and linguistic diversity may be central aims (Byram *et al.*, 2009), and the ideological dimensions of the ELT teaching – learning situation can be made explicit, situating them socially, culturally, educationally and politically. 'ELT conducted along such lines could make a break with anglocentric professionalism and serve to promote awareness of linguicism' (Phillipson, 1992: 263 – 264).

Can ELT constructively contribute to greater linguistic and social equality, and how could a critical ELT be committed, theoretically and practically, to combating linguicism (Phillipson, 1992)? In theory and practice, steps have been taken to address the kinds of problems associated with linguistic imperialism, yet Tsuda (1997) and Hatori (2005) both highlight the need to alleviate identity crises being caused by the hegemony of English in Japan. Tsuda (1997) sums up the problem rather accurately as follows, before giving in to slippery-slope argument by suggesting that some people discard their mother tongues and use English alone, questioning whether they can maintain their cultural identity and concluding that in the end, they will probably gravitate towards English anyway.

> Since language constitutes the core of cultural identity, the use of English generates a division especially in the personal identity of speakers of English as a second language. There is always a tension between one half of a person who speaks English and the other half who speaks his/her own mother tongue. In order to resolve the tension, people make choices. (Tsuda, 1997: 25)

But Tsuda's suggestion that the gravitation towards English is inevitable seems to deny the potential of critical approaches to education to empower people to take increased control over their choices that may otherwise take place unconsciously (Houghton, 2012; Houghton & Yamada, 2012; Tsai & Houghton, 2010). Despite Tsuda's (1997) incorporation of human rights perspectives into an Ecology of Language Paradigm, which is designed to counter the hegemony of English, this denies Japanese people the right to make conscious choices about identity development in response to English, which may explain why Tsuda (1997) does not take on board the use of critical approaches to ELT.

National and institutional policies and practices need to be addressed, but the sociolinguistic challenges being faced by the teachers themselves in the international workplace cannot be underestimated not least because of their potential impact upon the curriculum, which is supposed to equip students with the skills they need to function effectively in international society. Underlying fears of hegemony and linguistic imperialism need to be understood and addressed to prevent the vicious cycles of backlash they can set in motion if they are not. New directions in foreign language education are called for that carry the potential to overcome hegemony and linguistic imperialism. One part of this surely involves the development of intercultural communicative competence through critical approaches but Lazar *et al.* (2007) and Phillipson (1992) remind us that the development of intercultural communicative competence in students presupposes the intercultural communicative competence of teachers themselves.

Acknowledgement

Special thanks to Hartmud Haberland and Janus Mortensen from CALPIU for helping me develop an earlier version of this chapter.

5 Institutionalized Native-Speakerism: Voices of Dissent and Acts of Resistance

Damian J. Rivers

Imagine a workplace that welcomed dissent, celebrated and cultivated critical thinking and seeking alternative solutions, thanked those who pointed flaws in plans, and continuously solicited fresh ideas. In such an organizational culture an opposing point of view would merely be part of the normal way of doing business; it would be an integral component of everyday collegial conversation.

Matt and Shahinpoor (2011: 164)

Introduction

Through the juxtaposition of professional experience and interviews with colleagues, this chapter critiques the policies and practices imposed upon a collective of 'native-speaker' English teachers employed at a tertiary institution specializing in foreign language education in Japan. Within this particular site, the critique accentuates the intricate ways lived experience and professional integrity can become tainted by an institutional adherence to a native-speakerist framework, institutional demands which prioritize the financial marketability of foreign language education and institutional agents of oppression intent on maintaining the iniquities of unaccountable power and privilege. In drawing upon subjective professional experience and through sharing rarely heard minority voices, the data presented in this chapter is not intended 'to prove a statistical point through the statements of a representative sample, but to drill down into the workings of a professional discourse in order to critique established positions' (Holliday & Aboshiha, 2009: 674).

Consistent with the dominant masquerade of smiley faces and perpetual pleasantness decorating the veneer of 'native-speaker' English teaching, the adoption of a critical perspective by foreign language teachers is often ridiculed as being 'inherently disruptive, anti-authoritarian, and dangerous to those content with the way things are' (Snow, 1998: 30). Therefore, while the act of being critical (i.e. offering discerning judgements based upon some form of moral or intellectual standard) offers a felicitous method of professional inquiry, it also 'takes independence of thought and a certain degree of intellectual courage as one may find that one is not in agreement with the way one is expected or supposed to think about something' (Holliday et al., 2004: 159). The dangers posed to and by individuals embracing a critical perspective can be witnessed in the curious politics of mainstream intellectual culture and publishing which dictate that certain names and locations in this chapter, as well as throughout the wider volume, are represented by pseudonyms. Alderson (2009: 228) notes how 'other than for legal protection, anonymity serves no useful purpose, and is certainly not normal practice in the literature of politics and investigative journalism reporting the actions and motives of those engaged in political action'. Indeed, many institutions of foreign language education are often enthusiastic about flaunting their brand name in public but only when the discourse creates a gleefully positive reflection of their purified doctrines of best practice.

Part one of this chapter of this chapter describes and dissects the ideological and pedagogical parameters of the present research site, particularly those aspects most implicated by the institutional adherence to a native-speakerist framework. Part two shifts the focus towards detailing specific instances of professional experience within the research site and the struggles encountered with authority figures intent on maintaining the status quo. In point of fact, the struggles documented began only after attempts were made to assert a degree of teacher – researcher autonomy beyond the readily accepted boundaries of the dominant native-speakerist framework. Finally, part three reflects upon the turbulent emotions deriving from being imagined as a 'native speaker' of English and concludes with a general call for action.

Native-Speakerism as an Institutional Cornerstone

Contextual parameters of a native-speakerist framework

Officially positioned as an affiliated research institute of the International University (IU), the English Centre (EC) is represented by a stand-alone building on the grounds of the main university campus. When this project was undertaken during the academic year 2010 – 2011 the EC employment demographic was as shown in Table 5.1. Although the exact source of employment funding and individual department affiliation was not the same for all positions, within day-to-day operations all 63 positions (inclusive of the four managerial roles) were considered part of the EC collective.

Table 5.1 Demographics of the people employed in the EC during 2010 – 2011

	Employment category	Function	Nationality	Gender
Managerial	1 Professor (*kyoujyu*)	EC Director	1 Australia	Male
	1 Associate Professor (*jyunkyoujyu*)	EC Assistant Director	1 UK	Male
	1 Full-Time Senior Language Lecturer (*gogaku sennin jyoukyou koushi*)	EC Assistant Director	1 USA	Male
	1 Senior Lecturer and Learning Advisor (*jyoukyou-koushi/raninguadobaiza*)	EC Assistant Director	1 UK	Female
Non-managerial	9 Lecturers and Learning Advisors (*koushi/raninguad-obaiza*)	Provide services to encourage learners to become more autonomous	5 Japan 2 UK 1 Canada 1 Jamaica	2 Male 7 Female
	50 Full-Time Language Lecturers (*gogaku sennin koushi*)	Teach and develop English language proficiency courses	20 USA 12 UK 7 Canada 6 Australia 3 New Zealand 1 Japan 1 Japan/USA	33 Male 17 Female

Irrespective of institutional contributions or teaching excellence achieved during the two-year once renewable contract period (with the exception of EC management who are given longer renewable contracts or tenured positions), departing EC members are customarily replaced by younger, less experienced teachers. One motivation behind this conveyor-belt mentality can be found within the comments of Kitakyushu University Professor Shinichiro Noriguchi (2006: 14) who claims that 'native-speaker' English teachers who have lived in Japan for more than 10 years 'have adapted to the system and have become ineffective as teachers … their English has become Japanized and is spoken to suit the ears of their Japanese students'. Despite offering no empirical evidence, this mindset widely manifests through limited-term employment contracts and categories for 'native-speaker' teachers. This ensures that individual teachers are forever disenfranchised from an educational system which exploits them as a collective in order to sustain itself.

In having the terminal contract, the university is aiming to keep EC staff young which is a business model as they are selling young faces to students ... When I tell my students that I must leave after four years they are usually pretty shocked ... and I know that they would like to develop more meaningful and sustainable relationships with their EC teachers. If you keep bringing new people in then there will always be a kind of exotic relationship between the EC and the university, and between the EC teachers and the students. As a result, all parties are just left meddling in the exoticism of each other, rather than trying to understand our complexities as a form of intercultural education and experience. (Interview with Benjamin, third-year EC teacher)

As a documented teacher recruitment strategy, the EC promotes a policy that focuses on exposing students to the 'major varieties of English spoken throughout the world' (Torpey, 2006: 2526). In practice, this statement is exposed as rhetoric as the vast majority of teachers employed during 2010 – 2011 originated from within the Kachruvian inner circle (see Table 5.1). The teaching of inner-circle English(es) under the guise of being representative of the world's major varieties demonstrates an institutional contempt for what is now considered an irrefutable fact – that English has more 'non-native speakers' than 'native speakers' and is used predominately in situations where there are no 'native speakers' present (Haberland, 2011). Thus, the politics of EC teacher recruitment undermines 'the real linguistic needs of the learners, eclipses their education about the history and politics of English, and fails to empower them with ownership of English' (Matsuda, 2003: 721). Through neglecting factual complexities in preference to imagined simplicity, an act of self-deception further complicated by the racial dominance of white teachers (see Kubota & McKay, 2009), and an unwavering insistence that all students and 'native-speaker' English teachers adhere to an English-only language policy (see McMillan & Rivers, 2011; Rivers, 2011a, 2011b), it is apparent that teachers within the EC are recruited as 'badge[s] of authenticity for the environment that is being created ... employed as much for their status as cultural specimens as for their substantive work' (Seargeant, 2009a: 101).

The reliance of the EC on the native-English speaker is not at all consistent with the cultural realities of the world Japan is a part of. The way the EC is right now only acts to reinforce power differentials by saying to students the only way to learn is through a white native-English speaker from an inner-circle country. What is worse, it does this without giving students and teachers the skills or opportunities to understand and discuss this obvious power imbalance in a critical manner ... English teaching practices need to catch up and reflect the modern world and not the world of years gone by. (Interview with Benjamin, third-year EC teacher)

As described within the EC Handbook, written by EC management and distributed to all new recruits during a compulsory two-week orientation prior to the contracted period of employment, the official mandate of the EC concerns raising 'the English language proficiency level of students at the university in order to allow them to participate as global citizens' (Extract from the EC Handbook). Looking beyond the ostentatious nature of this mandate, notions of global citizenship are known to extend beyond those former colonial ideals and narrow boundaries reflected in the native-speakerist pedagogies of the EC. For example, it has been identified that one of the core virtues of global citizenship is a commitment to protect and uphold the cultural diversity of the global commonwealth (Turner, 2002). This necessitates the rejection of hegemonic or ethnocentric discourse identifying a circumscribed set of values as being universal (Guilherme, 2007). Therefore, as the EC advocates 'the reductionist movement of promoting the 'native-English speaker' as an embodiment of Western cultural norms, a view which affirms that nation and language are relative constructs (i.e. English belongs to those people of inner circle countries)' (Rivers, 2010a: 324), a powerful message is transmitted to students — in order to participate as global citizens (as defined by the EC) there are certain universalizing principles and values that must be adhered to. Consequently, like the hallucinatory foundations embraced by theists, accepting that the 'native speaker' is anything more than the product of a conditioned mind immediately binds all foreign language-learners to an eternal existence of servitude and a position of innate deficiency. Those institutions which preach the salvation to be found within this 'linguistic prophet' must also realize that student proficiency achievements will never be sufficient to assume the same celestial throne as that occupied by the almighty 'native speaker'. It is therefore utterly nonsensical and comically paradoxical to have the 'native speaker' as an 'authentic' component of any foreign language-learning initiative, least not 'the key to facilitating communicative competence, increasing awareness and knowledge of English-speaking cultures, and contributing overall to the university's mission of educating internationally oriented citizens' (Torpey, 2006: 2525). In such cases divine faith and paying ritualized homage to another mythical man in the sky would likely produce the same end result.

Paramount to maintaining their status as 'badge[s] of authenticity' (Seargeant, 2009a: 101) selected to function within the EC's monolingual environment, most EC teachers are hired direct from their country of origin rather than from within Japan as part of the EC Director's annual world recruitment tour. Almost certainly by design, new EC recruits therefore have no point of comparison between the practices espoused within the EC and those espoused within other Japanese institutions. As many teachers arrive in the EC 'knowing no better', the smooth imposition of those dominant social representations endorsed by the EC is facilitated as they appear unproblematic, unquestionable and entirely commonsensical. This form of indoctrination, where newcomers are adapted rather than integrated, is conducted in the first instance through the aforementioned newcomer orientation which functions as a rite of passage (Van Gennep, 1960) into the EC mode of existence. The various orientation rituals therefore work toward 'changing the consciousness of the oppressed, not the situation which oppresses them' (Freire, 2000, citing de Beauvoir, 1963: 34). Furthermore, the critical capacity of individual teachers to transform their new realities is removed, perhaps informed by an institutional understanding that 'the more the oppressed can be led to adapt to that situation, the more easily they can be dominated' (Freire, 2000: 74). Unfortunately, for many of the new EC recruits who are eager to make a positive impression upon EC management (who later act as judge and jury in the contract renewal procedure), the authoritative social representations of normality presented during the orientation period are internalized without question revealing exactly how 'the oppressed are "educated" into accepting their vanquished status as being inevitable and perhaps even honourable and desirable' (Van Gorder, 2008: 10).

Immobilized by static intergroup boundaries of existence

Beyond the classroom environment, the most common area for students to interact with EC teachers is in a space known as the EC lounge. The main focus of the lounge is an open-plan free conversation area where students and teachers must adhere to the same English-only language policy as enforced within their regular lessons. Throughout the IU's promotional literature, the EC lounge is advertised as a place to participate in the kind of edutainment synonymous with English conversation schools such as Nova and Geos (see Smart, 2010) where talk is primarily 'glorified for the sake of talk, rather than for the minds it opens up and the worlds it connects' (Van Lier, 1996: 148). Here, language proficiency improvements are a speculated by-product of playful interactions with the 'native speakers' of English who are positioned to enthral as opposed to educate their student audience. Significantly, there are no requirements or provisions made for teachers outside the EC community to participate in the lounge area activities or cultural events. Through 'positioning English outside the boundary of mainstream society [and mainstream academia] and creating purpose built enclaves within which to accommodate it [such as the EC], the perception is created that the language [like the 'native-speaker' English teacher] is forever foreign' (Seargeant, 2009a: 104).

One can only imagine the educational possibilities available if participation within the EC lounge was inclusive of teachers of different ethnolinguistic and cultural backgrounds. Students could potentially benefit from the provision of more realistic foreign language use role models and gain greater emotional support in acknowledging and managing the development of their evolving identity profiles as Japanese – English bilinguals. However, such an imagined future will never become reality within the EC for one reason—exposing the 'native-speaker' English teachers to workplace interactions alongside other forms of diversity threatens to unravel the institutional burden of authenticity upon which the EC is founded and maintained. It is therefore an absolute imperative that the 'native-speaker' English teachers operate in a space of captive isolation in order to retain their economic value to the university and supposed usefulness to the students in developing communicative abilities.

...from the very moment of venturing out into the wild from its idyllic 'natural environment', the native is condemned to lose its precious nativity progressively. For the native retains the amulet against 'contamination' from alien tongues only so long as it sticks to the confines of its hermit-like isolation and distance from members of other speech communities. As the supreme irony of it all would have it, the authenticity of the native speaker teacher (NST) can be guaranteed only to the extent to which she or he remains immune both to the contact with the alien tongue and to the influence it exerts as a result. (Rajagopalan, 2006: 295)

More inter-group boundaries designed to authenticate and protect the 'native-speaker' English teachers from contamination are maintained through the strict implementation of an EC dress code. The EC Director explains that 'as lecturers working within a Japanese university, members of the EC are expected to dress professionally throughout the working day (NOT just when in the classroom)' (Extract from the EC Handbook). The fact that no other department, affiliated research institution or first-language defined population has any such dress code enforced works to undermine the actual educational contributions of the EC teachers through reaffirming symbolic links between physical appearance, linguistic authenticity, institutional positioning and role capability within the minds of university management, regular faculty members and students. Yet, once a year when EC teachers are summoned for a compulsory promotional group photograph, the fixed parameters of the EC dress code are temporarily refashioned. Prior to this photograph, an email is sent by an EC Assistant Director requesting that all EC teachers introduce more colour into their shirts, ties, blouses and dresses.

Ignorant to the dehumanization of a process that ultimately reduces them to the role of designer mannequins, many EC teachers embrace this fun request by replacing their regular caliginous work attire with brightly coloured shirts, floral summer dresses and cartoon character ties.

> In many ways the EC is a glorified English conversation school. They are using the fact that there are so many native-English speaking teachers as their core promotional tool and this feeds into the English-only language policy and, the advertising campaign where we all have to dress in formal suits like business people and have pictures taken in front of attractive buildings. It kind of says 'look how many happy foreigners we have here'. It is bad practice from the very beginning and unfortunately many teachers also buy into the idea that they, as native speakers, are the best models for students, which maintains a long chain of poorly informed decisions and teaching practices. (Interview with Alex, second-year EC teacher)

The principles of captive isolation and the explicit illustration of difference are also promoted through the allocation of office space. Unlike all other IU employees, EC teachers (with the exception of the four members of EC management) are required to share office space with at least two other EC colleagues. This contributes toward the 'ghettoized expatriate professoriate speaking only to one another, remote from the pressing issues of education, viewed by their students as a bit of fashionable exotica' (Hall, 1998: 94). The fashionable exotica metaphor is given further life through the fact that all EC offices located within the main stand-alone building are entirely glass-fronted. These offices either face outward into either an open-plan computer centre or into the EC lounge area. Consequently, the workspaces and amusing anomalies of authentic 'native speaker' interaction are completely visible to students and the frequent tour groups (of potential students or potential affiliates) who come to sample the exotic ambiance of the distinctly foreign EC product. On such tours, physical segregation and exoticism are championed as attractive features of the EC package. Enthusiastic tour guides proudly showcase the offices and their foreign captives explaining how an entirely glass-fronted design makes communication with 'native teachers' easier. In warning of the potential dangers of such a practice, Klitzman and Stellman (1989) report that office environments lacking in adequate visual privacy hold serious implications for employee satisfaction and continued positive mental well-being. Indeed, the psychological discomfort of working within an ideologically cleansed fish-bowl manifests through numerous offices choosing to hang curtains or reposition furniture directly in front of the glass entrance as an attempt to block or partially restrict the all-access viewing.

Rewarding conformity and the purpose of research

As a contractual obligation, upon joining the EC all teachers are assigned to one of the EC's Research groups. The research groups serve an important role in creating staged opportunities for EC teachers to indulge in a kind of simulated role-play within the 'symbolically mediated lifeworld' (Pavlenko & Lantolf, 2000: 155) of the EC. These small groups usually meet weekly and are managed by one or two EC teachers selected by EC management to act as Coordinators. The EC management team describes the Coordinator positions as 'a valuable PD [Professional Development] experience, allowing people the chance to develop leadership and management skills that can be utilized in future jobs (and to get future jobs)' (Extract from the EC 'Guidelines for Coordinators' Handbook). The notable absence of any reference to research matters and the emphasis placed on developing leadership and management skills for use outside the EC marks the Coordinator positions as having a secondary focus on foreign language education research. The fact that no research competency assessment or support is given to Coordinators or regular research group members (with the exception of one research group exclusively geared toward proficiency testing as part of a departmental entrance examination) also supports this observation.

During the annual in-house Coordinator recruitment period, favoured EC teachers are often covertly approached by EC management and encouraged to stand against their equal-status peers based upon management's assessment of their potential. In addition to undermining the principles of equality of opportunity, how potential can be assessed within someone entering the second year of a two-year contract is never clarified or expanded on.

> The management will tell you directly that they often have to approach people that they think would be a 'good fit' in the position. However, being a 'good fit' is not necessarily synonymous with being the most experienced person from the research group. Nor does it reflect the amount of work done for the EC. It appears to be more connected with your personal relationship with management members. If you are willing to completely tow the line and never speak up against anything (at least not publicly), you are a 'good fit'. (Interview with Susan, third-year EC teacher)

In selectively rewarding EC teachers who are not the most professionally deserving of an elevated position and salary increase (even by their own admission) a 'kind of guilt reaction, which plays itself out in many ways, as well as compensation by overwork, lethargic confusion, or a secret, selfish joy in riding the English gravy train' (Fiyouzat, 2003: 58) is activated.

I was going to become a sound designer ... I was working in sound studios when I came to Japan to do some live concerts and stuff when I saw an advert for 'white person wanted to speak English' ... I went home to do a PGCE to train to be a media teacher, decided I was a bit bored of life in England, came back and this job was open. I am fortunate and grateful for what the EC has given me so I do not want to be overly critical of the system, I just want to get on and live my life. I know this may sound selfish but the EC system has benefitted me. I am appeased in my Coordinator position and I am grateful for it ... I see my teaching as a form of art and I really enjoy it, all the rest of it is just stuff that happens around me. Yes, I am a Coordinator and maybe I was a safe option, but that makes sense that they would choose a safe option. (Interview with Martin, third-year EC teacher and research group Coordinator)

In attempting to further understand why certain candidates are selected over others, and why the most appealing Coordinator candidates appear to be those individuals who possess a proven 'inability or unwillingness to grapple adequately with the social, political, cultural and ethical concerns that certainly come to bear on any applied linguistic context' (Pennycook, 2006: 287), it is possible to conclude that the EC research groups, despite official discourse, are not designed to be evaluated upon quality or quantity of the research produced or published. It is therefore important that those teachers entrusted with the responsibility of leading the research groups (i.e. Coordinators) are able to adopt a position of pathological apathy, thus strengthening the already established framework of majority oppression and minority power. Official evidence of this exploitative mentality can be found within a document made available only to EC management's trusted inner circle (i.e. Coordinators) in which the token value of the research groups is explicitly outlined and actively championed.

The brand recognition that comes to [the] IU from EC research is not to be underestimated. The annual JALT conference is a good example. [The] IU regularly ranks first of all universities for the sheer number of presentations given, and is very well-known in those circles as a result. EC research is one way [the] IU is able to 'fight above its weight' in a highly competitive educational environment. (Extract from the EC 'Guidelines for Coordinators' Handbook)

As regular EC teachers are denied access to this seemingly important information, it can be observed how the selective hierarchical distribution of knowledge functions as a means of empowering certain individuals and disempowering other individuals.

Lived Experience within the EC

Professional resistance to the Native-Speakerist framework

Shortly after beginning my employment as an EC teacher, a senior colleague and I came together to combine our shared research interests in a project aimed at exploring EC teacher attitudes towards first-language use in the classroom. We were aware of the large and growing body of research supporting the pedagogically principled use of the learners' first language as an important and effective tool for enhancing comprehension and use of the target language in the classroom. We also believed that such a research undertaking was further justified by the fact the EC teachers were working under similar conditions, making the project potentially beneficial for the evolution and advancement of EC language education pedagogy that had been almost stagnant since its inception as an experiment in the late 1980s. We were also motivated by a passage written by the EC management team in the aforementioned document made available only to those selected as research group Coordinators, 'the EC does not accept the idea that "some people are teachers" and "some people are researchers". It is assumed that any teacher who does not theorize about and experiment with their teaching is a poor teacher' (Extract from the EC 'Guidelines for Coordinators' Handbook).

Despite our sincere perception that we were therefore demonstrating good practice by theorizing about and experimenting with our teaching with a view to improving EC practice, it soon became apparent that the EC Director did not perceive our actions in this way and that we had overstepped the boundaries of our 'native-speaker' English teacher role. After administering an initial online survey to all EC teachers with the verbal permission of the EC Assistant Director in charge of research matters, my senior colleague and I were called to the EC Director's office and asked where we were going with such controversial research. The EC Director added that the chairman of the university had worked very hard to build the university's reputation and that he would be very upset if anyone did anything to damage it.

> Within the EC there is a lack of transparency in how decisions are made behind closed doors and are then imposed upon us. To be honest, I do not trust the people who are supposedly in charge of me from my Coordinator to my Director, and I doubt whether they are able to make competent decisions based on anything other than appeasing the demands of the university in terms of public relations. (Interview with Alex, second-year EC teacher)

In spite of this early warning, firm in our belief that we were pursuing well-informed research that could benefit the evolution of the EC, we decided to continue the project and collect the data. Several months later, after we began writing up our findings, and despite our data showing that many EC members believed the students' first language had the potential to be an important and effective tool, thus at least warranting an open discussion among colleagues, we were once again called back into the EC Director's office where we were confronted in a more authoritative manner as recalled by my senior colleague.

> We were told that if we published the paper with the true number of teacher participants it would be obvious that we were talking about the EC. He [the EC Director] asked why I, with two young children and about to start a new position at a sister university, would want to publish this research and risk being fired for it. He said there were Japanese faculty members who would read the published paper and alert the chairman and that as a result I could very well lose my job. I tried to assure the Director that our intention was not to harm the university's reputation, but to promote open discussion and improvements with respect to the English-only policy. I said that we felt there were problems that were not being officially recognized and that we should be addressing these issues rather than just trying to maintain the illusion that the program was perfect, that its curriculum and policies were informed by the latest research and founded on well-established pedagogical principles. (Interview with Steven, former EC teacher and research group Coordinator)

In addition to the ethical position of the EC Director using family members to stimulate fear and bring about conformity, the comments in relation to the Japanese faculty members illustrate how within oppressive social structures when weaknesses or problems are brought to the attention of authority figures, the most common reaction is to deny the existence of a problem by shifting attention away from the original issue on to the individual actors involved in challenging the status quo.

The pressures applied by the EC Director were eventually successful in making my senior colleague and I fear for our continued employment status. We published a diluted version of our findings within a domestic online conference proceeding. Furthermore, under instruction from the EC Director, the number of participants within the study was omitted. This seriously questioned the validity of our research, undermined our own academic abilities, and limited the wider appeal of the article. With the agreement of the EC Director, we also included a third decoy author from a different university in order to further reduce the chance that the research context could be identified as being the EC at the IU.

> Professional issues of reliability, validity and quality in research are totally overlooked in favour of using our classroom efforts, packaged as research to sell the school ... there is no incentive for the EC to better its practices as contributions do not extend beyond the EC. As the EC is only accountable to the university through a single foreign Director, it is easy to ignore calls for change and improvement. (Interview with Benjamin, third-year EC teacher)

Perhaps not completely satisfied that my own resistance had been fully quashed or that I was sufficiently conditioned into the EC mode of existence, a few months later I was again made to fear for my employment status on the basis that the EC Director had supposedly heard rumours among the Japanese faculty that I did not enjoy working at the IU. This accusation seemed bizarre as I had no direct contact with any members of the Japanese IU faculty and was unaware that a rumoured lack of enjoyment was sufficient legal grounds for dismissal. I asked the EC Director to either provide evidence of the rumour based upon my work or research performance (both of which were of a high standard) or to call to the meeting the faceless Japanese faculty members implicated as being responsible for creating the rumour. No evidence was presented and my request for a direct meeting was denied. However, the EC Director capitalized on this incident by instructing me to be more aware of how the Japanese faculty expected me to behave as a foreigner and to make extra effort to present a more positive public image of myself. It was explained that these actions were important to reassure the Japanese faculty that I was happy to be working in the EC as they held the ability to have EC teachers fired. The EC Director proceeded to recall an earlier incident in which he had personally saved another EC teacher from being fired despite widespread calls from the Japanese faculty to have the teacher immediately dismissed.

Such experiences highlight how the continuation of TESOL environments, such as the EC, which refuse to problematize the native-speakerist framework, are ultimately hinged upon keeping the 'native-speaker' English teachers in a short-term state of conditioned utopia. The use of short-term contracts is usually sufficient to ensure that these teachers never fully awaken to, or dare speak of, the ideological realities shaping their day-to-day employment experiences. On occasions when teachers do engage with these ideological realities, whether discovering them intentionally or by chance, the consequences are both revealing and traumatic.

You will be able to see for yourself how you are conditioned only when there is a conflict in the continuity of pleasure or the avoidance of pain. If everything is perfectly happy around you ... then you are not aware of your conditioning at all. But when there is a disturbance ... then you know you are conditioned. When you struggle against any kind of disturbance or defend yourself against any outer or inner threat, then you know you are conditioned. (Krishnamurti, 1969: 26)

Once the spell of my own conditioned utopia had been shattered, I represented a more significant problem for the EC management to the extent that one member of the managerial team began ignoring my very existence. This act demonstrates how invisibility can be used as an attempted form of governance once the incitement of fear, as a first and predictable option, is no longer deemed effective. The described events also serve to illustrate the simmering undercurrent of power and control resident within the grapevine culture used by faceless faculty members and also calls into question the principles of those middlemen who intentionally stimulate a sense of fear while simultaneously positioning themselves as sole figures of salvation. These middlemen often perform such acts based upon motives concerning self-preservation and a sense of obligation shrewdly puppeteered by their superiors. Sources of such gratitude may derive from the awarding of a long-term contract or tenure, the endowment of power and prestige through a higher academic position, or other benefits such as paid study leave, the awarding of an honorary degree or a lucrative consultancy position after retirement.

Reflections and Final Thoughts

The angst of being imagined as a 'native-speaker' English teacher

As a white European male, my innate physical attributes have undoubtedly been unfairly advantageous in securing employment within Japanese tertiary education. However, while advantageous at the pre-recruitment stage, at the post-recruitment stage the same innate physical attributes have been instrumental in limiting the contributions I am seen to be able to make and the scope of the roles I am expected to be able to perform. As demonstrated within the EC, these 'native speaker' roles typically parallel McLaren's (1993: 113) performance typology of 'teacher-as-entertainer and teacher-as-hegemonic overlord'. Although much of the existing TESOL literature dictates that individuals with such innate physical attributes are the ultimate benefactors of native-speakerist policies and practices, thus positioning people of other ethnicities or those from outside of the Kachruvian inner circle as the authentic victims of native-speakerism, present literature does not explain why some teachers despite being endowed with the so-called desirable characteristics also feel victimized, discontent and frustrated when imagined as a 'native speaker' of English.

> What many in the language teaching world seldom if ever pause to think is that the native speaker with all the attributes that are characteristically credited to this extremely powerful pedagogic totem is simply non-existent in the world of lived reality. A native meeting all the requirements of one hundred per cent authenticity and so on is a chimera that can only ever exist in the fertile imagination of an ivory tower theoretical linguistic. (Rajagopalan, 2006: 294)

This stance is compounded by the fact that institutions such as the EC are unable or unwilling to define the parameters of the 'native speaker' label despite making it a central criterion for employment (Rivers, 2011d). Therefore, although certain innate characteristics have forbidden me from assuming the role of an authentic victim of native-speakerism, associating positively with the aura of invisibility surrounding the 'native-speaker' English teacher status label presents an insurmountable challenge. I am therefore locked within a perpetual state of fantasized non-existence known by all for what I am imagined to represent moving through repetitive cycles of being 'treated like an illegitimate child who is sometimes loved, sometimes disowned' (Yngve, 1981: 37).

Conclusions and call for action

Juxtaposed alongside professional experience this chapter has shared the voices of a small number of EC teachers. During the data collection process several other EC teachers refused to participate in this project or discussions relating to the topic of native-speakerism. While it is important to acknowledge that this is acceptable as research participation should always be on a volunteer basis, the reasons given for not wanting to participate are significant enough to be mentioned. The reasons given can be divided into one of three categories:

- *Native-Speakerist Fear*: Despite the guarantee of anonymity, several teachers expressed concern with being identified and punished for expressing opinions that conflicted with official EC rhetoric.

- *Native-Speakerist Subscription*: Several EC teachers expressed agreement with the EC Director's view (explicated to the entire EC in a general meeting soon after this volume was contracted to Multilingual Matters) that native-speakerism was a 'personal interest topic' unconnected to the development of good language-learning practice in the EC.
- *Native-Speakerist Denial*: Several EC teachers stated that they did not want to get involved explaining how they preferred to remain neutral on the issue of native-speakerism.

Such varied refusals to engage in the struggle for self-determination can act only to further empower institutions such as the EC to 'adamantly oppose any form of coming to terms with the political and ideological nature of the discipline' (Kabel, 2009: 12). While the first two reasons offered concern power and position, the third reason offered is more complex as 'it is not possible to be neutral under an unjust status quo ... neutrality is usually if not always a cowardly cover for conservatism' (Hagos, 2011: 37). Consequently, those teachers who expressed a desire to remain neutral were in fact empowering the already dominant native-speakerist framework of the EC to continue unchallenged. It appeared to be something of a default position within the EC that the majority of teachers were content to embrace the norms of 'native-speaker' English teaching which cast the individual teacher as an expendable commodity, sold by the institution and consumed by the student in a transaction bereft of educational morality. Many such teachers, seduced by an unhealthy groupthink mentality of endless optimism, remained semi-conscious throughout their short employment experience, conditioned to the point of ignorance by the alleged benefits afforded to them by their 'native-speaker' English teacher status label, regardless of its mythical foundation or the educational disservice done to themselves and their students.

If marginalized voices of resistance and dissent are to ever become part of 'everyday collegial conversation' (Matt & Shahinpoor, 2011: 164), 'native-speaker' English teachers must become more actively engaged in the fight to transcend the limitations of their conditioned status without fear of being labelled as an in-group deviant, losing position within the social hierarchy, not having a contract renewed or being fired. Although an admittedly painful process, activism does not rest on hope, it rests on action, meaning that failure to drive forward by succumbing to institutional pressures to accept the dated status quo parameters of 'native-speaker' English teaching represents a significant threat to the already shredded integrity of the TESOL profession in locations such as Japan and can only see the trail of human collateral and missed opportunity remain.

Acknowledgement

Sincere appreciation is offered to the small group of EC teachers who gave personal and professional support during the documented experiences and who subsequently provided encouragement and critical feedback in the course of writing of this chapter.

6 Negotiating a Professional Identity: Non-Japanese Teachers of English in Pre-Tertiary Education in Japan

Joe Geluso

Introduction

Teaching English to Speakers of Other Languages (TESOL) is a burgeoning field. This is reflected in the number of TESOL-related degree and certificate programmes that exist today. TESOL, Inc., a leading organization in the field of TESOL, for instance, had approximately 450 such programmes listed on its website at the time of writing this chapter (TESOL Directory of Degree and Certificate Programs, n.d., para. 1). Johnston (1997) notes that with this growth of the field, discourse on careers in TESOL has become commonplace. As the number of professionals in the field has increased, so has the research examining their careers and subsequent constructions of professional identity (see Amin, 1997; Casanave & Schecter, 1997; Johnston, 1997, 1999; Simon-Maeda, 2004; Tang, 1997). This chapter aspires to add to the literature on professional identity among professionals in TESOL by focusing on the experiences and perspectives of non-Japanese teachers of English working in pre-tertiary education in Japan.

Background information

Much research on professional identity in the field of TESOL to date has focused on the dichotomy of 'native speakers' and 'non-native speakers' of English. This is evidenced in the numerous publications devoted to the topic throughout the 1990s and today (e.g. Barratt & Kontra, 2000; Braine, 1999; Breckenridge, 2010; Medgyes, 1992; Tajino & Tajino, 2000). To aid in understanding discussion with respect to native and non-native speakers in TESOL, readers should be familiar with Kachru's Three Circles model of World Englishes (see Kachru 1985, 1986; Kachru & Nelson, 1996). Sung-Yul Park and Wee (2009: 390) note that while the Three Circles model has come under criticism in recent times as it does not account for the heterogeneity and dynamic use of English across the three circles, it is still relevant 'as a representation of dominant ideologies that constrain speakers' performativity in English in local contexts. It is through this lens that Kachru's terminology will be employed in this chapter.

The native speaker and the non-native speaker

A substantial portion of research that has been carried out on the topic of 'native speaker' versus 'non-native speaker' has been aimed at dispelling the myth that NESTs are inherently superior English teachers simply due to their 'native speaker' status (e.g. Braine, 1999; Medgyes, 1994; Nemtchinova, 2005). This is likely in response to the considerable amount of research that has shown that NESTs are, in fact, widely perceived to be the ideal teachers of English, especially in Inner Circle countries. Amin (1997), for example, interviewed NNEST colleagues who were teaching ESL at a university in Canada and found that the NNESTs believed their students wanted native speaker teachers, or 'real Canadians', to teach them.

It is important to remember, though, that identity and perception are dynamic and change with location. Mackie (2003: 32) expounds: '... identity categories are sometimes false constructions ("the Japanese woman," "the oppressed student," "the white teacher") and ... location or situation is a crucial part of how we see and how we are seen'. There are a number of social practices which will be reviewed in more depth in this chapter that serve to include or exclude social actors in a given context (see van Leeuwen, 1996) and perpetuate dichotomies such as that of the 'native English speaker' versus the 'non-native English speaker'. Such practices can be used to disempower non-native speakers of English in TESOL in Inner-Circle countries, and, as this chapter will argue, their native speaker counterparts in Expanding Circle countries.

While the experiences of 'native speaker' English teachers in Japan will be explored in this chapter, it is worth mentioning that neither is the 'native speaker' label limited to the English language nor is the employment of 'native speaker' teachers unique to Japan. In the United Kingdom, for example, the employment of 'native speakers' of French, German, Spanish, Japanese, Chinese, etc. as 'Foreign Language Assistants' is commonplace at the pre-tertiary level.

Foreign teachers of English in Japan

Foreign teachers have been teaching English in Japan through small-scale government-organized programmes since the 1950s (see McConnell, 2000). Since its inception in 1987 and for the decade that followed, however, the JET Programme was the primary route for foreigners to teach English in primary and secondary schools (McConnell, 2000). According to a JET Programme pamphlet, the majority of participants in the JET Programme are ALTs, teachers who team-teach with JTEs. Out of the 4334 participants in the JET Programme in 2010, 3974, or about 92%, were ALTs. Over 90% of all JET ALTs come from an Inner-Circle country, and over 50% come from the United States alone (CLAIR, 2010b). Therefore, the vast majority of foreign English teachers in Japan can be assumed to be 'native speakers'.

The JET Programme website declares that the aim of the programme is 'to promote grass roots internationalisation at the local level by inviting young overseas graduates to assist in international exchange and foreign language education in local governments, boards of education and elementary, junior and senior high schools throughout Japan' (CLAIR, 2009a, para. 1). Indeed, the JET Programme appears to seek out young individuals to teach for very finite periods of time. Current participants in the programme can teach for a maximum of 5 years and should, in principle, be under 40 years of age as 'one of the main purposes of the Programme is to foster youth-to-youth exchange between Japanese youth and young professionals from the countries participating on the JET Programme' (CLAIR, 2009b, Section 2.15). This trend of temporariness among young foreign language teachers in Japan largely persists today.

In 1999, a change in Japan's Worker Dispatch Law (*roudousha haken hou*) allowed private companies to provide ALTs to both public and private schools, affording school districts with alternatives to the JET Programme. Since then the number of ALTs working through JET has dropped, while the number of ALTs working through dispatch companies has skyrocketed (Takahara, 2008). Hashimoto (Chapter 11) not only explains that many boards of education now prefer using dispatch companies as providers of foreign teachers to their schools, as it is typically the most economical, but also notes the murky legal aspects that accompany this method of employment.

Professional identity

Dictionary.com defines *professional* as 'following an occupation as a means of livelihood or for gain; of, pertaining to, or connected with a profession; engaged in one of the learned professions'. Few would dispute the classification of teaching as a profession or *teacher* as a professional. The word teacher rests in the title Assistant Language Teacher, which is one of the most prevalent positions for foreigners working in TESOL in Japan. Simon-Maeda (2004) notes that more and more foreigners, including professionals in the field of TESOL, are settling in Japan and starting families. Naturally, many of these individuals begin to look for long-term employment with benefits, opportunities for upward mobility and satisfaction of being recognized and identifying oneself as a professional. I too fall in this category.

I have roots in Japan, plan to be here for the foreseeable future and hope to secure stable and long-term employment in the not-too-distant future. I identify myself as a teacher and professional in the field of TESOL now and did so while working as an ALT. Personally, however, during my time as an ALT, I wasn't confident that I was perceived as a 'teacher' by my Japanese colleagues or students, and was frustrated by lack of upward mobility. I felt that I had to leave pre-tertiary education if I wanted to move forward with my career. Meanwhile, the Japanese teachers working alongside me had what I perceived to be a stable and long-term career path. They enjoyed incremental salary increases, potential life-time employment and benefits such as health insurance and a pension plan. Working through a dispatch company, I was kept at 29.5 hours or less per week in the classroom to maintain the veil that I was working part-time. Consequently, the dispatch company I worked for had no legal obligation to provide me with the benefits my Japanese colleagues enjoyed (Takahara, 2008). These working conditions and perceived lack of acknowledgement that I was a 'teacher' did not seem befitting or fair.

Methodology

In an attempt to arrive at a deeper understanding of the experiences of foreign teachers of English in Japan, interviews were conducted with seven non-Japanese teachers of English. As I was more concerned with the stories of teachers with considerable experience in Japan, who have, perhaps, entertained the idea of settling down in Japan, participants with at least five years of teaching experience were selected. I aimed to include both men and women teachers from a number of different countries in the interviews. Some participants I knew from previous jobs, one I met at a professional conference on TESOL and others I was introduced to through mutual acquaintances. Participants are referred to by first name throughout the chapter; a few chose to use pseudonyms.

The participants took part in extensive email interviews, an increasingly common method of conducting interviews in qualitative research (Duff,

2008: 135). Interviews took place over the course of four months and followed a standard semi-structured format (Dörnyei, 2007: 136). Questions were decided upon after an extensive literature review (see reference list) and included topics ranging from admiration to professional identity in the workplace. I tried to leave the questions broad and open-ended in an attempt to refrain from leading participants to answer in a certain way, and to allow for the emergence of unpredicted responses.

Given my history in Japan, I could not help but draw on my experiences as an ALT while researching and writing this chapter. In fact, it was my own quest at constructing a professional identity during my time as an ALT that provided the impetus for this work. The questions arrived at were not only representative of broader themes prevalent in the literature but also struck a chord with me. For example, I could understand the notion of being the recipient of student admiration simply for not being Japanese, and therefore more likely than not, a 'native speaker' of English; I felt like I had something to say about not being viewed as a legitimate teacher by colleagues and students; and I felt as though I could contribute to the discourse on professional identity of teachers in TESOL from the perspective of Japan. It was with these themes in mind that I set out to gather the perspectives of other non-Japanese teachers of English at the pre-tertiary level in Japan.

In the sections that follow, the participants' voices will be related to and expand on existing reports of foreign teachers working in Japanese pre-tertiary education and concepts of identity and professional identity. Because my aim was to frame the participants' voices within the existing literature, it was necessary to brief them with relevant background information before asking questions. For example, participants were informed of terms like Inner Circle, NEST and NNEST; when asked for their thoughts on topics like admiration of NESTs in the classroom, I provided them with quotes from and references to the literature that inspired the question.

The participants wrote over 25,000 words of insightful commentary, and the more I read over their responses, the more I felt that I was reading their personal narratives as opposed to answers to questions. In this sense, the study took on an air of narrative analysis (Casanave & Schecter, 1997). As I read, links and commonalities between their stories became apparent. For example, they all believe that they are the recipients of admiration from their students, that they are sometimes essentialised and stereotyped, viewed as representative of an entire group, and that there is a dissonance between their self-constructed identities as teachers and how they believe they are identified by their Japanese colleagues, school administration and subsequently by their students.

Reception and Role Allocation of NESTs

Kubota and McKay (2009: 62) argue that 'teaching English in Japan is a raced practice with preference for white native speakers'. Indeed, as will be discussed below, there appears to be a trend toward associating 'native English speaker' with non-Japanese and most likely white Westerner. While this perception may open up teaching positions for NESTs, the positions made available are often peripheral and serve to marginalize the teacher in relation to the larger learning community or school. NESTs are frequently pigeonholed into pre-determined constructs, such as that of language verifier or linguistics model, but seldom that of 'teacher'. Hashimoto (Chapter 11) presents a compelling deconstruction of how 'native speaker' and 'ALT' are defined and positioned in relation to English-language education in Japanese government publications.

Admiration

Admiration of native English-speaking Westerners among Japanese students is well-documented. Miyazato (2003) provides an example of this through interviews with 13 Japanese students of EFL, which examined issues of anxiety and admiration with respect to NESTs. The students in the study believe that NESTs have better pronunciation and the desire to understand and replicate that pronunciation motivates them to listen more attentively to the NESTs than they do for the JTEs. Email informants for this chapter find their students' reactions to be similar to those in Miyazato's (2003) study. Chris and Nick, who are both white males from Canada and the United Kingdom, respectively, and both long-term residents of Japan with plans to stay indefinitely, had this to say:

> There is absolutely a degree of racial profiling. As a Caucasian male, initial impressions are usually that I am a good teacher. (Chris)

> In a way, I can get a sense that they [students] appreciate everything that they have done with their NNEST, but that speaking with the NEST can give them a sense of achievement, from discovering that they are able to put into practice what they have learned. The challenge of actually communicating with the NEST shows the student that their English actually 'works', giving a great deal of motivation and hence admiration for the NEST. (Nick)

Comments of this nature appear to corroborate the above-mentioned notion of Kubota and McKay (2009), in that English teaching in Japan is a racialized practice from which white 'native speakers' benefit the most; NESTs are viewed as the ideal language model in terms of pronunciation and providing 'authentic' English input. Veritably, Matsuda (2002: 488) reveals that Japanese 'students' idea of English speakers is limited mostly to those from the UK and US', This is hardly surprising when representations of 'foreign' cultures in Japanese junior and senior high school English textbooks are taken into account. Yamanaka (2006: 72) notes that 'there is a marked lack of emphasis on nations in the Outer Circle in comparison with countries in the Inner Circle'.

What are the implications of this for teachers who are foreigners and come from a country where English holds an official status, but may not be labeled 'native speaker'? One informant for this study, Rizza, who is a Filipina and has demonstrated a continual positive attitude about teaching English in Japan, remarks on how she perceived the reactions of some JTEs upon seeing that she would be their team-teaching partner: '... at first some teachers stare at me as if they want to question everything about me ... I feel that in some certain ways, they don't appreciate me at first'. Rizza explained that she took this perceived challenge of her authenticity and used it as fuel to motivate herself to prove to any doubters that she is a legitimate and skilled teacher of English. Rizza believes that her teaching has squelched the flames of uncertainty and comments that 'now I have a good relationship with some of those who doubted me'. Nevertheless, Rizza's experiences again lend support to Kubota and McKay's (2009) argument that there is a preference for white 'native speakers' in Japan.

From admiration to othering

> In some countries (Japan and Saudia Arabia come to mind), although expatriate teachers are well-paid and enjoy relatively high status, their very identity as foreigners renders them marginal in social and often professional terms... (Johnston, 1999: 257)

An interesting dialectic emerges when NESTs teach in a context like Japan. It is true that they may enjoy the perceived linguistic capital that accompanies being a 'native speaker' of English, and students may additionally admire them for 'their exotic nature', or their 'friendly' and 'approachable' image (Miyazato, 2009: 46). However, there are other social practices used in the process of allocating roles to social actors that can disrupt a teacher's attempt to construct a professional identity. A number of these social practices have been identified and labeled by van Leeuwen (1996: 59); among them are *genericisation* and *impersonalisation*. The former is when an actor is stripped of his/her individual identity and seen as representative of a particular category (i.e. essentialised and stereotyped), while the latter is characterized 'by abstract nouns, or by concrete nouns whose meaning does not include the semantic feature "human"'.

Instances of the genericisation of foreigners in Japan are well-documented. In McConnell's (2000: 220) seminal publication on the JET Programme, it is noted that 'Because JET participants were visible as members of a category, their actions carried extra symbolic consequences; their behavior was interpreted as representative of that category indicating not their individual personalities but "the way their nationality is"'. Participants in the email interviews for this chapter found truth in McConnell's comments.

Lauren, a white American, had been a resident of Japan and working as an ALT for five years when this study began (she has since moved back to America). Lauren believes that her students projected their perceptions of what an 'American' is on her before she had a chance to present herself to them on her own terms:

> With my students, I do feel that they view me as an 'ambassador from America' and thus project their previously formed opinions about Americans onto me. For example, they are surprised that I have no brothers or sisters or that my family doesn't own a gun... After finding out that the children would respond like this, in my second-year teaching (at a different school) I started the year off with a presentation about America, not only showing them where I am from but also showing how different the regions of the US are. I also make bulletin boards and posters about the different areas of the US. This strategy has worked very well and the children understand that I am from the Midwest and things in California are different. (Lauren)

As illustrated in the quote, Lauren developed a number of strategies designed to dispel such generalizations about Americans in her first lessons with new groups of students. Her hope was to nurture a more anti-essentialist understanding about foreigners in her students, that is an understanding of diversity within a group (Kubota & Lin, 2006).

In addition to genericisation, the impersonalisation of NESTs has recently received attention in the literature in TESOL. Breckenridge (2010) adopts van Leeuwen's (1996) conceptual framework of role allocation and analyses how the term 'native speaker' is used in three corpora: *The Corpus of Contemporary American English* (Davies, 2008) and two more corpora compiled from electronic versions of articles from the journals *TESOL Quarterly* and *ELT Journal*. In the analysis of concordances containing the term 'native speaker' in the two journals, Breckenridge (2010: 176) found that 'in the ELT corpus native speaker was used as a generic category in 81% of the instances it occurred and 88% in the *TESOL Quarterly* corpus'. The impersonalisation of 'native speaker' was also found to be quite common. In the corpus generated from the *ELT Journal*, 'Of the 202 concordance lines that contained native speaker/s, there were only 38 instances where "native speaker" referred to actual people, rather than a generalized category or concept...' (Breckenridge, 2010: 147); and in the *TESOL Quarterly* corpus, 'Only 48 concordances or 12% of the concordances referred to people' (Breckenridge, 2010: 155). Breckenridge (2010) found the term 'native speaker' was most often used to describe one of the four constructs: (1) a characteristic, (2) a verifier, (3) a language learning model and resource or (4) a person failing to meet expectations.

After being presented with these four constructs, the majority of participants in the interviews for this chapter believe that they are viewed most prominently as verifiers and/or language learning models and resources. James, a white British man, notes the friction his allocated role creates with respect to how he identifies himself:

> I think from the start of my time in the Japanese school system I was quite aware that I was being viewed as the third of Breckenridge's constructs (language learning model and resource), and if anything, experience has only reinforced that opinion. The only problem I have with this is that I am viewed as a model, a resource, but not as a teacher in the Japanese sense (the equivalent of a JTE, for example), and a teacher is how I define myself, and would like to be seen as, not merely a model or resource of language, neither of which I feel is very flattering. (James)

Ultimately, though, it is irrelevant which construct a teacher is viewed as because the bottom line is that they are not being viewed as 'teachers'. Like James, many of the teachers interviewed for this chapter believe that they are viewed as something other than a teacher by their colleagues. Jess, a participant in this study and an ALT through the JET Programme for five years (2005 – 2010), in fact, attributes his decision to return to America in 2010 instead of pursuing more teaching opportunities in Japan to the dissonance between his self-constructed identity as a teacher and his perception of how he was defined by his colleagues and administration. Jess is not alone in this opinion. Jack, who like Jess is also a white American working as an ALT, substantiates:

> I do say I am a teacher since I do teach at other locations, but feel my status as an ALT is not really a teacher. I feel that other teachers see me as an outsider.

Even where I sit in the teachers' room, I am not seated with the other teachers, but off with the nurse's desk and the administrative assistant. (Jack)

Participants also believe that their students are quick to pick up on cues that the non-Japanese teachers are not allocated 'teacher' status and that it affects students' attitudes toward them. Chris notes that '… [students] unabashedly ask personal questions and joke with me in ways that would probably get them reprimanded from their regular teachers'.

It has been suggested that perhaps Japanese schools are not concerned about an NEST's qualifications and that by not hiring individuals with teaching credentials, schools can assuage JTEs' feelings of inadequacy when standing next to a 'native speaker' (McVeigh, 2002; Miyazato, 2009). By making 'native speaker of English' the most important qualification, teaching positions are trivialized and the NEST rendered little more than a highly replaceable commodity, 'sold by the institution and consumed by the student' (Rivers, Chapter 5). This creates circumstances that may be ideal for recent college graduates who are looking to experience Japan for a year or two while making a decent income and then return to their respective home countries to pursue their careers. But what of those who have more invested in the country, such as spouses and families, plan to be in Japan for the long term, are motivated to construct a professional identity as a teacher in Japan and subsequently seek long-term, stable employment? Of the seven teachers interviewed, five appear to be in Japan indefinitely and four have families. Takahara (2008) suggests that one way to increase job security and benefits for those who plan to be in Japan for the long haul and pursue careers in TESOL is to promote direct hire by boards of education.

A sense of permanency

Ostensibly, there is some common ground between the goals of the MEXT and teachers looking to forge a professional identity within a long-term career in Japan. Tanabe (2004) notes that MEXT offered a plan on its website to promote the hiring of ALTs as full-time teachers:

Promotion of the hiring of ALTs with advanced abilities as full-time teachers
From 2003, by making an additional quota to the fixed number of teachers at junior high schools, the aim is to appoint 300 people as full-time junior high school teachers over the next three years with the future goal of appointing 1,000 junior and senior high school teachers. (Section 2.6)

James and Nick are apparent examples of the type of NESTs that MEXT had in mind for being appointed as full-time teachers. Both have many years experience teaching in Japan, Nick holds teaching credentials from Britain and the *Cambridge Certificate in English Language Teaching to Adults* (CELTA), and James has earned a master's degree in education in TESOL. Both enjoy direct employment from what they describe as prestigious schools with an international aim, and solo-teach their own Oral Communication (OC) courses. MEXT (2003b) states that the objectives of OC courses are 'To develop students' basic abilities to understand and convey information, ideas, etc. by listening to or speaking English, and to foster a positive attitude toward communication...' (para. 2). According to James and Nick, the implicit understanding of the OC courses is that they meet once a week, are taught by an NEST (as opposed to a JTE) and emphasize giving students oral practice of grammar structures encountered in the JTE's classes, which consist of four to five lessons a week.

Despite this seemingly improved integration of NESTs into their respective teaching situations, both James and Nick make explicit points about where students still see a marked distinction between NESTs and JTEs:

> The goal for almost all students (all students in my current school) is to use English to pass the university entrance exams, not to use English as a tool for communication. JTEs are viewed as having a better knowledge of the tests and what is needed to pass them (communicative competence in English certainly is not needed!) (James)

> I'd say the majority of students in Japan are focused more on passing their university entrance exams. Being in the Expanding Circle, English has no official role in their day-to-day lives, but it is a requirement for entering a good university and possibly getting a good job in the future. (Nick)

The value students place on the English taught by NESTs versus the English taught by JTEs that James and Nick are describing here has been reported on before. McVeigh (2004: 215) describes the different approaches to English education in Japan noting that there is a 'Japanese version of English, or "Japan-oriented English" (*eigo*) ... English for climbing the examination-education ladder' and there is '"non-Japan-oriented English" (*eikaiwa*) ... "English for communication"'. The fact of the matter is that regardless of how far removed from 'real' or communicatively useful English university entrance exams are, that is precisely the English that is most important for Japanese students who aim to study at university. Nick shares an illustrative anecdote:

I had a vocabulary question in a recent class, and it was asking the difference between 'no less than' and 'not less than', apparently quite a typical question for exams in Japan. Many of my NEST friends were unable to distinguish between the two. Most of the JTEs on the other hand could answer straight away. (Nick)

Where does this leave native English speaking teachers who are charged with improving students' communicative competence when the actual emphasis of foreign language education is placed on dissecting and analysing the foreign language as a static code? Many of the interviewees in this study believe that their classes are, in fact, stripped of academic value in the eyes of their students, and seen as more for fun than for any real academic purpose.

When teaching high school students, I have often found that students see the NEST class as more of a fun time to relax with little academic value. It is definitely weighted with less importance than the NNEST class. (Nick)

As most teachers know, motivation is key to acquisition of knowledge. The motivation for most students is grades. With no grade given for a class, there is likely to be no motivation to learn, or even behave yourself … This brings me to the point that our classes are seen as being for fun, not for real studying, and the real English study, the study that helps you pass the entrance exams, can only come from the JTE. (James)

The perception among students and Japanese faculty that the NESTs' class is for fun and lacks tangible pedagogical value is at odds with teachers who identify themselves as teachers. However, as long as the emphasis of English education is placed on passing university entrance exams that test abstract rules of English more than the communicative aspect of the language, students and administration may see little reason to invest more in increasing students' communicative competence. The implication for foreign English teachers in Japan being that their classes and their role in the students' education is of secondary importance.

Concluding Remarks

While it is true that NESTs enjoy many opportunities for employment as language teachers in Japan, the positions made available to them are located on the periphery of the institutions in which they teach. This is reflected in the facts that most NESTs do not teach their 'own' classes, rather they visit another teacher's class; sometimes, they are even physically seated apart from their Japanese colleagues; and in most cases NESTs have no say in assigning grades, and if they do, the weight and significance are often ambiguous. While it is true that NESTs are often the recipients of admiration, sometimes unfounded, they are also pigeonholed into certain constructs, and seldom feel as though they are viewed as 'teachers'. More often, they function to serve as models as to what their students can achieve in terms of English proficiency, entertainers and/or windows into a mysterious and exotic culture embodied in English.

Through a model diagramming the prototypical exemplar of the 'native speaker' English teacher in Japan, Rivers (2011e: 845) asserts that there are various ideologies centered around linguistic, racial, behavioural and cultural attributes often seen as commonsensical by the majority meaning that 'a large number of EFL learning environments within Japan are still dependent on "native-speaker" English teachers who best conform to a rather narrow set of pre-defined characteristics'. The ever-increasing interconnectedness and dynamism of the modern world, however, has rendered traditional definitions of 'native speaker' antiquated and stereotypes too often inaccurate; to cling to such hackneyed representations will only serve to impede one's own progress in a rapidly evolving international community.

The positioning of 'native speaker' teachers at the pre-tertiary level of English language education in this way may lead to the unfortunate consequence of setting an accepted standard or precedent that could, and may already, influence students' perceptions of 'native speaker' teachers as well as hiring and employment practices at the tertiary level (see Rivers, Chapter 5; Simon-Maeda, 2004). While beyond the scope of this chapter, further inquiry into this hypothesis could provide for an illuminating and critical discussion on the positioning of 'native speaker' English-language teachers and scholars in Japanese universities.

To conclude, I'd like to reiterate Mahboob's (2010: xiii) call for the progression of 'the applied linguistics and TESOL profession in a direction where one's mother tongue, culture, nationality, and race do not define one's professional identity and position'. This is a noble call and one that should be taken seriously with respect to all participants in all contexts. It can be difficult, even uncomfortable, to simply recognize (much less reconcile) that a situation perceived by many as 'normal', or even 'privileged', may be perceived by others as unfair or unjust. The field of TESOL, however, and all professionals in the field, regardless of location, 'native' and 'non native speaker' alike, will benefit by being judged on their merits rather than their mother tongue, nationality or race.

7 Forming Pathways of Belonging: Social Inclusion for Teachers Abroad

Joseph Falout

Introduction

When teachers choose to work abroad, they might anticipate learning about local cultures, making friends and contributing to mutual understanding, appreciation and acceptance among people across the world. Then after moving to a land of strangers, clumsy if not illiterate in the local language, far from home and the people who know and care about them, they experience culture shock and may eventually find themselves misunderstood, unappreciated, unaccepted and wanting one fundamental human need – the feeling of belongingness. When this need is not satisfied, mental and physical health can deteriorate. Those who feel rejected can react unintentionally with self-defeating behaviours – they lose cognitive and self-regulatory capacities, meaning they are less able to solve their problems, and become anti-social and aggressive, possibly contributing to ostracism from a broader community and perpetuating a vicious cycle of exclusion. Teachers may be further at risk of interpersonal detachment due to workplace incivility, ignorance of local labor laws and human rights, and lack of access to or knowledge of social support systems. This chapter will explain from a social psychological perspective why teachers need to nourish their fundamental need to belong, how it can be denied and what might form their pathways of belonging.

The Need to Belong

According to the belongingness hypothesis (Baumeister & Leary, 1995), humans require frequent companionship and enduring mutual care of others for their overall well-being. They are motivated to satisfy this fundamental need by seeking out and regularly spending time with a minimum number of people, usually no more than several, who share reciprocal concern throughout long-term relationships. This need to belong is hardwired into our species and universally each person shares it to a certain extent. Hence, our own adaptive responses may be determined by how we adopt practices of working and living that relate to this innate need within us and every person we meet (Finkel & Baumeister, 2010).

The motivation to connect with others can be spontaneous and powerful. It operates without precondition, ulterior motive or material advantage. Social interactions shape our cognitions and emotions. Acceptance from others brings feelings of warmth and elation, and the formation of social bonds becomes marked as high points in our lives. Some of the most acute negative emotions, jealousy, grief, guilt, anger, anxiety and depression, result from strains and tears in bonds deeply established. People tend to resist attenuation and dissolution of relationships, even those that are destructive. The way individuals feel about their sense of belongingness depends on their inner perspective, not by what might be casually observed. What matters is the qualitative sense of shared intimacy (Baumeister, 2005; Baumeister & Leary, 1995).

The feeling of belongingness can help keep stress levels low, and related psychological and somatic health systems in check, such as immunity, coping and healing. Conversely, a wide range of adverse consequences can arise when the need to belong is deprived. Loneliness and social isolation can predict a wide variety of unfavorable outcomes, from unhappiness to risk-taking to criminality. Baumeister (2005: 108) concludes: 'The need to belong is literally a vital matter of life and death, health, welfare, and sanity'.

Social Exclusion

Both the anticipation and experience of social exclusion lowers the abilities to think intelligently, feel emotions and behave pro-socially. Across differing situations of exclusion and intelligence measures, people who feel rejected show dramatic impairments in speed and accuracy in answering questions, learning, logical thinking, reasoning, extrapolating and performing other higher cognitive functions. Social exclusion largely hinders self-regulation, with sufferers seeming to lack a willingness to exercise self-control to improve their situation (Baumeister *et al.*, 2005; Baumeister *et al.*, 2007).

Those who feel socially excluded likely behave anti-socially potentially towards anyone interacting with them, even those innocent of the rejection. Not only do rejected individuals tend to stop interacting with others pro-socially, they can lash out for little apparent reason. On a brighter note, those rejected often respond positively towards someone offering them praise, and their anti-social downturn can be restored when enough positive social contact, such as connecting with the acceptance of family, enables them to feel socially included (Baumeister et al., 2007; Twenge et al., 2008; Twenge et al., 2007).

Another way rejected individuals might reconnect socially is through an unconscious coping process of searching for positive thoughts. For example, rejected individuals, compared with socially accepted individuals, view people's faces as friendlier, kinder and more inviting. Such impressions possibly help excluded individuals to open up socially, as long as they don't feel anxious about negative evaluation. In other words, excluded individuals may experience heightened interest to engage with others, but their readiness to interact is marked by cautiousness and passivity (Baumeister et al., 2007; Maner et al., 2007).

Belonging for Teachers Abroad

The belongingness hypothesis and the reactions to social exclusion pose crucial implications for teachers abroad. To satisfy the need to belong, humans need four to six close people, seemingly just about anyone would do, who can have frequent interactions in an ongoing relationship of mutual care (Baumeister, 2005). Are environments for teachers abroad conducive to meeting these requirements? The move abroad automatically separates them from regular contact with whoever they were just recently close to, be it family members, life-long friends or newer companions at the school where they recently studied or taught. They may have frequent interactions with students, but unlikely in deep bonds of mutual affection within long-lasting relationships. After school, teachers are busy with class preparation, leaving little spare time to build social networks from scratch. And for newcomers, finding where to socialize can be challenging even in one's own country.

Isolated due to differences in local language and cultural codes of conduct, teachers abroad may also be precariously close to feeling excluded. Whether this exclusion is actual doesn't matter, perceived exclusion can bring about the same ill-effects as from intentionally harmful interpersonal behaviors in the work environment (Thau et al., 2007). It took little in laboratory experiments, compared to stresses in the outside world, to induce states of rejection; for example, a prediction that one would be alone in the future, criticism on one's written essay and a lack of expressed interest for working together on a project. Retaliations to these insults included giving poor evaluations for job applications and painful physical punishment via computer game-settings – aggression that was also targeted at bystanders who had no connection with the acts of exclusion (Twenge et al., 2008).

These laboratory experiments relate analogously to the everyday environments of teachers, who can be expected to interact in classrooms, committees, team projects and extra-curricular functions, and to undergo evaluations from students, colleagues and supervisors. Moreover, teachers give their opinions on hiring, form curricula, make tests, manage classrooms and grade students. Through these avenues, teachers are open to both receiving and administering unfavourable treatment. However, they can take pro-active measures by practising ways of belonging to increase their inclusion within their immediate social environments, prevent the sense of social exclusion from arising and prepare a social network base plus a cognitive, psychological and behavioural readiness for reconnecting socially during hard times.

Forming Pathways of Belonging

Teachers abroad can overcome social exclusion and succeed in forming pathways of belonging. Wenger (1998) provides a theoretical framework of belonging with three mutually constitutive modes that influence our identities and learning: *engagement, imagination* and *alignment*. These modes describe ways interrelationships flow, develop and transform between individuals, between individuals and communities, and between communities, involving interrelationships within and across local and global domains.

Engagement

Engagement refers to a process of ongoing mutual practices that bind people together in time and place. It is the source of shared experiences and histories, and a medium for identities and competencies to manifest. Through concerted action, interpersonal relationships develop, their boundaries are managed and mutual goals are negotiated and embarked upon. Enterprises, visions, lessons and identities become tactile and vivid when intermediated and transformed through engagement – thus more learnable and transcendent on the positive side, although on the negative side more limiting of possibilities and insular of practices. Engagement can be blocked through lack of professional experience, lack of common histories, communication breakdown and toxic environments conducive to incivility (Wenger, 1998).

The JET Programme receives much attention as a potential crossroads of interaction for learning about languages, cultures and identities. It recruits native speakers from abroad, many without formal teacher training, and places them into ALT positions to help JTEs at junior high and high schools across Japan. In 2010, the programme was in its 24th year, and it employed 4334 ALTs from 36 countries (CLAIR, 2010b). Often, ALTs feel disrespect in, and disconnected from, their professional practices (see Geluso, Chapter 6). They report about being partnered with JTEs who provide little direction or cooperative lesson planning; required to make appearances in costumes or otherwise act in silly ways; given the role of 'human tape recorder', meaning they just provide example pronunciation; and given roles to entertain but not educate. When they do get their own chance to teach, usually with communicative language teaching methods, they are not taken seriously (McVeigh, 2002). A former ALT named Mike (Falout et al., 2008: 238 – 239) lamented:

> I remember being made to feel that I wasn't a "real teacher" when I was a high school ALT because I brought my guitar to class, sang with my learners, played and laughed with them. "Just an entertainer," was whispered in the teachers' room; they would get back to the serious business of drilling English after the *Mike Show* left town. I let the whispers bother me, and I put my guitar away years ago.

JTEs might rely on ALTs to motivate students, especially in large classrooms, and they may be aware of the ALTs' plight; however, JTEs may not have the resources to deal with the pressures and complexities they face in their jobs while taking on the additional responsibility to provide professional development to their team-teaching foreign counterparts. As teachers of a foreign language, JTEs may be stigmatized by their colleagues as having foreign ways of behaving that are overly assertive and selfish. School administrators and students' parents pressure them to cram enough information into the students' heads to pass high school and university entrance exams, particularly through a method known as grammar-translation – marked by extensive grammar drills, long vocabulary lists and rote learning – while the Japanese government sets mandates for more use of communicative methods. Meanwhile, with the presence of ALTs in their classrooms, JTEs can feel both their English capabilities and their teaching competence under question (Crooks, 2001; Gorsuch, 2000; McVeigh, 2002).

Considering this intricate system of cross purposes, it is curious to find that the more meaningful professional contact JTEs have with ALTs, the more JTEs seem to appreciate the opportunities to learn together, with greater approval of communicative methods and greater confidence in their own English (Gorsuch, 2002). Many JTEs express an interest in more training for working cooperatively with their partnered ALTs, and although such programmes have been offered, JTEs' schedules are often filled from morning through evening with classes and extra-curricular programme responsibilities. Taking a partial day's leave from work, even for professional training, might mean castigation by colleagues, including senior faculty and administrators: JTEs partnered with ALTs are considered to be already privileged enough, and seeking additional opportunities for educational advancement would be shirking their teaching duties at school (Crooks, 2001).

These reports provide only a glimpse of ways that learning through interactive professional engagement can be hindered for many teachers by lack of time, tact, prudence, understanding, respect and support from colleagues and administration for continuing professional development. Nevertheless, productive professional engagement can be sought by those who exercise their own collaborative agency and creativity to engineer schedules and spaces for interaction.

Recognizing common purposes and similar interests, teachers might cooperate to improve their interrelationships and teaching practices by asking for suggestions about lessons, techniques or problems; opening their classrooms for observational visits or team teaching; arranging workspaces, offices and classrooms in ways that make them linked or adjacent to one another. Information technology might be employed for interacting, such as through online bulletin boards and discussion groups; sharing references and resources, such as web links and educational articles on pdf files; conducting project work on electronic files, such as co-authoring curricula or research papers; and expanding their social networks of like-minded colleagues (Habhab-Rave, 2008).

When unprovoked psychological violence happens at work, it is recognized as bullying (see Rivers, Chapter 5). It encompasses verbal abuse, humiliation, intimidation and threats; typically starting from one perpetrator and potentially escalating into group bullying, known as mobbing. Usually, victims – targets – remain silent, while management, if alerted, becomes an accomplice either passively or actively. Targets can fall ill both psychologically and physically, quit or lose jobs they love, strain and lose relations with friends and family and in extreme cases, turn to murder and suicide (Namie & Namie, 2009).

Vickers (2001), a university teacher daring to share her own story, describes how each perpetration might be passed off by others as inconsequential. But she aggregated and contextualized the incidents into patterns showing relentless, deliberate and directed acts of aggressive abuse. Apart, they appeared seemingly innocuous, petty offences and demands involving the use of a fax machine, a parking space, an office key; then stalling on joint project work, refusing to meet or communicate, speaking offensively in private and public, and through deception and lies, provoking others into becoming unwitting accomplices. With her own documentation and analysis, Vickers eventually helped unveil these ploys as nefarious tactics to induce physical and emotional exhaustion, cause self and public degradation, enforce trivial demands as a means of totalitarian control, and spark feelings of anxiety and despair through threats. Her report prompted a formal investigation leading to the perpetrator's resignation.

Vickers offers first-hand advice for targets of bullies. Record incidents by including date, time, place and potential witnesses. Confirm potential witnesses by checking whether they view events the same way as you do. And most importantly, the earlier you get legal advice, the more likely you can produce a favourable outcome. Legal counsellors outside the organization can provide you with options of how to respond to your particular situation. This may protect you from further damage and keep you out of court.

Equally important is learning how local laws can define, protect and give you recourse from work-based abuse. If you can't read in your host country's language, then perhaps a friend can help you consult a local human rights organization to understand the situation you may be in and find possible solutions. For example, in Japan bullying is known as power harassment and moral harassment, and social support is available at http://www.jinken-net.com/ and http://www.morahara.com/. Here are more suggestions for protecting yourself from bullies (in Falout, 2010: 30; garnered from Kohut, 2008; Lubit, 2004):

(1) Don't blame yourself, blame the bullies – you just happen to be the target at the time;
(2) avoid them – despite appearances, bullies don't have the capacity to empathize or cooperate;
(3) avoid provoking them – bullies excel at setting people up, distorting facts, spreading rumors and manipulating others;
(4) document each act and how it made you feel – not only does this help you vent but you can also analyze the situation more objectively when you are calmer;
(5) don't let them see, hear, or smell your weakness or pain – they feed on it and their attack escalates;
(6) seek friends and allies for support, and for knowing that the school does employ kindhearted people; and
(7) daily cherish your little victories.

In summary, teachers can engage by asking for teaching tips, sharing materials, visiting classrooms, connecting their physical and virtual workspaces, and collaborating on projects. Protection from social aggression is possible, especially by seeking help from your social and legal resources. Figure 7.1 lists more suggestions for engaging.

Imagination

Imagination expands our notions of self, the world and possibilities through creative processes that transcend time and space. Whereas engagement situates inter-subjectivities, imagination relates disparities into broad systems and patterns, and generates connecting outcomes. It provides us with allegories from stories, extrapolations after descriptions and reinterpretations of experiences and events. With imagination, we see new images of ourselves, perspectives from another's point of view and the connections of past, present and future for understanding the continuity of emerging identities of self and communities. Imagination helps us to take risks and explore the exotic, make the meaningless meaningful and try to become someone new. While it can help reify previously inconceivable possibilities, imagination can drift awry toward assumptions, stereotypes and disconnections, misinforming practices that exhibit incompetence and lead to ineffectiveness. Imagination can be blocked by lack of creativity, playfulness, goals, energy, hope, mentors and vicarious experiences; plus bias, stereotypes and preconceptions (Wenger, 1998).

Teachers coming to Japan may have first heard the profession is highly respected in the society, then start picking up on the stereotypes about them that limit their professional roles. They feel viewed as tokens from another-culture world, overlooked as educators with true value, unrecognized as mature people and treated as scapegoats (McVeigh, 2002). It may seem wise to ignore such inappropriate attitudes and try to move on, but their insidious effects can trail you – through co-constructive, subconscious processes of both 'stereotyper' and 'stereotypee', stereotypes become self-fulfilling prophecies. That means despite conscious resistance you can begin to act as you are perceived (Brown, 2000).

Another deleterious stalker of teachers is burnout (Falout *et al.*, 2012). Potter (DiPardo & Potter, 2003) began her short-lived career as the only English teacher for grades 10 – 12 in a primary school of 400 pupils in an impoverished rural area of the US Midwest. She made a turnaround of her students' low self-expectations and soon they were writing for readers outside the school. With a full load of writing classes, plus after-school volleyball coaching, play and musical directing and more, she spent a few years between bouts of depression, headaches and fatigue – classic symptoms of stress – and bursts of effort, organization and palliative strategies such as walks and rest. Her colleagues were empathetic but disengaged. Beginning one new academic year, listless and despondent, Potter quit teaching.

Research suggests teachers who can weather stress and last in the profession had two things early on: hope and a role model (Wilhelm *et al.*, 2000). Role models promote the development of adaptive thinking and behaviours through social learning (Bandura, 1997). Deacon (2003), fresh into Japan and teaching English at a university, sought advice from his colleagues about immediate concerns such as classroom management. His informal queries led to systematic classroom observations in a long-term professional mentorship. Deacon visited his mentor's classes regularly, participated with students, asked them about their learning and took notes in a reflection journal. Following observations, the pair went to lunch for debriefings. No doubt, Deacon also learned in more subtle ways – maybe by envisioning his future possible self (Markus & Nurius, 1986; see Yphantides, Chapter 15) when watching his mentor – about goal-setting, plan implementation, time management, self-conduct and dignity. The mentor himself developed through reflection, articulation and intensification of self-awareness brought about by Deacon's observations and questions.

Groups engender imagination and mentor their members through whole-group interactions. A multi-disciplinary readers and writers' group of teachers at a British university reported their self-apprenticeship (Herrington et al., 2008). By encouraging fluid and permeable boundaries of membership, forming and reforming, sharing individual motivations and energies, they eventually created a safe intellectual and emotional space for challenging, resisting and playing. Individual's learning, identities and lives changed by cross-disciplinary research collaborations that eventually propelled the group's professional activities and identities outside the university. Through their collective imagination, Herrington et al. (2008: 197) formed a space where they could reinvent themselves:

> Some saw it as a physical emptiness, free of things, and into which we could write ourselves but others felt so viscerally in the space that they could not see it as empty. One member discussed it as a space with glimmers and flashes; one as a home ground space from which the routes to the bigger discourse were created; and one as a refuge. Some did not see it spatially at all, rather as about lack of constraint, unmonitored cognitive freedom and intellectual stimulus.

In short, interacting with other people gives you the stimulus for expanding your imagination. Get connected with people outside of your discipline or organization. Seek their wisdom and be prepared to connect emotionally. Figure 7.1 contains more suggestions for nurturing your imagination.

Alignment

Alignment combines energies from smaller parts into larger unifications within social systems. Imagination helps us to see how all the parts fit and alignment assembles the parts into a broad framework. Alignment allows the care to direct and manage personal energies into coordinated systems, styles and discourses – through a shared ethos, ideal and affinity – to change the environments around us. When we join forces with something larger than us, we sense an increase in power and purpose. Alignment occurs through giving and following prompts or commands, defining procedures, communicating needs and proposing criteria. It is superlative when inspiring and morbid when stealing our agency via coercions, confrontations, corruptions and literal interpretations, violating our investments and damaging our identities. Alignment can be blocked by lack of shared languages, discourses and values; lack of compliance and persuasion; and dis-identification (Wenger, 1998).

The only expatriate teacher in a department at a Japanese university fell out of favor after a newcomer began a smear campaign based on lies. Any discrepancy between the expatriate and the faculty brought scrutiny. Changes were made in her work conditions, both official and covert, including the tapping of her office phone. In the end, she out-survived her conniving colleague, who resigned in shame, with a few basic strategies. First, she withheld from defensive behavior that might foment the situation. Then, she developed relationships with various colleagues and sought advice from different sources. And finally, she made every effort to mirror and exemplify, as could be understood within that specific sociocultural environment, the most conscientious work behaviours. For instance, teachers weren't required to be on campus when out of class, but she stayed at her desk, working diligently (Wordell, 1993). Abiding by implicit norms, passing other's unspoken judgements, detecting the social vibe and entering its flow – alignment goes beyond using a book of rules.

At another Japanese university, Murphey (2004) attained a tenured full professorship before he was required to do something against his morals: chair the entrance exam committee (see Toh, Chapter 13). He could accept the responsibility if he were allowed to ameliorate the unfairness of his university's entrance exams. The statistical evidence indicated how its exams unreliably measured the English abilities of the exam takers, whose futures were at stake. Murphey's suggestions included changing part of the exam in a way that might beneficially influence the educational system at large. However, his superiors were unwilling to improve the unsound construction and unfair use of the exams. Murphey concluded, 'I would not feel healthy, happy, or sane working under those conditions, and I did not want a long disagreeable fight. So I sent a letter of resignation' (Murphey, 2004: 705). Teachers may need to opt out of aligning altogether to preserve their values.

To summarize, aligning can mean conforming to both explicit and tacit social rules and cultural norms. And it goes deeper, finding a lifestyle that is compatible with your well-being and that of others within your work environment. Figure 7.1 below suggests more for aligning.

Figure 7.1 Forming pathways of belonging

Conclusions

Teachers abroad may be at risk of not fulfilling the fundamental psychological need of frequent contact with several people in ongoing relationships of mutual care. When feeling socially excluded, most cognitive, emotional and behavioural reactions that arise exacerbate social withdrawals, lead to wider detachments and block formation of potential alliances. But it is worth remembering that from the need to belong, people of every nation and culture are motivated to connect with others. This motivation is both spontaneous and powerful. It operates without precondition, ulterior motive, or material advantage, and can pre-empt opposing motivations that exclude individuals from out-groups (Baumeister et al., 2007). Teachers abroad can take pro-active advantage of this. Engaging, imagining and aligning form co-constructive means to gain and maintain the social relations you need to thrive, learn about local cultures, make friends and contribute to mutual understandings, appreciation and acceptance among people across the world.

Acknowledgement

Special thanks to Tim Murphey for comments on an earlier draft of this chapter.

Part 3

Employment Policies and Patterns in Japanese Tertiary and Secondary Education

8 Communicative English in Japan and 'Native Speakers of English'

Ryoko Tsuneyoshi

Introduction

Various attempts have been made to enhance the English communication skills of Japanese in recent decades. Various reforms were introduced to this end, such as English activities in elementary school, the establishment of English medium courses at the higher education level and the introduction of listening comprehension in the Center Exams (*senta shiken*) at the university entrance examination level (Erikawa, 2011; Tsuneyoshi, 2005). Communicative English is seen as moving away from a reliance on grammar and translation to acquiring English which is usable in the real-world context. The key term in this discourse has been 'communication', a term that emphasizes using English as a tool to express oneself, to understand others and to gather and convey information. The Japanese version of communicative English has emphasized speaking and listening. Given that becoming competent in oral English communication involves interactive situations in which English is used, this has created an increased demand for the so-called 'native speakers of English'.

For example, 'communication' is now explicitly part of both the secondary school English language curriculum and the goals of the elementary school foreign language (English) activities introduced with the 2002 revisions to the *Course of Study* (i.e. the national curriculum), and which is required for fifth and sixth grades (aged 10 – 11 and 11 – 12, respectively) starting from the year 2011. Foreign (English) language activities in elementary school were to develop a foundation in 'communication' abilities (MEXT, 2008a: 1). The revisions to the secondary school Course of Study in 1989 added the word 'communication' to the foreign language education goals (MEXT, 1989).

Such reforms worked against the widely held belief about Japanese that although they have studied English for years, they are not able to use it as a tool of communication (MEXT, 2002, 2003).

What is ironic about this communicative English focus, especially oral focus, however, is that English is a language that is used in daily life neither by the Japanese nor by any of its major cultural minorities, such as the Koreans and Chinese. In other words, it is not a language that is actually necessary for daily 'communication'.

Being a colonizer, Japan has never been colonized by a foreign power, though it experienced a period of occupation by the United States and others after World War II; even then, English was never forced upon the public. Thus, Japan's language situation is very different from, for example, South East Asian countries in which a colonial power (or powers) of the west left relics of its (their) domination, such as language, even after the colonized country had won its independence (Gopinathan et al., 2004).

The descendants of Korean and Chinese in Japan who reside in Japan because of Japan's colonial policies are now in their fourth and later generations, and under pressure to assimilate, Japanese is their everyday language. As for more recent inflows into Japan (e.g. foreign labourers), their mother tongue is not English. The mother tongue of (public school) students of Japanese as a Second Language are Portuguese 9477 children (33.2%), Chinese 6154 (21.6%), Filipino 4350 (15.3%) and Spanish 3547 (12.4%), constituting over 80% of the total number of the JSL students; English native speakers were a mere 717 (2.5%) in 2010 (MEXT, 2011a). Therefore, if using a foreign language was emphasized as a tool of 'communication' with foreign language speakers *within* Japan, the natural choices would be Portuguese, Chinese, Spanish, Filipino and, adding the language of the old-comers, Korean – not English.

Thus, we are faced with the paradox that though English has little to do with everyday life, it is linked to 'internationalization' and occupies a special position relative to other languages in Japan as an exam and school subject, the language of the global economy, the global science and the international community at large.

Thus put, the function of communicative English is twofold in Japan. First, there are those who actually need it because they are at the forefront of contact with the outside world where English is largely used as the language of communication (e.g. business persons sent abroad, international athletes, tour guides, etc.). I will call these 'needs-driven' English learners. For this population, there is a real need to use English as a tool of communication.

Second, there are those for whom English communication is in effect unnecessary for the large part, but the need to use English, mostly English reading comprehension, translation and grammar, arises in certain areas at a certain stage of life. These constitute the majority of the Japanese population. For the majority of Japanese, the 'real' need for English arises as a school subject in junior and high school, entrance examination subject for high school and college, and for some in college classes, and then largely disappears.

Though the entrance examinations for high school and higher education have moved somewhat toward emphasizing usable English like material from the internet, or less emphasis on grammatical questions, the usual requirements to pass the examination are still to read passages in English and to answer questions in a limited amount of time, to translate into Japanese and answer grammatical questions. In some instances, English listening skills, like conversation and short passages, are tested. However, the tests are still predominantly written comprehension and grammar based rather than hearing or writing based, and speaking is nonexistent. Thus, 'native English language teachers' find themselves teaching the so-called language of 'internationalization' in a context in which communicative English is emphasized in principle, but is not really an immediate necessity for the majority of Japanese.

This chapter will focus on two illustrative examples at the top and bottom of the English language education link in Japanese education: the foreign language (English) activities at the elementary school level and English in the higher education context. For the latter, I use the case of the University of Tokyo. Between these two points is English as a subject in secondary school.

By focusing on communicative English and the role of the so-called 'native speakers of English' in two contexts at opposite ends of the educational pole, this chapter tries to contextualize some of the themes advanced in this volume.

This chapter argues that the context, especially the framework within which the 'native speakers of English' is positioned in an organization, is crucial to understanding how they are perceived. Here, I focus specifically on the case of English activities in which 'native speakers of English' tend to be seen as representatives of both the English language and their 'foreign' national culture, and the case of higher education, which illustrates that 'native speakers of English' may or may not be identified with culture, depending on their positioning in the organization. When the 'English native speaker' is seen as both the representative of language and the representative of language culture, this invites native-speakerism which is understood here as 'a pervasive ideology within ELT, characterized by the belief that "native speaker" teachers represent a "Western culture" from which spring the ideals both of the English language and of English language teaching methodology' (Holliday, 2006: 385).

English Activities: 'Native Speakers of English' as Bearers of English and Culture

First, the chapter will focus on the case of English activities at the elementary school level. Here, I argue that though there may be commonalities that transcend specific contexts, the context is crucial in how 'native speakers of English' are understood. I specifically focus on how language and culture are nearly identified in the definitions of elementary school English activities in Japan, thus defining the role of 'native speakers of English' as agents of both the English language and of a foreign culture in international understanding. Later, I take the example of a highly research-oriented university, where this definition is applied to part of the foreign faculty, but not to others. Where and how the 'native speaker of English' is positioned is crucial to understanding the different definitions of who that person is. Both cases point to the need to contextualize.

Now, the Japanese government definition of elementary school foreign language (English) activities is very clearly orally communicative; speaking and listening, not writing and reading, are emphasized. According to the new *Course of Study*, the goal of foreign (English) language activities is defined as follows:

> To form the foundation of pupils' communication abilities through foreign languages while developing the understanding of languages and cultures through various experiences, fostering a positive attitude toward communication, and familiarizing pupils with the sounds and basic expressions of foreign languages. (MEXT, 2011b)

It is assumed that pupils should engage in communication in a foreign language and acquire cultural understanding simultaneously.

English activities in elementary schools gained momentum with the 2002 revisions to the *Course of Study* when the period of integrated studies was established as an interdisciplinary period. The period was to provide self-initiated, 21st-century types of activities such as international understanding, information, environment and welfare/health, which could not be contained in a single existing subject. The *Course of Study* mentioned that 'foreign language conversation etc.' could be brought in as part of international understanding during this period (MEXT, 1998), which led to the emergence of language (English) activities as we see it today. From 2011, a period for foreign language activities is provided for fifth and sixth graders.

'Foreign' language was basically identified with 'English' language, this in itself being a problematic slippage, and elementary school English activities, consisting of, for example, songs and games to 'get used to' (*shitashimu*) English, hands-on activities to acquaint the child with English and foreign cultures and simple conversation/pronunciation, spread across the nation.

There is a clear reliance on the Assistant Language Teacher, the ALT, who is seen as the agent of the above-stated goals of the activities (MEXT, 2008b). In a Benesse survey, over 60% of classroom teachers answered that the ALT was the main figure in these activities (Benesse, 2006). It is useful to note that a teacher's certificate is not required to become an ALT, and yet the ALT is positioned as an agent of English communication and 'foreign' culture in these activities. Indeed, the present situation in which Japanese elementary school teachers do not have a certificate in English teaching, and can rarely manage communicative English, almost necessitates ALTs to assume a major role. In addition, the framework of introducing language (essentially English) as part of 'international understanding' (*kokusai rikai*), not English as a subject in the *Course of Study*, advances the view that 'native speakers of English' are representatives of both English and their 'foreign' national culture.

'Native speakers of English' are often referred to as simply 'native speakers', since the dominance of English in these activities and the society at large is given, which in itself is a notable slippage. Advancing communicative English is important since

> ... it is a good opportunity to learn living (*ikita*) English and to become acquainted with foreign languages and foreign culture, etc., and to feel a sense of accomplishment that one's English was understandable to a native speaker, and thus become more motivated to learn English... (MEXT, 2003: 5)

There are more issues here. First of all, the meaning of 'native speaker' is not uniform and subject to controversy (Davies, 2003). The 'native English speaker' in the above-stated context is someone who bears a 'foreign' culture and who has fluency in English. One can further venture to say that the term 'native' implies that fluency is associated with the fact that English is the person's first language or mother tongue. Since Japanese government documents often use the words 'foreigner' to imply 'a native speaker of a foreign (in this context English) language', the ideal image of the 'native (English) speaker' in this context is someone who grew up in and comes from a foreign country in which English is the dominant language. The government action plan for developing 'Japanese who can use English, in elementary school English activities' recommended that foreign teachers, someone fluent in English, or junior high school English teachers, be utilized about one third of the time (MEXT, 2003: 11).

Second, placing English activities under the framework of international understanding has the danger of promoting the very biases, such as favouring English-speaking cultures, that education for international understanding should be critical of.

For the purpose of international understanding, one does not have to be a 'native speaker' of English. Indeed, an identification of the 'native speaker' with 'native speakers of English' with being foreign, and assuming that the 'foreigner' is someone from abroad, primarily from an English-speaking country, excludes the long-existing 'foreigners' within Japan such as the Koreans in Japan, and is in itself problematic from the perspective of international understanding.

In summary, the focus of elementary school English activities emphasizes communicative English, especially speaking, listening and experiencing within an international understanding framework. Thus, the period emphasizes both an exposure to English and an exposure to a 'foreign culture', especially through the ALT. Since language is basically identified with English, by definition the ALT is in most cases an AET, who is seen as representing both the English language and a 'foreign' culture.

English Activities and Minorities in Japan: Issues of Language and Power

As was seen in the previous section, the present definition of English activities almost necessitates the AET to assume a double role as an assistant English language teacher and a carrier of a 'foreign' national culture. This framework also gives a clear advantage to people from English-speaking countries. For example, the JET Programme plays a major role in providing ALTs to Japanese secondary and elementary school classrooms (CLAIR, 2010a; Tsuido, 2007). Though JET Programme participants came from 36 countries in 2010 – 2011, with the vast majority operating as AETs, there is an overrepresentation of speakers from the United States of America, the United Kingdom, Australia, New Zealand and Canada (constituting 86.5% of nationalities), and countries where English is the official language or daily language (CLAIR, 2010b).

Another example can be found in district A in the southern Kanto area, a district with a strong ethnic movement, where the author of this chapter was the adviser for international (understanding) education for the district education centre from 1997 – 2002. As elementary schools started to introduce English activities as international understanding, they started to ask not only for 'foreigners' but also for foreigners who can speak in

English. For example, Latin Americans who had served as guest speakers in the schools mentioned that more and more schools asked for foreigners who could speak in English, which excluded them (Tsuneyoshi, 2010). There was a naiveté on the part of the school teachers in that they did not realize that by emphasizing English as a requisite for a guest speaker to introduce a 'foreign' culture, they were in effect sending a very skewed message from the perspective of international understanding: that foreigners from English-speaking countries (e.g. the United States, the United Kingdom and Australia) and, secondarily, from former colonies of English-speaking countries were preferred.

The dominance of English in the international society and in Japan relative to other languages is behind this (Tsuda, 1990); the fact that the activities are justified on the grounds of introducing a 'foreign' culture, not just language, helps to justify the advantage of English. Here, we see how the identification of foreign language with English with culture, in effect, works to exclude the colonized populations such as the Koreans in Japan.

Native English Language Teachers in Higher Education

The case of English activities (*eigo katsudo*) in elementary school provided a case in point in how the definition of the role of the 'native speakers of English', in this case the near identification of language, English, and 'foreign' culture, could lead to a preference to 'native foreigners from English-speaking countries'. In this section, I will approach the question from the other end that originates from the higher education level and moves down. Traditionally, this line of English education has emphasized grammar and reading comprehension, with little focus on communicative skills. In recent years, there have been more attempts to strengthen communicative English at this level as well. Here, I will focus on the two popular methods, using English as a medium of instruction and increasing 'foreign faculty'.

Establishing courses in English to 'internationalize' Japanese higher education has repeatedly been advanced by the government, such as the establishment of English-medium short-term exchange programmes in the mid-1990s, under the auspices of the Association of International Education, Japan (AIEJ, Nihon Kokusai Kyouiku Kyoukai; Tsuneyoshi, 2005) and the more recent project for establishing core universities for internationalization (Global 30). The latter contained the requirement that candidates were to establish courses in which students could graduate taking lectures in English and to increase 'foreign' faculty members.

Well-known private colleges or departments at the undergraduate level now offer English courses in humanities and social sciences (e.g. Waseda University, Sophia University, etc.). All of these universities use strategically English medium courses, opportunities to study abroad and the high percentage of foreign students and/or foreign faculty members to appeal its 'international' nature for marketing. On the other hand, national universities tend to be at the other end with an emphasis on graduate school and research. A case in point is the University of Tokyo.

The University of Tokyo Case

Overview

The following is the case of the University of Tokyo, which can be seen as a case in point in examining how the positioning of 'native speakers of English' relates to their role. The case calls for the need to contextualize.

The University of Tokyo has one of the largest numbers of foreign students in Japan, totalling 2966 in the year 2011. The majority of students are from Asia (82.0% of the foreign student body), 90.7% are at the graduate school level and are thus academically advanced (The University of Tokyo, 2011a).

English is acknowledged as a means of 'internationalization' in official university statements. In its action plan for the presidency that started in 2009, one of the means to realize a 'global campus' is to increase the number of courses in which students can earn degrees taking lectures in English (The University of Tokyo, 2010a). The strong position of English relative to other languages as a 'common language' can be identified here, as is the case in the elementary English activities, language education in secondary school, and in the entrance examinations.

The divided functions of foreign faculty

When looking at the figures for foreign faculty at the University of Tokyo, there is a trend. Many of the foreign faculty are specially appointed researchers (*tokutei yuki*), often hired for a certain purpose (e.g. participating in a certain project) and on a limited term. Many are of Asian nationalities and junior researchers (The University of Tokyo, 2004).

The following categories constitute the research staff: professor (*kyouju*), associate professor (*junkyouju*), lecturer (*koushi*), assistant professor (*jokyou*), research associate (*joshu*) plus the category of specially appointed research fellows, and foreign research fellows. In 2010, there were 3764 persons in the 'researcher' category at the university excluding research associates,

Table 8.1 Foreign researchers by selected departments at the University of Tokyo (2007)

	Full-time*	Specially appointed (tokutei yuki)	Total**
Law	1	2	3 (2%)
Economics	3	8	11 (8%)
Arts and Sciences	23	9	32 (7%)
Frontier Sciences	4	15	19 (6%)
Medicine	13	17	30 (3%)
Engineering	11	42	53 (8%)

Notes:
* Foreign full-time researchers (*seiki*) faculty include professorship, associate, assistant professor, assistant (*jokyou, joshu*) and research fellow (*kenkyuin*). and foreign teacher (*gaikokujin kyoushi*).
** The total number of the categories of foreign researchers above, and the percentage within the total faculty of the department.

Source: The University of Tokyo (2010b)

and 2.3% were of foreign nationality. In contrast, if we take those 'specially appointed', there were 1761 (excluding one foreign fellow) faculty in 2010 of whom 16% were foreign nationals, the majority of foreigners, 77.3%, are specially appointed (*tokunin*). The geographical areas from which this faculty come most are Asia (especially China and Korea), constituting 56.1% of foreign research staff, North America (12.8%) and Europe (24.6%). Just two nationalities, Chinese and Korean, make up 42.2% of the total (The University of Tokyo, 2010c: 1). Official figures including all foreign faculty of whatever category show 100 full-time, and 245 specially appointed, resulting in 6% of the total faculty (The University of Tokyo, 2010b: 407).

Engineering, a highly globalized area, is a case in point. Most (31) foreign researchers in the field are categorized as 'research fellows etc.' (*kenkyuin nado*), 13 are assistants (*jokyou*, of which eight are specially appointed), indicating the project-based nature of foreign researchers' employment. On the other hand, the department received a total of 404 visiting researchers in 2006, indicating that there is an active flow of foreign visitors (The University of Tokyo, 2010b: 47).

The division of liberal arts in this university is obviously the exception in its high rate of full-time foreign faculty. This is because it provides the first two years of language education at the university. In the liberal arts division, 23 of the 32 foreign faculty members are professors or associate professors, mostly operating as language teachers. The regions of origin reflect the languages taught: 8 Asian, 16 European, 5 North American, 2 Oceanian, and 1 Latin American (The University of Tokyo, 2010b: 147). Thus, when we focus on foreign English language teachers, we are talking about a very small minority within the total faculty, and a segment in the language faculty.

It is thus easy to predict the situation that would arise in this kind of placement of native language teachers. Foreign visiting scholars come frequently, invited or supported by university faculty as researchers. They would be linked to projects, to their collaborators in Japan, or might be 'distinguished' visitors. If they are known scholars in their field, they would give presentations at the university, often with an interpreter. These scholars are identified for their research, not for their language; in fact, language may be an obstacle in attracting an audience since the Japanese audience would have difficulty understanding the content.

As can be seen above, there are some full-time foreign faculty within the university, especially as language teachers, but most others are 'specially appointed' researchers hired for a specific purpose and for a fixed term. The 'native speakers of English' operating as language teachers are concentrated in the liberal arts division and are part of a body of various language specialists. Given their small numbers, it is natural that any of the foreign language faculty would be held as representatives not only of their language but also of their country and national culture. It is this population that is likely to be the object of 'native-speakerism' discussed in this book. The division of labor between 'native speakers of English' and Japanese faculty is rooted in the native speaker's advantage in communicative English (e.g. speaking fluently, writing naturally, etc.) and familiarity of a 'foreign' country.

Discipline-based Positioning

In addition to the differentiation of roles between the 'native speakers of English' and the Japanese, a major axis of differentiation, this time among the foreign faculty, is whether one's role is language based or discipline based. An example is the set of courses targeting science majors. The undergraduate science majors are identified as a special group since they require 'needs-driven' English. For this population, the liberal arts division offers communicative English called the 'Active Learning of English for Science Students' (ALESS) (The University of Tokyo, 2011b). Here, 'native speakers of English' are defined differently from the AETs in the English activities in elementary school; the 'native English speakers' are not carriers of English language identified with a 'foreign' culture, but transmitters of the strategies to survive in an English-dominated international science community. Indeed, the international standard of presentation at conferences, the format of writing articles in English, for example, may be a Euro-American standard, but it has become a 'world standard', a reflection

Table 8.2 Number of courses in English at the University of Tokyo (2006–2007)

Law	5 (graduate/professional level)
Economics	17 (6 at undergraduate level and 11 at graduate level)
Arts and Sciences	58 (31 at undergraduate level and 27 at graduate level)
Frontier Sciences	50 (at graduate level)
Medicine	16 (at graduate level)
Engineering	152 (majority at graduate level, 14 at undergraduate level and 3 for foreign students only)

Note:
The variety of foreign language education is a major characteristic of the arts and sciences division, and also leads to the need for native speakers of various languages (see numbers of foreign faculty). In addition, the large number of courses in English for undergraduates is a reflection of the English-medium exchange programme at this department, and the department's focus on undergraduate education. Some courses above may mix Japanese and English.

Source: The University of Tokyo (2010b)

of the global English/cultural domination of English-speaking countries. However, unlike in the elementary school English activities, native-speakerism is not built into the definition of the role of the 'native speakers of English', and is somewhat different from the language teachers in the general education courses since there is a stronger focus on method. Here, we see a variation in the theme of 'native-speakerism'.

Another example is the specialized courses in English. According to Table 8.2, courses using English as a medium of instruction are provided mostly in the science departments at the graduate school level. These same departments provide lectures in English for academic writing in their specific fields, since the research areas are 'internationalized' and using English is required to present and publish in competitive journals. Here, we see how Japan, as a country using a minority language in the world, is led to compete in English in areas that are globalized (Altbach, 2004; Altbach, 2005; Crystal, 1997; Tsuda, 1990).

We can see clearly that the English medium lectures target what I called the 'needs-driven' learners of English, graduate school science students who must use English to publish and present their findings to the world. Only the College of Arts and Sciences has general foreign language education.

Thus, these English medium courses are purpose-specific, acquainting students with area-specific science English language skills (Tanaka, 2007), rather than the more general English language teaching that has traditionally been the norm in general education. For example, the Department of Frontier Science (*sentankagaku*) has a large number of courses in English in the sciences. According to a press release of one of its programmes, it notes that it has pioneered the type of internationalization strategies that are outlined in the government plan to increase the number of foreign students. In the past, English lectures by foreign staff were used in Japan to quickly absorb (and imitate) western knowledge (Erikawa, 2008).

However, as seen in the previous section on the numbers of foreign faculty members hired (about 6% of total), it is the Japanese scientists that are teaching academic content in English at the graduate school level, not 'native speakers of English'. Thus, the role of 'native speakers of English' weakens as their positioning calls for a more discipline-based role in the organization. Moreover, hiring foreign faculty in regular positions assumes that they fulfil the 'regular' chores accompanying the 'regular' faculty position in the university. However, committees in most departments use Japanese, and the committee material is often written in formal bureaucratic language. There is also a lack of secretarial support staff in comparison to the leading Western universities (The University of Tokyo, 2009: 1).

For foreign faculty members to operate as full faculty members in this sense, they would have to have high Japanese reading skills and be willing to sit in on hours of committee work. According to a 2008 survey by the university's Division of International Affairs of the foreign scholars at the university, the largest work-related obstacle mentioned was the Japanese language-centred environment (Funamori, 2009: 65). The positioning of foreign faculty members would most likely change considerably if, for example, English was a medium of committee work, materials were bilingual, the number of committees was limited or if teaching was the main job content.

Conclusions

In this chapter, I have examined the Japanese version of communicative English and the role of 'native speakers of English' from two different ends; from the very communication-oriented elementary school English activities; and from the specialized end of higher education using the case of one of the most research-oriented university in Japan.

Both indicate that the framework of the way in which the 'native speakers of English' is defined and positioned influences the manifestation of how the speaker is understood. The case of English activities nearly identifies language with culture, and its definition basically invites the application of native-speakerism. The case of the university implied that depending on the positioning of the 'native speakers of English', there were variations to the theme. English activities provided an example of a very naïve understanding of language and culture, which in effect could work to disadvantage the colonized populations in Japan in preference of those from English-speaking countries. The very fact that culture and language can be so identified is in itself an indication of the language situation in Japan. English activities emphasized attitude, getting 'used to' English and interacting with the ALT. If communicative English was immediately necessary in daily life, such a mild approach to acquiring English competency would probably be regarded as too weak.

On the other extreme was the case of the University of Tokyo. There, we find a population whose needs are not fully met by the conventional general language education. The English medium courses there pointed to the requirements of the 'needs-driven' English learners. These students faced a special need to acquire field-specific English in order to meet the demands of their globalized fields (Tsuneyoshi, 2005). Members of the teaching staff are predominantly Japanese, seen qualified to teach the English-medium courses because of their competence in a particular field, not for their 'native' language skills.

I have used the above-stated examples to examine the issue of communicative English and 'native speakers of English' in varying educational contexts. It is possible to see commonalities, but the role of 'native speakers of English', how they are situated and the need of those being taught produce vital variations. Educational reform needs to address both such contexualized factors and the common currents.

9 Hiring Criteria for Japanese University English-Teaching Faculty

Blake E. Hayes

Introduction

Japanese universities have been described as attractive to foreign academics. Teaching conditions, working conditions, salary and the seniority system have been identified as some of the reasons (Yonezawa, 2009a). Visiting professors and invited professors may feel like they are treated well and are respected (Lie, 2001), but it may be less rosy for those who are building their careers while in Japan. Tensions have surfaced in the ELT labour market that is dichotomized as Japanese/non-Japanese. When it comes to the right to employment, the stakes are high, and conflict between dominant and non-dominant cultures inevitably has emerged.

In addition, conflict may arise that is related to what native speaker status supplies and what it demands, and the question of *who* has the right to ELT employment has been widely theorized both explicitly and implicitly (Holliday, 2005a; Kachru, 1992; Kubota, 2002a). The study described in this chapter confirmed anecdotal evidence of structural labour market constraints that ghettoize foreign teachers into non-standard employment due to the lack of pipelines to standard employment. Ideological constraints related to nationality, race, gender and native speaker status also surfaced. Such structural and ideological factors conferred disparate benefits and constraints.

The Japanese university labour market provides an interesting context of a non-English dominant country with strong national pride that may make it less prone to the 'colonizing' ideologies that have been assumed in much of the critical theory analysis of ELT. Lack of agency in determining the trajectory of English education can hardly be assumed, and the historical processes that have contributed to English hegemony have been tempered by Japanese national and regional educational policies of MEXT. The qualitative study described in this chapter explored the hiring processes in Japanese universities for ELTs, and examined the benefits and constraints in relation to career opportunities for those from inside and outside the dominant culture.

Employment terminology contrasts standard (tenured, lifetime employment) with non-standard (limited term contracts and part-time employment). Part-time positions were usually filled through networking and résumés being sent in for approval. For contracts and standard employment, the hiring process was more formalized, though rarely entailed more than résumé and publication scrutiny, a short interview process and sometimes a quick model lesson, all assessed by appointed committees of faculty. Reliance on proxies was paramount due to time management concerns.

It can be problematic when supply skills are conflated with demand requirements (Tahlin, 2006). Supply-side skill sets are what teachers offer as potential candidates. Skills required by those who are hiring are demand-side skills. Proxies, with all their inherent inaccuracies and generalizations, are commonly used to determine candidates' expertise and these included formal qualifications and publications, native speaker status as well as Japanese nationality, which was an implicit proxy for Japanese language and cultural competence. By clearly defining demand-side skills of the ELT labour market, a coherent analysis of the right to employment can avoid conflating supply and demand.

The Japanese Context

The need for foreign academics and their ability to contribute their international academic knowledge to Japan has a historical base. Japan, like most countries, has had foreign influences on its educational systems, and from the Meiji era, international knowledge and expertise have been embraced. The need for non-Japanese to teach languages has 'ebbed and flowed' and English has been proposed more than once as a national language – in the Meiji era due to the many dialects and inability to communicate across regions (Lie, 2001) – and more recently, to enhance international communication.

Non-Japanese have a higher representation as teachers in universities than their percentage in the Japanese population in general. Foreign university teachers (not including part-time, research fellows and post-doctorates) were 3.5% of all full-time university faculty members (MEXT School Basic Survey, 2008, cited in Yonezawa, 2009a), though no information is available indicating either the number of tenured versus limited term contracts or the numbers of foreign part-time ELTs. Yonezawa (2009a) found that approximately 38% of foreign teachers were citizens of the Organisation for Economic Cooperation and Development (OECD) countries that have predominantly English-speaking populations. His research did not specifically demarcate ELTs, but half the foreign teachers from

OECD countries were found in the categories of linguistics, education or area studies (the United States, 50.0%; the United Kingdom, 48%; other OECD countries including Singapore, 50%). The remainder were mostly in humanities and social science, which is where ELTs might also be, including those teaching content *in* English. However, not all of those from OECD countries who are teaching in these fields would consider themselves to be ELTs. Nevertheless, extrapolating from the above, full-time non-Japanese teachers in ELT-related teaching would be approximately 27% of all full-time non-Japanese university teachers. This researcher estimates there were roughly 1600 non-Japanese ELTs in full-time employment, either tenured or limited term, throughout Japan (no data was available on the large population of part-time ELTs).

There are no official statistics on the number of non-Japanese women ELTs. Overall, women were only 19% of university teachers nationally (MEXT, 2009b). Yonezawa (2009a; personal communication, 11 March 2010) found that of those who taught social science and humanities or language-related subjects (linguistics, education and area studies), Japanese women were approximately 28% and non-Japanese women were 29%, compared to 72% and 71%, respectively, for Japanese and non-Japanese men. A recent survey of 192 non-Japanese women in Japan found that for those teaching in higher education, 74.6% were in non-standard employment and 25.3% in standard employment (D. Nagatomo, personal communication, 11 January 2011). A quick survey of faculty profiles of ELTs from university web pages combined with information from published and internal university documents found that non-Japanese women were roughly 11% of full-time non-Japanese ELTs, with the majority in limited term contracts. Extrapolating from the above broad range, this researcher estimated the number of non-Japanese women ELTs in full-time employment (mostly limited term contracts and some tenured) to be between 175 and 470 out of the approximately 1600 non-Japanese full-time ELTs.

Age-dependent causal mechanisms are a central determinant in Japanese labour markets that keep women out of the workforce once linear career paths have been interrupted. Since women accrue no human capital when their careers are interrupted due to strong societal pressures (child care, elder care, accepting peripheral employment), they will rarely be the 'best candidate' in the hiring process where success depends on having the time, for example, to publish and attend conferences. The exclusion of non-paid labour in socially constructed skill sets is not the only glass ceiling. Cook and Waters (1998) argued the requirement of an uninterrupted linear career is also a glass ceiling. Charles and Grusky (2004) found the intersection of gender and age is a lethal combination for women who have had interruptions in their careers and the United Nations has warned Japan that this practice is a form of indirect discrimination against women (S. Koedo, personal communication, 7 October 2007).

Skill Set Assessment: Supply versus Demand

The job search process is competitive, and therefore potential candidates' self-assessments will emphasize the positive, sometimes at the expense of reality. Skill-set evaluation through self-assessment is 'subject to considerable social esteem biases, and also to measurement error if people are unable to judge for themselves how good they are' (Felstead et al., 2007: 8). Supply-side skill-set evaluation for job candidates would be complex and extremely time consuming, so proxies are used instead; however, accredited qualifications or length of education are only somewhat objective measures of skill sets. Using 'educational attainment as a measure of job skills' is problematic because it is only a loose measure of actual workplace skills (Felstead et al., 2007: 7).

Relying on qualifications to determine candidates' skills is specious, even though 'qualification is perhaps the widest used proxy for both skills and knowledge' (Warhurst & Thompson, 2008: 791). For expertise, degrees and publications were used as proxies, but they were also used as proxies for, and sometimes prioritized over, one's teaching expertise. In the aggregate, there is a correlation between accredited qualifications and actual skills (Felstead & Gallie, 2002), and this somewhat supports their use. However, it is evident that expertise as reflected in degrees and publications is a fairly weak predictor of whether someone is a competent, skilled teacher, and it is no predictor of administrative competence or one's potential. Another weakness of using formal qualifications as a proxy for determining individual skill levels is its gender bias. Felstead (n.d.) argued that formal qualifications are the last bastion of male privilege.

Critical theory has challenged both the definition and the primacy of skills attributed to native speakers, problematizing the use of the term native speaker as a proxy for supply-side skills. Felstead et al. (2007: 6) stated that skills are socially constructed, are not static and are contestable. Attempts continue to be made to redefine and realign job skill demand (skill requirements of the job) and skill supply (educational and expertise attainment), to counteract the inaccurate assumptions of proxies. At the same time, Japaneseness was found to be used as a proxy for Japanese language skills, administrative skills, as well as local cultural knowledge, empathy with students and being a role model. The problem of essentialism arose for both proxies of Japaneseness and native speaker status.

Methodology

Snowball sampling was used to interview 24 full-time faculty members: 12 Japanese and 12 non-Japanese, 13 women and 11 men who have been in hiring positions in the Kansai area. Unstructured interviews were conducted, transcribed and analysed. Anonymity was ensured and was especially important as participants expressed concern because the hiring process is quite secretive, thus pseudonyms have been used in the data presented here.

All participants were from universities that had programmes with a strong English component, and all were involved in hiring for both Japanese taught and non-Japanese taught positions. Without exception, all non-Japanese interviewees had been the *sole* non-Japanese when hiring for standard employment, and often the *main* faculty member involved in hiring non-Japanese for non-standard positions, usually in consultation with Japanese faculty members.

Results and Discussion

Three dichotomies emerged in describing recruitment and hiring: Japanese/non-Japanese, Japanese/foreigner and Japanese/native speaker. These three bifurcations contrasted Japaneseness with 'otherness'. It is significant that the dualism used in much of the critical theory literature on native speakerism – native speaker/non-native speaker – was not used, and native speakers of Japanese ELTs were never referred to as non-native speakers of English but rather simply as Japanese. Lie (2001: 147) wrote, 'When I asked about what kind of people live in Japan, almost everyone answered by dividing people into Japanese (*nihonjin*) and non-Japanese (*gaijin*)' and he argued that Japaneseness is a conflation of race, ethnicity and nationality. The terminology that emerged in this research substantiated this, positioning those who were not Japanese as 'other', suggesting fundamentally racialized hiring practices. Some points of comparison are presented in Tables 9.1-9.3.

Non-Japanese ELTs: Benefits and constraints

One benefit mentioned by interviewees for non-standard employment was that formal qualification requirements might be relaxed in lieu of native speaker status. Apart from the assumed language skill expertise that is attributed to those with native speaker status, there was value placed on the diversity that would be added to a department by having non-Japanese teachers. In general, a master's degree in any subject would be sufficient, though there has been a recent trend towards also requiring publications for part-time teaching. These less stringent requirements

Table 9.1 Benefits and constraints for Japanese in the hiring process

	Benefits	Constraints
Japanese (see Table 9.3 for further racialized and gendered constraints)	Conflation of nationality with administrative competence and assumed smooth adjustment to corporate culture (S) More positions allocated to Japanese (S) Focus on passive language skills (S and N) Speaking skills not prominent, generally irrelevant (S and N) Accented, even highly accented English, not problematic for NSJ (S and N) Essentialised empathy and cultural understanding as teaching related skills (S and N)	NSJ positions competitive (S) Stricter requirements of publications (S and N) Stricter formal qualifications, such as degrees in ELT specialization, required (S and N) Fewer part-time classes (N)

Note:
S: Standard employment (tenured, lifetime); N: Non-standard employment (limited term contracts and part-time employment)

benefitted non-Japanese ELTs, though not uniformly as this was racialized and gendered.

> We have a whole group of guys, who were hired before I got here, because they could speak a tad of Japanese, mostly bar language, with MAs in whatever, medical technology, not related to language teaching. (Michael, non-Japanese male)

Another benefit interviewees mentioned was that foreign teachers were often forgiven for their poor Japanese language skills, which allowed them to be hired with limited ability to do administrative work, though some stated this has been changing. Regarding lack of Japanese language ability, Lie (2001: 173) stated there is 'remarkable indulgence accorded to white academics and

Table 9.2 Benefits and constraints for non-Japanese in the hiring process

	Benefits	Constraints
Non-Japanese (see Table 9.3 for further racialized and gendered constraints)	Essentialised language skills from native speaker status (S and N) Assumption of adding diversity which was valued for programmes with international focus (S and N) Less focus on formal qualifications (N) Master's in any field generally acceptable (N) Publications often not required, though getting more specialized (N) Functional Japanese usually sufficient (N)	Few positions allocated to non-Japanese, and dichotomy of Japanese/non-Japanese precluded crossovers (S) More strongly scrutinized or discounted regarding skills of being able to get along and cultural harmony (S) Japanese language skills automatically assumed to be insufficient as language skills largely conflated with Japanese nationality (S)

Table 9.3 Racialized and gendered benefits and constraints

	Benefits	Constraints
Racialized	Candidates who were visibly Japanese (e.g. *Nisei* – second-generation Japanese) or partially Japanese (e.g. *hafu* – half Japanese) sometimes beneficial, as it was assumed the candidate would have cultural empathy, especially if they also had Japanese language skills (S and N)	Candidates who were visibly Japanese (e.g. *Nisei* – second-generation Japanese) or partially Japanese (e.g. *hafu* – biracial) sometimes constrained as they didn't fit the native speaker image, and weren't *foreign* enough to be considered native English speakers, though they were (S and N)
		No positions available at some universities for those who did not fit into the Japanese/Other dualisms (e.g. Korean, Chinese nationals, teaching English) (S and N)

(Continued)

	Benefits	Constraints
Gendered	None	Japanese and non-Japanese women – women's work/life cycle conflicts with age-normative demands, women too old at 40 or 45 (S) Non-Japanese women had less chance of being hired for part-time teaching, which is essential for career building, diminishing chances to move up to standard employment (S)
		Non-Japanese women disadvantaged (Japanese women not mentioned, but may be the same for them), because patriarchal attitudes endowed males with skills and attributes men didn't actually have and made invisible women's skills that are traditionally attributed to maleness (S and N)
		Non-Japanese women not fitting dominant native speaker image of white males (S and N) Assumptions that students would prefer male non-Japanese teachers (S and N)

Note:
S: Standard employment (tenured, lifetime); N: Non-standard employment (limited term contracts and part-time employment)

intellectuals'. Some recruitments specifically earmarked for non-Japanese tenured positions accepted functional Japanese.

Structural constraints for non-Japanese were situated mostly around the shortage of tenured positions. Hiring for tenured positions occurred when someone retired and therefore candidates had to be able to teach classes that were defined as 'Japanese taught' classes, automatically excluding non-Japanese. The number of allocated non-Japanese positions has been extremely limited and interviewees stated that almost no new ones had been created over the decades. Three exceptions for new positions added were one in an existing department, one for a new department and one for a new programme. Regarding English teachers,

> There has been a huge increase in part-time and *ninkisei* (limited term full-time contracts) positions over the decades but not even one tenured position for foreigners. We started having *ninkisei* a while back and that is just foreigners, all have been men. No Japanese at all ... We have a few dozen tenured Japanese ... just one tenured foreigner. (Midori, Japanese female)

All other things being equal, the lack of excellent or perfect Japanese language skills emerged as a strong reason for eliminating most non-Japanese candidates, since it was deemed necessary for administrative duties. Yonezawa (2007: 488) argued the lack of proficiency in the Japanese language was one argument given for the small number of foreign university faculty as 'Japanese language largely dominates daily academic and social life in every field', and the use of English in university administration is rare. This contrasted with part-time positions that required little or no Japanese proficiency. Yonezawa (2009a) found that many language teachers have fair, basic or no Japanese language skills (around 42%), and while only around 32% describe themselves as fluent, another 20% or more describe their proficiency as good. An interviewee mentioned that their department might be open to a non-Japanese with excellent Japanese language skills filling a position normally allocated as Japanese taught, but their colleague was not as optimistic. Japanese interviewees saw the requirement of being a Japanese native speaker as reasonable, though non-Japanese participants felt it was unfair.

> It is normal to want a Japanese. We know the culture and the language. In your country, imagine if someone couldn't speak English. (Keisuke, Japanese male)

> Over the years I've heard every excuse, especially language, even when someone is fluent. I've given up trying (to get non-Japanese hired). (John, non-Japanese male)

Personality has been increasingly viewed as a skill (Payne, 2000). Cultural compatibility, such as 'getting along' and 'being able to work on a team', along with a knowledge of how things work in Japan and an understanding of how to function with Japanese staff and faculty were further cited as demand-side criteria by interviewees. Participants, Japanese and non-Japanese, indicated that this might, at times, unfairly preclude non-Japanese. Japanese interviewees thought the possibility of having to function in another language might be unconsciously perceived as being disruptive to some Japanese. Harmony was viewed as an ideal and how one's personality fits in, as Payne's (2000) 'Unbearable Lightness of Skill' has shown, has become a common, though potentially precarious, development.

Japanese ELTs: Benefits and constraints

Age normative hiring has traditionally benefitted Japanese men (Charles & Grusky, 2004) and interviewees described age normativity as a very strong indicator of success. Demand-side criteria included not having gaps in employment and having the age-appropriate amount of qualifications, publications and work experience. A common comment was that the hiring committee members were suspicious of résumés that were out of the ordinary. While eventually non-Japanese may learn successful job-hunting strategies based on knowledge of uniquely Japanese hiring criteria such as the importance of internal university publications (*kiyo*), many of these criteria may be unknown to non-Japanese during the age-appropriate times. Strong adherence to hiring norms generally advantaged Japanese men; it severely disadvantaged those with breaks in their careers (mostly Japanese and non-Japanese women as they tended to have different work/life cycles).

Another benefit was that Japanese ELTs were the preferred teachers because of their knowledge of the local student population. According to interviewees, hiring committee members often articulated the importance of a successful job incumbent as: being concerned for their students' learning; having knowledge of specific grammar weakness that sprang from their Japanese language and; being familiar with Japanese students' learning styles. Another stated cultural consideration was that the students would feel more comfortable with a Japanese teacher. Japanese teachers, therefore, benefitted in this regard, for both part-time and full-time positions. However, some interviewees did mention that this essentialising was problematic.

Accented English of Japanese ELTs was not problematic, and speaking skills and 'native-like' English were generally irrelevant. It was uniformly acknowledged by participants that a lot of Japanese was used in the classroom for all English levels of students, though the wisdom of this was questioned by some Japanese and all the non-Japanese interviewees. When one candidate who had low overall English skills was being considered, a Japanese interviewee reasoned:

> We couldn't say that (the candidate's) English wasn't good enough, and we had been advised to hire someone who could not only do administrative work in Japanese, but someone who also could understand the complex corporate culture (at this university). We had no foreigners who could do that. (Yuichi, Japanese male)

Interviewees mentioned that students' speaking and listening skills were, at times, clearly higher than the candidate's.

> The hiring committee members said Japanese could be used to teach in the class even though many of the students had better English, were returnees (Japanese returning from abroad) and non-Japanese. (Estelle, non-Japanese female)

Racialized constraints

Non-Japanese ELTs who did not fit into the prevailing native speaker ideology were particularly marginalized, though this was far from universal. Interviewees mentioned they had seen candidates from countries like the Philippines, Korea, Taiwan and South Africa receive desk rejections. However, it was not monolithic, as others mentioned their departments had hired Vietnamese, Australians, Indians, Singaporeans and Québécois. For the most part, classes were bifurcated into Japanese taught or native-speaker taught, and there was no other category when recruiting; no non-native English speakers except Japanese nationals. Non-Japanese, who were not native English speakers, could not be hired for the Japanese-taught category or the native speaker-taught category. Those marginalized in this way were highly disadvantaged.

Being visibly different was found to be both beneficial and constraining. Two interviewees mentioned half-Japanese (*hafu*) teachers being hired because they were 'as close to Japanese as can be without looking totally Japanese'. One interviewee mentioned an African-American candidate not being hired because of race:

> They took one look at him and said they wanted a 'real' American. (Stephen, non-Japanese male)

It was proposed by participants that those used to being on the top of a racial hierarchy might not recognize that their frustrations in the workplace come from their unwarranted sense of entitlement being challenged. Tensions from the dichotomies also created apprehension before and after the actual hiring process.

We have a big group of part-timers. They are all American men. No, one is Australian, I think. When a job comes up, these foreign guys act like the job is theirs and afterward (when they don't get the job) a bad feeling occurs between us. (Keisuke, Japanese male)

The foreign men, they sometimes stop working hard when they get passed over. We Japanese don't like this. We have a few foreign women, and they work really hard, so we are learning that women fit in much better. Maybe because they can empathize with us Japanese. (Takao, Japanese male)

While the Japanese/'other' dualism was problematic in that it contributed to racialized constraints, interviewees in general expressed concern that without a category for non-Japanese, Japanese faculty would be prone to reverting to hiring only Japanese nationals, and both diversity and language skills would be hard to maintain.

Gendered constraints

The Japanese labour market is highly gender segregated, and biases in recruitment and hiring, which disadvantage women, may arise from assumptions of 'male as breadwinner' and 'female as caregiver'. Consequently, age emerged as a formidable force of segregation, and Japanese and foreign women were similarly penalized for employment gaps or assumptions that gaps would inevitably occur. Skills gained by women outside the paid workforce, such as time-management, mediation and people-oriented skills, were never viewed as building human capital to add to women's skill sets, and there was certainly nowhere to put these skills on Japanese résumés, inevitably excluding highly qualified women candidates because they were, at the age of 40 – 45, considered too old.

Interviewees witnessed gender discrimination during hiring. A number of participants mentioned that they were told expressly that foreign men would be preferable.

Most of the students are women, so we should hire a male because students would like that. (Yumiko, Japanese female)

One participant mentioned that he was told explicitly that the administration didn't want to hire any foreign women. Another mentioned a candidate was discounted because they felt she would not fit in, as the Japanese faculty thought she was too aggressive, though the non-Japanese woman interviewee found her to be the opposite.

The lack of female foreign teacher applicants has often been mentioned anecdotally as the reason there are so few women faculty members. This, however, was contested on many levels.

One interviewee said they had to do nothing special to get a gender balance.

> It just happens naturally, as equally qualified women and men apply. We want female role models. We get way more males applying but they are mostly highly under-qualified. Once weeded out, few survive and we have equal numbers of qualified women and men. (Yoshiko, Japanese female)

Some programmes managed to always have a fairly even gender balance.

> We (now) have about 50/50 because we now make sure qualified women are also hired. Before I came they (the university) had only one foreign woman ... I have no idea why others insist there are no foreign women who want to teach in Japan. (Saori, Japanese female)

> I am so tired of the lament that there are no foreign women applying ... Meanwhile, some young guy with an MA in anything, and they start salivating, like the Japanese women and men have a crush on them! Then this male homosocial thing happens. (Ellen, non-Japanese female)

The tensions of gendered work relations were apparent, as was the accompanying discrimination, and this study confirmed anecdotal evidence that foreign women are comparatively disadvantaged and may choose to exit the Japanese labour market rather than adapt.

> Japan is patriarchal. No doubt about it, and foreign women keep leaving. (Tony, non-Japanese male)

> Japanese academia is a hostile environment for women, especially for foreign women academics. I don't blame them for leaving. (Yoshiko, Japanese female)

The complexity of the contested gender workplace, according to the data, resulted in many tensions. Interviewees mentioned that a hiring system based on networking left women out of the loop, taking longer to build human capital (see Hicks, Chapter 10). Nonqualified men got contracts and part-time jobs, then quickly moved up the ladder because they were then able to put teaching experience on résumés. Women were inevitably left behind.

Conclusions

This study, which focused on recruitment and hiring of ELTs, found that there were different benefits and constraints for Japanese and native speaker ELTs, with further constraints for non-native speakers who were not Japanese. It seems that the recent trend of removing (Japanese) nationality or native speaker status from recruitment postings, as well as the removal of gender and age, has not resulted in changes in practice. The role government policies have played in this bifurcation needs to be examined in relation to educational goals, such as diversity in the teaching population and diversity in the language skills that students may need, especially given MEXT's stated desire of 'internationalizing' universities.

Japanese ELTs benefitted more from the higher allotment of positions, though job searches were highly competitive, and hence they were generally required to be more qualified. Japanese gained from hiring practices that emphasized cultural norms and being a native speaker of Japanese, though age normative hiring harshly penalized women (both Japanese and non-Japanese), as their work/life cycles generally do not fit age normative career expectations. While essentialisation of both Japanese and non-Japanese led to tensions, interviewees generally voiced concerns that removing the dichotomy, and not having non-Japanese (native speaker) positions, would lead to fewer ELT positions for non-Japanese, resulting in less diversity.

Much of the existing literature on native speakerism focuses on the struggles of non-native teachers (Medgyes, 1994). This research, for the most part, found that for English teaching in Japanese universities, Japaneseness was favoured over native speaker status, and it was native speakers of English who were struggling, being generally relegated to non-standard (precarious) employment. Native speaker status was further mitigated by inequality regimes (Acker, 2009) of gender, race and age, and the intersectionalities (Crenshaw, 1989) highlight the complexities and nuanced nature of native speakers in the Japanese context.

However, native speakers benefitted from the well-developed part-time and contract positions that often required little more than a master's degree. These precarious jobs may be viewed as embodying more than the language, and may include a taste of 'foreignness', much as Tsuneyoshi (Chapter 8) suggests regarding non-tertiary language teaching.

There were constraints in hiring native speakers who did not fit the image of white (Caucasian) males, though there were inconsistencies if candidates were of Japanese heritage. ELTs who were non-native speakers of English and not Japanese were particularly disadvantaged, receiving desk rejections when it could not be conceptualized how they might conform to the Japanese/'other' bifurcations that assumed 'others' to be native speakers of English.

This research confirmed the existence of tensions between the various teaching populations. University hiring structures to a certain extent dictate the nationality of who is being hired. Without a pipeline to standard employment, tensions are inevitable when the segregated labour market fails to embrace long-term residents. Yonezawa (2009b: 209) stated that 'Japan has a long history of utilizing foreign workers as a buffer against economic fluctuations', and this was confirmed to be problematic for long-term residents building academic careers. Recent initiatives by MEXT (n.d.) though, aim to increase the number of foreign academics through non-standard employment.

Individuals deal with the processes that structure hiring in a variety of ways: sometimes avoiding change; sometimes embracing diversity by hiring those outside the ideological norms – those from countries not normally considered to be English-speaking countries, non-Japanese women and those with accented English. Potential flexibility is afforded in how the actual hiring process proceeds due to the generally decentralized nature of Japanese university hiring. Structural and ideological constraints can potentially be circumvented and there is room for flexibility to embrace those who fall outside the conventional criteria.

Acknowledgement

Sincere appreciation is offered to all the professors who agreed to participate in this research. I would also like to thank Robert O'Mochain for reading an early version and sincere gratitude to Salem Hicks for all the feedback and support.

10 On the (Out)Skirts of TESOL Networks of Homophily: Substantive Citizenship in Japan

Salem Kim Hicks

Introduction

> On a previous contract job everybody gushed about the male teacher (so handsome, so wonderful, etc.) who never came to meetings, extra activities or did any extra work. I did all of the extra jobs, but it didn't result in anything positive for me. (Interviewee # 9)

The pervasive ideal conceptualization of the native speaker TESOL professional has traditionally been racialized as typically 'white' (Grant & Lee, 2009) and from *Inner-Circle* countries historically deemed the cultural and linguistic bases of English (Kachru, 1992). Much of the literature on native-speakerism falls short of delineating the gendered complexities and realities but tends to erroneously position the English native speaker in a rather gender-neutral way. Women and men's agency tends to be undifferentiated, misrepresenting the benefits, realities and hardships of native English speakers as being similar, if not equal. When native-speakerism intersects with other social dimensions such as race (see Kubota, Chapter 14) and gender, the 'multidimensionality' of power relations (Crenshaw, 1989) illuminates a less essentialised and much more complex agency of the native speaker.

Recently, much research on immigrant citizenship rights has been published in Japan (Chung, 2010; Douglass & Roberts, 2000; Shipper, 2008; Tsuda, 2006). Many immigrants in Japan, while not formal citizens, have access to certain social welfare systems and benefits via substantive citizenship. Following improvements and changes in policies and laws, foreign residents in Japan have better access to national health insurance, have easier eligibility to pension benefits and have increased protection against discriminatory practices in housing (Tsuda, 2006). In addition, protection of equal employment opportunities is promised by the Labour Standards Law (*roudou kijun hou*) and the Equal Employment Opportunity Law (*danjo koyou kikai kintou hou*). However, as many foreign TESOL professionals in Japan are in non-standard employment and often not enrolled in health or pension plans via their employers, access to these welfare benefits, though legally protected, is not necessarily easily affordable, especially for women.

Furthermore, foreign female TESOL professionals must negotiate the dual stratums of the masculine Japanese culture (Hofstede, 1983, 2001), which does not generally envision women as either leaders or as candidates for standard employment, and the male-dominated TESOL sub-culture, which in many ways similarly subscribes to discriminatory ideologies and structures, placing further constraints upon equal employment opportunities for women. The interview data of foreign female TESOL professionals presented in this chapter makes salient the discriminatory barriers to equal employment, and the resulting effects on substantive citizenship benefits. The data adds to previous literature, though sparse, regarding gendered difficulties for foreign female TESOL professionals in Japan (Simon-Maeda, 2004), in other Asian contexts (Appleby, 2010b) and women faculty members of color working in TESOL (Lin *et al.*, 2004).

Equal Access to Substantive Citizenship

It is now widely accepted that citizenship is gendered (Lister, 1997; Walby, 1994) and that the public – private dichotomy is at the core. Despite all the legal gains towards gender equality, in Japan there is still a 'huge gap between *de facto* equality and *de jure* equality' (Kinjo, 1995: 355). As women, to varying degrees world wide, are still ultimately responsible for unpaid private care giving and domestic labour duties of citizenship, and men are linked to the status of public citizen worker, this type of citizenship model distinctly disadvantages women. Although women's equal access to employment opportunities is legally protected in Japan, women still encounter ideological and structural gendered constraints often resulting in lower wages, lower status and precarious employment (see Hayes, Chapter 9). Lower wages ensure that women in general make lower pension contributions. Limited contract work results in only short-term access to benefits such as health care, pension membership and maternity leave. Part-time employment often means limited or no access to paid maternity leave, with health care and pension membership entirely at the expense of the employee. If a woman in precarious work is unable to continue, the lack of benefits and employment security can be devastating.

The amount of wages lost over a working lifetime due to the gender wage gap has been calculated by economists to be very substantial. Because women on average earn less than men, and pension benefits are calculated based on lifetime contributions, the labour market inequalities and constraints continue to exert a negative impact on financial security well into retirement. In this way, citizenship is not equal as women are disadvantaged by a system that often awards more immediate benefits in the labour market to men, and then more pension payments at retirement. As elderly women make up the majority share of people living below the poverty line in Japan (Tachibanaki, 2006) and around the world, the losses are not inconsequential.

Foreign and Japanese residents are required to enroll in the social insurance system under the Health Insurance Act (*kenkou hoken hou*) and the National Pension Act (*kokumin nenkin hou*). However, since residents of Japan engaged in part-time employment are usually not enrolled by their employer in the Employee Health and Pension Plan (*shakai hoken/shigaku kyosai*), they must pay out of pocket for the less comprehensive National Health Insurance (*kokumin kenko hoken*). The monthly premiums can represent a heavy burden for teachers without secure employment.

Pension, another important benefit available to residents in Japan, is payable after contributing payments for 25 years. The government has improved the eligibility system for some foreign residents by signing bilateral agreements allowing employees to apply pension contributions between certain countries. Teachers in standard employment contribute a percentage of their salaries and their employers pay an additional percentage into a teacher retirement fund. Besides medical insurance and survivor annuities, the major retirement benefits usually consist of a lump sum cash payment upwards of two years salary, and an annual pension upon retirement.

Layers of Cultural, Social and Employment Contexts

In order to situate the data presented in this chapter, it is necessary to describe in some detail the double layer of the dominant Japanese culture and the TESOL subculture from a gender perspective. Japan is a patriarchal culture, with women experiencing discrimination at most levels of society. Schultz Lee *et al.* (2010: 199) showed that despite modernization, economic development and a stable democracy, gender beliefs in Japan have not 'become more egalitarian'. The World Economic Forum's Global Gender Gap Index ranked Japan as being well behind the majority of the industrialized nations in gender equality, at 94 out of 134 countries (Hausmann *et al.*, 2010: 174).

Although recently Japanese women have been pursuing a broader range of life trajectories (Miller, 2003), the prevailing ideology that women should be ultimately responsible for domestic work and care giving is still pervasive. Lebra (1985: 100) argued that the gendered roles in Japan feed 'into unequal social status that dictates women to be inferior, submissive, more constrained, and more backstage than men; that they may be lower in status, power, autonomy and role visibility'. Assessing the prospects for gender diversity in Japanese employment, Benson *et al.* (2007: 903) concluded that the male-dominated culture that exists in many Japanese companies serves to 'restrict the opportunities available to women'. Indeed, foreign women often express that the distinct gender roles and expectations in Japan are in many ways a throwback to past generations in their own countries. McVeigh (1996: 328) observed that in Japan 'Western women are often portrayed as "liberated" or "assertive"', though unfortunately these are not qualities that are culturally viewed as appropriate for women in Japanese society.

TESOL sub-culture in tertiary education

'How extraordinary, and I thought the majority of English teachers were women?' And he said, 'Oh that's absolutely true: something like eighty per cent of the teachers are women'. I ... commented on the large number of men at the meeting, and he said 'Oh yes. But you see these are *head* teachers!' One had the impression that these men had crawled out of the woodwork at the 'head' level. I think that there is a similar very prevalent view in TEFL. (Brown, 1989: 171)

The teaching profession in general is highly feminized (Acker, 1994; Rots *et al.*, 2002). It would then seem women should be successful as academics; however, they are often seen as 'other', marginalized in the lower status, lower paid positions (Acker, 1980). Although women are dominant in teaching in primary education, women remain seriously under-represented in senior teaching and administrative positions. TESOL is no exception (Sunderland, 2000). Pennycook (1989: 612) acknowledged the segregation of the male TESOL academy maintains inequalities between male academics and female teachers. The Japanese Ministry of Education, Culture, Sports, Science and Technology (as cited in Gender Equality Bureau, 2009: 39) found that the number of Japanese female university faculty members was much lower than for males, and were concentrated in the lower status positions: 11.6% professors, 23.2%

associate professors, 18.9% assistant professors and 27.1% for lecturers. Yonezawa (2009a) found foreign faculty in the area of linguistics/education/area studies as being 72.4% male and 27.6% female, although the data does not distinguish between job status.

Japanese universities have a long history of utilizing networking for recruitment purposes. Foreign TESOL professionals have been traditionally asked to recommend other foreigners for teaching jobs, essentially assigning them as gatekeepers to potential employment. It is still not uncommon for language teachers to 'pass on' their entire teaching schedules and for new teachers to be hired primarily on the recommendation of an existing teacher. Perhaps, Japanese faculty members feel they do not have easy access to the foreign community, so they entrust recruitment to 'known' foreign teachers. Even though native speaker status endows certain benefits that are not based primarily on expertise or qualifications (Holliday, 2005a; Kubota, 2001), this corporate culture of networking has for the most part not worked in favour of women.

Pertinent to the male-dominated TESOL profession in Japan, research has shown in other contexts that women are not included in the male-led occupational networking (Crompton, 2006; Kanter, 1977; Walby & Olsen, 2002) which often leads to 'positions of leadership and decision making' (Usui et al., 2003: 114). Kanter (1977) showed that women in organizational work settings lack access to, or are excluded from, networks. While women pursue a differentiated network, Ibarra (1992) found that men were more likely to form homophilous ties based on gender and reap greater network returns.

Women are excluded from these networks in part because they are not seen or valued as leaders. According to a report by the International Labour Organization (2007: 2), 'The largest barrier to equality in career development remains male-biased recruitment procedures and criteria' and '"camouflaged" stereotypes concerning their suitability for leadership roles'. Carli (2001: 735) found resistance to female-influenced leadership is 'particularly pronounced in men'. In addition, reports from the Japanese Gender Equality Bureau (2010) confirm that the number of women in leadership and decision-making positions is still pitiably small in most sectors.

To compound the difficulties, when women do enter the male-dominated university environment, there are few protections against harassment or hostile work environments. Although some of the larger universities have created harassment guidelines and committees, Creaser (2012: 24) explains the complexity of trying to define different types of power and academic harassments and writes that many universities are 'unwilling to create official policies on academic harassment for fear floodgates would open up and advisory services would be inundated with complaints'.

The wider social environment in Japan continues to portray an atmosphere of foreign male sexual activity entangled with the English teaching industry. Japanese women's desire for Western white men (see Kelsky, 1999, 2001; Piller & Takahashi, 2006) and comments on numerous blogs and websites about the sexual perks for foreign men while teaching English in Japan are pervasive. In some ways, the recently reissued 1990s comic book series 'Charisma Man' (Rodney & Garscadden, 1998), which portrays a white, Western, male English teacher in Japan as transformed into a 'super man', at least in eyes of Japanese women, sheds light on the sexualized nature of the TESOL environment. In interviews with Australian men who had taught in Japan, Appleby (2010a) found that none of the men identified themselves as a charisma man but knew of *other* men who fit the description. The comic, sadly, portrays Western women as the 'arch-enemy' of Western men.

Methodology

As someone who has lived in Japan and worked in the TESOL profession for a number of years, I have spoken with several women and men about their lives as foreigners in Japan. In many ways, foreign women have a very different experience in Japan from their male counterparts. Despite creating rich and rewarding lives for themselves and their families, many women speak of loneliness, exclusion and discrimination not only based on being foreign but also because of gender.

In this preliminary research project, semi-structured email and/or face-to-face interviews of 13 foreign women teaching in higher educational institutions were conducted. Participants were asked to answer a questionnaire with open-ended questions about their experiences and perceptions as foreign female TESOL professionals in Japan. Purposive sampling using preselected criteria to identify common areas of experience among the women was used. All of the women were living in, or had lived in, the Kansai region and had worked their way up the TESOL ladder. They had a schedule of part-time classes, had secured a full-time limited contract position or had a tenured teaching position. They were from various ethnic backgrounds, held post-graduate degrees, considered themselves native speakers of English and had years of teaching experience.

Results and Discussion

Ideological structures as obstacles

These interviews illuminated how some foreign women experience the unique gendered structures and systems within the Japanese culture, as well as the male-dominated foreign TESOL sub-culture. It became clear from the interviews that not all foreign men participate in actively discriminatory behaviour; however, there was a general perception among the interviewees that foreign men would nonetheless benefit, directly or indirectly, from these structures and ideologies.

In general, interviewees did not feel optimistic about their job security and their ability to collect pension benefits in the future. Some expressed feelings of stress, uncertainty and frustration at being in a cycle of limited contract work or part-time work and were not confident that they would be able to secure stable employment in the near future despite their efforts.

All of the women interviewed were the main earners in their family units, contributing 85 – 100%. Seven were married to Japanese men and had children. These women reported that attitudes often existed among Japanese and foreign men regarding their role as earners, and in some cases had severe negative consequences:

> I was told … off the record … afterwards that although we had similar qualifications, I didn't get the job because the other candidate … a guy …. had young children to support. I was so angry because I do too … I am the main earner in my family. (Interviewee #5)

> I have been told directly that they (male teachers) need the jobs to support their families and women don't need these jobs. (Interviewee #9)

Also emergent in the interviews were the effects of the ideology of 'women as the main caregiver' on their career advancements and access to financial stability:

> I think it is almost impossible for a woman who has home responsibility with kids to progress. I do not have the time to devote to reading, working on a PHD. I see my male counterparts hanging out at the office till late, working on papers, while I have to continually rush home to my responsibilities as a mother. (Interviewee #11)

The lack of paid maternity leave for women in part-time employment sheds light on the realities and consequences of the ideology of private versus public citizenship. Some women reported losing classes or having to go on unpaid leave because of having to take time off for care giving, which impacted negatively upon their family's financial welfare.

Another common theme that emerged was the feeling of invisibility, exclusion and isolation in academia. When attention was drawn to the lack of gender diversity in faculty, there was often little recognition of the problem:

In general, however, there is still a dearth of females. For example, in some departments of universities where I have worked, 85 – 90% of the instructors are males. And worse yet, when some foreign males look at this ratio, they say, 'Well, what are those women complaining about? Look, there's one women right there!' They really seem to think that this ratio is acceptable. (Interviewee #3)

In instances when women do become visible, interviewees related stories of male colleagues opining that foreign women secure highly competitive employment because of their gender, inferring that their gender is valued above qualifications, thus giving them some sort of advantage:

Some guys think for some reason that it is easier for women to get teaching positions here. Unbelievable in a country that is notoriously sexist … plus wouldn't there be more women here if it was so easy? (Interviewee #12)

The normalization of male dominance and female subordination in Japanese employment seems to foster the invisibility of foreign women as well, even in the eyes of foreign men.

Social Structures as Obstacles

Networking and nepotism

All of the women interviewed spoke of a system of male networking and nepotism that ultimately excluded them. Some women reported that they had been hired for teaching positions through the recommendations of male colleagues but, for the most part, women had acquired their jobs through the help of another female colleague or through open job postings. On average, they had worked at five different universities over the course of their careers, all of which were dominated by both Japanese and foreign male faculty.

Accessing the structure of networking is often important in securing part-time employment in Japanese universities. The problem for women is that it is primarily a system based on in-group networking in which men tend to recommend other men. As the need for personal recommendation is still preferred by many Japanese administrations, especially at the part-time faculty level, it means that women often remain outside the network loop:

All of my university positions have come about through the recommendations of female colleagues. There is a boys' network which is stronger and tougher than the girls' network, so I feel lucky and thankful to my friends who helped me get university positions. Given that 80 – 90% of positions are held by foreign males already, some of whom are Neanderlithic, it is tough for women to get positions. (Interviewee #3)

Some women reported cases of outright, systematic exclusion based on gender:

I know of one prestigious university in Kansai that has 3-year contract positions. The Japanese administration only accepts recommendations from known teachers. They accept anyone recommended, even with no M.A. Women for the most part can't even get an interview, even if they are qualified. The men just recommend each other. Those contracts are like a pipeline to other contracts in other universities ... so it's not a small thing. (Interviewee #10)

Others reported general negative attitudes toward foreign women:

Had there been any foreign men involved in my hiring I absolutely never would have got this job given my experience here with foreign men. I know it's not about me, or my qualifications, but it's rather about their attitudes towards foreign women. I do feel that having a Japanese woman on the hiring committee did benefit me, however. (Interviewee #5)

Being socially excluded marginalizes women's networking and potentially creates tension in the work environment. Most women reported they were rarely, if ever, invited out for drinks or socializing after work with male colleagues, further leaving them out of both workplace networking and human capital building:

I have been in many situations where I am the only foreign female and I have been ignored and isolated. For example, walking into the teacher's room and no one acknowledging you – I have heard this from many women. The guys often arrange to go out but the women are not included. The male teachers often work together to produce articles/presentations, etc., but we are not usually asked to join. (Interviewee #9)

While some women did report being sociable in the staffroom with male colleagues, further clarification found the communication was often initiated by the women, that the schools were either exceptionally small, or did not have a highly competitive environment. A notable exception to the social and networking exclusion was expressed by the interviewees who were tenured faculty members. Lin (1982) found that individuals are likely to prefer interaction with others who have a higher status in order to gain access to valued resources. All of the women who had increased their status to tenured professor and were in hiring positions said that they noticed a difference in how they were being treated by many foreign male teachers, especially those in the job market. The increased social interaction initiated by the men was thought by the respondents to be related to the shift in their power status.

Power and sexual harassment

A workplace environment that is free from objectionable conduct and is socially inclusive is desirable. Sexually-oriented discussion and conduct creates an atmosphere that makes it uncomfortable, inaccessible and in some cases hostile to women professionals. Interviewees seemed quite dismayed at the participation of some foreign male TESOL professionals in offensive conversation and conduct that would not be legal in their own countries, but was sanctioned or at least tolerated in Japanese culture:

> It seems that as a Western woman I have had to leave behind expectations of equality that I had in my own country. Here, it's like a step back in time. Whereas the guys seem to be able to get away with anything almost and thrive here ... they love all this ego boosting ... they have no problem going back to the good ol' days. They couldn't act like that back home. (Interviewee #5)

The following data comment on the attitudes of some foreign male teachers toward Japanese female students:

> It has really surprised me to see foreign males whom I thought were enlightened drooling over their students in public and engaging in very questionable behavior out of class. (Interviewee #3)

> I see male teachers flirting with female students all the time. It seems to be the way they relate to them ... not as guardians of their education and well-being but rather as perks of the job. Young women often wear fashion here that is cute and 'sexy' and some of these guys somehow think it is for their pleasure. (Interviewee #8)

Interviewees also reported comments from male colleagues about 'short skirts being a perk of the job' (Interviewee #13), male colleagues asking their female students to 'sit at the front of the class in case they spread their legs and offered a peek' (Interviewee #2), a male colleague who 'routinely referred to female students as "fuck-me types" during faculty meetings' (Interviewee #6) and numerous incidences of foreign male colleagues asking students out on a date, flirting and accepting presents. All of these comments indicated the sexualized nature of language education, at least for some foreign men, in the university environment.

Some interviewees also related experiences of direct sexual harassment. Two women working at the same school reported that their supervisor, a foreign male tenured faculty member, would often stare at their breasts while talking with them about work-related issues and tasks. Each of them felt uncomfortable but powerless to confront him for fear of negative repercussions and their lack of confidence in the school's sexual harassment policies and practices.

These types of harassment create an environment that is hostile to women and has the potential to have serious adverse affects on their employment and access to equal substantive citizenship. Several women reported they just teach their classes and leave. Two women reported having had to terminate their employment as the atmosphere was so uncomfortable.

Furthermore, women reported some male colleagues who were required to attend harassment awareness workshops thought it was unnecessary for them but that the workshops were necessary for many of the Japanese male professors. Several of the interviewees reported foreign male colleagues making light of and being dismissive of these types of anti-harassment workshops.

Conclusion

The rich interview data provided by these foreign female TESOL professionals illustrates how 'native speaker' is a gendered status. The data further elucidates the negative effects of gendered ideological and structural constraints on equal employment opportunities and the costly effects on substantive citizenship benefits, such as pension. Several ideologies and structures operating within the dual layers of culture were identified in the data: the male as breadwinner model of citizenship, representation of male as normative, informal homophilic networks linked to nepotism in hiring, social and professional isolation and exclusion and permissive attitudes towards power and sexual harassment. Despite laws promoting equality, many women still experience these very real barriers to equal employment and thus equal citizenship. Though the sampling of interview participants is limited in size and scope, it is nonetheless worthy of consideration and begs further research into what may be occurring in the wider context of the TESOL community in Japan for foreign female TESOL professionals.

Acknowledgements

I would like to thank the women who generously shared their time, personal and professional experiences, and insight with me. Also a special thanks to Blake E. Hayes who was instrumental in helping me organize and conceptualize this research, and to Roslyn Appleby, Joanna Hosoya and Ellen Webber who gave helpful feedback on this chapter.

11 The Construction of the 'Native Speaker' in Japan's Educational Policies for TEFL

Kayoko Hashimoto

Introduction

In Japanese government publications, the term 'native speaker' usually takes the form of the loanword 'ネイティブ スピーカー' (rather than the Japanese equivalent '母語話者', which literally means 'mother tongue speaker'. The crucial difference between the two terms is that the loanword is often used based on the assumption that it refers to foreigners who speak English, while the Japanese word does not specify the language or the speaker's background. This view that an NSE is a foreigner has played a crucial role in the Japanese education system, and has contributed to restrictions on the functions of NSEs within the system.

While NSEs have an ambivalent position in Japanese society, Holliday (2005a: 6) proposes a term 'native-speakerism' that is defined as 'an established belief that "native speaker" teachers represent a "Western culture" from which spring the ideals both of the English language and of English language teaching methodology'. Holliday also argues that the native/non-native dichotomy that gives rise to negative perceptions of NNSE is a political construction. This situation is certainly not limited to English. In Asia, where the proportion of native speakers of Japanese among teachers of Japanese language is lower than in other regions where Japanese is taught, the nature of 'nativeness' and 'Japaneseness', combined with the history of Japanese occupation during World War II, has resulted in an inferiority complex among Japanese teachers who are non-native speakers of the language, despite the fact that they are in the majority (Hirahata, 2008). In Japan, however, the native/non-native dichotomy has impacted on NSE and NNSE teachers in a different way. This chapter examines how NSE is described, defined and discussed in educational curricula and policy documents in Japan, and argues that 'native speaker' is a political construction that seeks to utilise NSE in the Japanese education system for the purpose of TEFL.

For the textual analysis, I have used both the original Japanese and the English versions of texts where available, and have compared them for wording and rhetoric when significant gaps existed, applying critical discourse analysis (CDA) as a methodological tool. CDA is concerned with the conscious or subconscious production and reproduction of dominance through discourse (van Dijk, 1993), and has also been seen as an approach to language use that aims to explore and expose the roles that discourse plays in reproducing or resisting social inequalities (Richardson, 2007). There are many studies of Japanese policy documents in the field of education (Beauchamp & Vardaman, 1994; Kawai, 2007; Okuno, 2007), and their approaches to policy texts predominantly involve content analysis. While content analysis assumes an interpretation of a text identical to the one intended by the policy maker, CDA allows us to see beyond the reading of policy documents that was intended by the policy maker, which is crucial to connect seemingly unrelated texts. In this way, CDA is likely to be an effective tool for revealing the mechanism for constructing the 'native speaker' within educational policy documents.

Current Political Climate Surrounding NSE Teachers

First of all, I will discuss the latest political moves in relation to TEFL in Japan, which have the potential to significantly affect NSE teachers. On 11 November 2009, in Round One of the Japanese Government Revitalisation Unit's (GRU, 事業仕分け) screening process, a panel advised to abolish the total plan for English education reform proposed by the MEXT. This plan included a budget for introducing 'foreign language activities' (外国語活動) in elementary schools. The panel stated that the proposed budget could not be justified because the plan was merely a continuation of the existing school curriculum, with no concrete plan for the future of TEFL (all documents relating to the GRU screening are available on the Cabinet Office website: http://www.cao.go.jp/gyouseisasshin/contents/01/shiwake.html).

In Round Two, on 21 May 2010, another panel of the GRU advised that the JET Programme, which is administered jointly by the MIC, the MEXT and the MOFA, should be reviewed, expressing concerns about the programme's relevance and the funding. The JET Programme has offered three types of positions to foreigners since 1987, ALT, CIR and SEA, and more than 90% of JET participants are employed as ALTs. The panel pointed out that the programme itself had not changed since its inception, and that the breakdown of responsibilities between central and local governments in terms of cost was unclear. In relation to the lack of substantial change to the programme, the panel observed that the ambiguous relationship between language education and international exchange had resulted in the ineffective practice of accepting ALTs who did not possess qualifications in language teaching. Behind the scenes, there was a frustration, in the business sector in particular, over the lack of success in the delivery of TEFL, even though English has been a key element of Japan's internationalisation movement since the 1980s (Funabashi, 2000; Torikai, 2010).

The overlap between language education and international exchange in the programme is reflected in the name of the project itself. The name 'JET Programme' has been widely used in both Japanese and English. It should be noted, however, that the original Japanese name for the project did not exactly correspond to 'Japan Exchange and Teaching', for which JET is the acronym. The original Japanese was the lengthy 語学指導等を行う外国青年招致事業, which literally means 'project to invite foreign youth who conduct language teaching etc'. The main part of this expression relates to inviting foreign youth, and the first part, 語学指導等を行う (to conduct language teaching etc.), is often omitted. The issue of confusion between language teaching and international exchange was also pointed out at a separate meeting of the ministerial review conducted by the MOFA on 15 June 2010. It was revealed that MOFA believed that the main purpose of the JET Programme was still international exchange, whereas local governments saw it as a provider of ALTs, which has created a gap between provider and receiver in terms of the selection of ALTs. According to the report (MOFA, 2010), MOFA sought to select ALTs with diverse backgrounds, but schools preferred ALTs from the United States of America and the United Kingdom.

Even though the GRU screening was driven by the financial necessity to reduce ministerial spending and was not legally enforceable, the outcomes of the screening are likely to have an immediate impact on NSEs who are directly involved in both the JET Programme and the elementary school education. It should be noticed that the screening also highlighted various problems surrounding TEFL, which has involved not only the MEXT but also other government offices such as the MIC and the MOFA that have been engaged in promoting TEFL according to their own political and economic agendas. In the following section, I will examine how NSE are described and defined in educational policies.

ALTs and Team Teaching

Just as there is a gap between the Japanese and the English versions of the name of the JET Programme, there is a crucial difference between the term 'ALT' and the original Japanese: ALT stands for 'assistant language teacher', whereas the Japanese 外国語指導助手 literally means 'foreign language teaching assistant'. In other words, in English they are teachers, but in Japanese they are assistants. Like 'JET Programme', the term 'ALT' is also commonly used by Japanese. The origin of the misleading English term is unknown, but this double standard has been a cause of legal issues in relation to the employment of ALTs.

The JET Programme is no longer the sole provider of ALTs to local schools; many local governments now prefer to outsource ALTs as contract workers (業務委託 or 請負) because of the lower costs compared to hiring ALTs through the JET Programme under the scheme of worker dispatches (労働者派遣事業). Under the Worker Dispatch Law (労働者派遣法), a local board of education or school is not allowed to instruct ALTs to carry out team teaching as assistants to JTE if the ALTs are outsourced contract workers. Contract workers hired by private agents must carry out their work independently, without direct supervision. In fact, in August 2009, the MEXT (MEXT, 2009b) wrote to the MHLW, seeking legal advice on 'the use of ALT through contract agreement', accompanied by a document that specified that the role of ALTs in team teaching was to support the teachers in charge (担当教員) and that under the School Education Act only the teachers in charge could conduct classes. After receiving advice from the MHLW later the same month, the MEXT sent a notice to local boards of education, outlining the MHLW's view that team teaching could not be conducted with outsourced ALTs and urging them to review the employment conditions of ALTs. Nevertheless, problems surrounding the employment of ALTs as contract workers have continued to be reported (*Asahi Shimbun*, 2010). ALTs' perceptions of their involvement in schools are discussed by Geluso (Chapter 6).

MEXT's view that the role of ALTs is to support JTEs, and that only JTEs can conduct classes, is consistent with the description of 'native speakers' in the Course of Study (学習指導要領). 'Native speakers', as a loanword, appears in the section on 'Curriculum Design and Treatment of the Contents' of the new Course of Study for foreign languages in senior high schools. The term 'native speakers' is mentioned in relation to teachers' use of innovative teaching methods and styles, along with information and communications technology (ICT). The item that refers to 'native speakers' appears last, after items relating to teaching materials, pronunciation and dictionaries:

(4) In the instruction of each subject, teachers should innovate in terms of teaching methods and styles, incorporating pair work, group work, etc. as appropriate and utilizing audio visual teaching materials, computers, communication networks, etc. Moreover, *team-teaching* classes conducted in cooperation with *native speakers* etc. should be positively utilised to develop students' communication abilities and to deepen their international

understanding. (MEXT, 2010b; author's translation and emphasis based on the English version of the old Course of Study provided by MEXT)

This statement highlights the fact that the team teaching in question is not between JTEs and NSE teachers but between JTEs and 'native speakers', and that the team teaching itself is not rated highly in the syllabus. ALTs, who are sent to schools under various schemes, are not recognised as 'teachers' but as 'native speakers', which indicates that the relationship between JTEs and NSEs in team teaching is not equal. In the new Course of Study for foreign language activities in elementary schools, 'native speakers' are no longer mentioned in relation to team teaching:

III. SYLLABUS DESIGN AND TREATMENT OF CONTENTS

1. (4) Homeroom teachers or teachers in charge of foreign language activities should make teaching programs and conduct lessons. Efforts should be made to get more people involved in lessons by inviting native speakers of the foreign language or by seeking cooperation from local people who are proficient in the foreign language, depending on the circumstances of the local community. (MEXT, 2009a, original English version. Emphasis by author)

In elementary school settings, 'native speakers' are people who JTEs should make an effort to involve in classroom activities, which means that their involvement is optional. Contrary to the assumption that the new policy for introducing English in elementary schools would increase the presence of NSEs, it has actually encouraged Japanese homeroom teachers to conduct classes by themselves rather than engaging in team teaching (NHK, 2011). The original Japanese Course of Study, however, reads differently from this English version. The second sentence, which includes the word 'native speakers', suggests a different approach to native speakers:

For class delivery, efforts should be made to enhance teaching by *utilizing native speakers* and by seeking cooperation from local people who are proficient in the foreign language, depending on the circumstances of the local community. (MEXT, 2008c. Author's translation)

In the original Japanese text, the expression 'to get more people involved' does not appear, and 'native speakers' are not 'invited' but 'utilised'. The instrumental description of 'native speakers' is toned down in the English version, but it is the same rhetoric used in the above-mentioned MEXT document about the role of ALTs that was sent to the MHLW. Describing NSEs as resources to be utilised is a common practice in both the private and the public sectors in Japan, and the rhetoric of 'utilisation of native speakers' is predominant throughout the government documents produced by the cabinet, the MEXT and the MIC.

Native Speakers as Resources

To describe native speakers along the same lines as other resources is also a common practice in Japan. For example, in 2006, at a sectional meeting on the foreign language curriculum in elementary and secondary schools of the MEXT Central Council for Education, a table entitled 'Examples of characteristics of native speakers and ICT' was distributed (MEXT, 2006). Despite the highest rate of infrastructure development in the world, Japan has not had a coherent approach to the introduction of ICT (Elwood & MacLean, 2009), and MEXT begun to organise a support system for the implementation of ICT in schools in 2007.

The table lists the 'current situations', 'merits' and 'challenges' of 'native speakers' and ICTs side by side, as if the aim of distributing this material for discussion was to compare the merits and shortcomings of 'native speakers' and ICTs and decide which was more useful in TEFL. Only one 'merit' is listed for 'native speakers', whereas there are four for ICTs. Likewise, four items are listed as challenges in relation to 'native speakers', while only one is given for ICTs. The summary of the table is as follows:

(Native speakers)
Merits:
- Children can have two-way communication with native speakers

Challenges:
- Pronunciation and quality of teaching vary according to the individuals
- Have difficulty in conducting repetitions according to children's ability
- Restrictions in terms of time and space
- Need time for induction and meetings with teachers

(ICT)
Merits:
- Children can experience high quality pronunciation of the standard English of native speakers anywhere in Japan

- Can be repeated according to children's ability
- Available in regions where it is difficult to secure native speakers
- Possible to conduct flexible classes with a variety of materials

Challenges:
- In general it is difficult to have two-way communication (it is possible, however, to have two-way communication by distant mode)

This suggests that JTEs would prefer to use cassette tapes, CDs or videos rather than actual 'native speakers' because ICTs are easy to use, reliable and authentic, and that 'native speakers' might be desirable for a two-way communication but are not necessarily indispensable for TEFL. The view of 'native speakers as resources', however, contradicts or questions the way in which team teaching was described in the Course of Study for senior high school foreign languages; team teaching was seen as facilitating the development of students' communication abilities and deepening their international understanding. If 'native speakers' are seen as resources and are considered less desirable than ICT by JTEs, what kind of 'international understanding' students are expected to deepen? The next section examines the new Course of Study for senior high school English, which has been discussed for its aim to conduct English classes in English.

The New Course of Study for Conducting English Classes in English

The new curriculum for conducting senior high school English classes in English presents some pedagogical issues in relation to the treatment of native speakers. As Rivers (2011a) points out, pedagogical motivations are often compromised at the altar of political ones when language policy is implemented, and this applies to this new curriculum.

The new Course of Study for senior high schools will be fully implemented from 2013 as part of the government's policy to cultivate 'Japanese with English abilities', which was announced in 2002. It should be noted that the Course of Study, which has been revised roughly every 10 years since the early 1960s, is binding on public schools, and that textbooks must be written to conform to the Course of Study (Horio, 1988). The new curriculum aims to increase the exposure of students to English and to create classrooms that are a place for communication (MEXT, 2009c). The expression used in the new curriculum, '言語活動は英語で行う, to conduct language activities in

English', brings us immediately to the notion of English as the medium of instruction. The wording or rhetoric is crucial here because issues of medium of instruction are both political and educational. Over the past 10 years, particularly in regions where English has played a significant role in shaping cultural and political independence, medium-of-instruction policies have been considered in terms of educational, political and economic agendas as a reflection of globalisation in communication (Tollefson & Tsui, 2004). In the new Course of Study, however, no equivalent expression to 'medium of instruction' in Japanese, such as '指導言語' or '教授言語', is used.

If the new curriculum is, in fact, a medium-of-instruction policy, one obvious concern is overlooked: the impact on both NSE and NNSE teachers. Usually, those who are most affected by a medium-of-instruction policy in school settings are NNSE teachers and students. When MEXT announced its plan to revise the Course of Study in December 2008, it caused a stir in public circles, including among JTEs in senior high schools. It has been reported that JTEs felt it placed them under greater pressure to perform, but MEXT did not consider this a problem because 'teachers are supposed to be experts' (Katayama et al., 2008: 34). From MEXT's point of view, JTEs probably did not need to worry about their performance in comparison to NSEs because there would not be any NSE teachers, only 'native speakers' or ALTs.

The expression 'to conduct language activities in English' appears in the Language Activities section of the Course of Study for senior high school English. The same wording is used for the instructions for all English subjects except for 'Communication English Basic', which serves as a bridging course between junior and senior high school English:

> The following *language activities should be conducted in English* by setting actual scenes for language use so that students practise receiving and sending information, ideas etc. (Translation and emphasis by the author)

An important point here is that this instruction is actually about students' language activities. No distinction is made between learning items for students and teaching items for teachers. Another section that includes a reference to conducting classes in English is the clause on 'Content common to each subject in English':

> In terms of each English subject, because of its specific nature, in order to provide students with ample opportunity both to have contact with English and to make classes an actual place for communication, *in principle classes should be conducted in English*. In doing so, consideration

should be given to using English appropriate to the level of the students' understanding. (Translation and emphasis by the author)

It is not clear what 'English appropriate to the level of the students' understanding' means here. Does it mean that teachers can switch to Japanese if students do not understand the instructions? Or, are students allowed to use Japanese if they do not understand the task? Is Japanese banned in classes? If all activities should be conducted in English, shouldn't textbooks be written in English? What about dictionaries? Do students use English/English dictionaries? What about assessment? Are tests to be conducted in English? And more important, how does this affect team teaching with native speakers?

It must be pointed out that the curriculum design and treatment of content, including the description of team teaching involving native speakers mentioned earlier, is almost identical to the version in the old Course of Study. In other words, the new approach to conducting English classes, in fact, has very little effect on the curriculum itself. This leads us to conclude that the new curriculum actually has nothing to do with English as the medium of instruction and does not change the way NSEs are treated.

Conclusions

The recent TEFL curriculum changes such as the introduction of English in elementary schools and the new approach to conducting senior high school English classes potentially provide opportunities for NSEs to expand their roles in TEFL at schools, but this potential has not yet been realised because of problems and restrictions in the areas of employment, curriculum and pedagogy. Ongoing financial difficulties have forced the Japanese government to review ministerial programmes, including projects relating to TEFL. The review concluded that the government could not afford to spend money on projects that did not have clear and attainable goals. The JET Programme, which has been a major provider of ALTs to schools, was one such project, and lack of change to the programme's content and continued selection of ALTs who do not have language-teaching qualifications in the name of international exchange were criticized for failing to meet regional demands. The conflict between language teaching and international understanding at the tertiary level is discussed by Tsuneyoshi (Chapter 8).

An examination of the legal issues surrounding the employment of ALTs reveals the reality of local demands for ALTs: local schools prefer the less expensive and less committed option of 'utilising' NSEs for team teaching with JTEs. The gap between the original Japanese term and its

English version symbolises the ambiguity and confusion surrounding the issue: an ALT is not a teacher but an assistant, and NSEs are therefore not recognised as independent teachers within the education system. No effort has been made to change this situation, which is in marked contrast to the government's move to change the regulations to allow junior high school teachers to teach English in elementary schools to facilitate the successful implementation of the new curriculum of 'foreign language activities' in elementary schools. It should be noted that there has been systematic exclusion of foreigners from full-time employment in the public education sector: the central government's advice to local boards of education to limit the employment of Japanese-speaking Korean nationals is a well-known case in point (MEXT, 1991).

The initial purpose of the JET Programme was to promote international relationships (McConnell, 2000), but even before its inception, there existed a scheme of inviting British teachers of English to Japan, which was introduced in 1978 (MOFA, 1980). The transition to the JET Programme in the 1980s, which coincided with Japan's growing internationalisation, can be interpreted as a shift from importing teachers, presumably accompanied by pedagogy, to cultivating NSEs to fit into the Japanese education system. Teaching qualifications and Japanese proficiency are deliberately *not* sought in the selection process for ALTs, precisely because these would render them equal to or better than JTEs. It could be said that this constitutes Japan's answer to the 'monolingual fallacy', the 'native speaker fallacy' (Canagarajah, 1999b; Phillipson, 1992), or the 'inferiority complex' to NSE (Jenkins, 2000).

Space does not allow a detailed examination of the elementary school curriculum for 'foreign language activities' in this chapter, but the deliberate ambivalence towards or disrespect to the professionalism of teachers of TEFL is evident in various forms: the use of 'foreign language activities' rather than 'English' in the subject title, the lack of assessment for language components, the fact that teachers can conduct the 'foreign language activities' classes without being English teachers, the 'English notes' that MEXT distributes to schools rather than using a textbook and so on. Certainly, the new curriculum was not designed to embrace the expertise of NSE teachers. Whether the recommendations that resulted from financial necessity during the GRU screening process have an actual impact on the way in which programs and schemes for promoting TEFL operate remains to be seen, but it merits close consideration, because responses of the various government departments to the recommendations could signal a new environment for 'native speakers' in Japan.

12 The Meaning of Japan's Role of Professional Foreigner

Evan Heimlich

When is racial inclusion preferable to racial exclusion? In a landmark study of the Bell Telephone company's professional role for operators (Green, 1991), from 1965 to 1970 segregation and White supremacy hardly worked less powerfully after Bell hired Black operators. Before 1965, Bell had invested its professional, career position of 'telephone operator' with considerable privilege and prestige, and had excluded Black women from it. When Bell at long last moved to integrate its workforce of telephone operators, within a few years it filled a majority of its positions as telephone operators with Black women, but subsequently Bell degraded its own position for operators. New policies claimed this role no longer deserved the privilege and prestige that Bell previously had invested in it. Such devaluation of the professional role of operator served to mark, categorize and oppress the status of the organization's own Black workers. That is, Bell defended the White supremacy that structured the organization and American society from the threat posed by the presence of Blacks in honored roles in the workplace. In order to mark the integration as not too threatening, Bell redefined it as much less substantial, by degrading the position it now had designated for Black women.

In this chapter, this story of the operator role at Bell matters for its dynamics of backlash, by which impetus towards segregation countered the impetus towards racial integration. Policies shaped the roles for employing the feared outsiders, in order to police the status barrier between White and Black workers. Although any analogy between Whiteness and Japaneseness is inexact, the dynamics of Japan's employment of non-Japanese workers tends to follow a congruent pattern: policies categorically regulate employment of the socially low outsider, reserving normal status for insiders. Bell's dis-esteeming of its own operator resembles Japanese school systems' degradation of the role for their non-Japanese teacher, during a period when more outsiders were infiltrating. As it charts the meaning of Japan's role for the 'native speaker' in terms of xenophobic backlash in Japan, this chapter will refer particularly to three incongruous yet related events: the landmark 2000 *Gallagher* ruling against a terminated teacher, the 2004 termination of the national *gaikokujin kyoushi* (literally, 'foreigner experts') programme and the 2009 effort to repatriate the *Nikkei*. Finally, the chapter turns to an illustrative, televised satire of Japan's xenophobic use of its role for the 'native speaker'.

In order to frame the professional role in Japan of the 'native speaker' as teacher, this chapter will first briefly examine a key framework in which Japan's national policies have retained non-Japanese workers for roles as professional foreigners. Japan's policy-makers (circa 1860) created the template within Japan's national university system: a prestigious, national position for the *gaikokujin kyoushi*. Japanese officials brought thousands of non-Japanese into these national positions at Japan's national universities. It was the model for both the eponymous position at Japan's prefectural universities and similar positions at many Japanese cities' universities. More broadly, it helped shape the role of the non-Japanese professor at private universities, the role of the JET Programme teacher and most populously, the role of the non-Japanese conversation schoolteacher.

Why did policy-makers re-cast Japan's foreign teacher merely as the 'native speaker'? 'Native speaker' in Japan is primarily a category of social roles in the workplace, best understood in terms of the policing of hierarchized role boundaries. This newer schema of the 'native speaker' serves to mark boundaries more clearly: the role of the professional foreigner henceforth officially is not to serve as any sort of scholastic expert per se, but instead merely to represent the category of 'native speaker'.

Of course, it is also a kind of professional, economic role, with economic and legal contexts. Indeed, in order to contextualize this role's development, it fits to mention the global economic downturn's squeeze of the labour market, not least in the teaching profession, and particularly the professionalization, specialization and squeeze on TESOL globally. Meanwhile, Japan's semi-privatization of sectors of what was its government, including the national university system, is not irrelevant. But such explanations cannot suffice to explain what has been happening in Japan with the role of the 'native speaker'.

Always, when attempting to say not only how but also why Japan maintains or adapts its use of the 'native speaker', one courts controversy. The challenge largely stems from broad issues in the sociology of knowledge, concerning rational choice theory and Orientalism. Do people generally make choices that accord with strategies for maximizing material interests? Although such a notion has lost favour in academic economics and in other fields, few writers on Japan have developed facility with alternative frameworks of interpretation for reading social policies in terms of social logics. So on the one hand, the standard fallback is to insist that Japanese policy-makers, like almost anyone, must be making choices aimed to protect finances or to obey the rule of law. On the other hand, when a writer focuses on social pressures to explain Japanese policies, they should expect charges of Orientalism. So a disclaimer is in order: to wit, not only Japanese but also non-Japanese policy-makers implement policies that make the most sense according to a logic at variance with their own society's reigning sense of rational choice. Actually, such rational-actor models of behaviour, which are based on neoclassical economics, cannot go very far towards explaining social policy or any social behaviour. As Bigelow (2005: para. 20) has articulated, 'because the neoclassical theory emphasizes calculations made by individuals, it tends not to focus on the impact of external and social factors'. Moreover, if Japan exemplifies a society in which social contexts not only always matter but also are supposed to matter, then surely the neoclassical model of the actor as maximizer of material resources is particularly unfitting here.

The explorations of this chapter arose first in the context of a 2005 debate over why Japanese colleges increasingly were outsourcing their 'native speaker' positions. In an internet-based discussion group affiliated with JALT, Robert Aspinall and other leading voices contended that a concern for the financial 'bottom line' motivated institutions to save money by outsourcing. I countered that the social pressures to join in xenophobia were more salient. Meanwhile and moreover, according to a common, nationwide, semi-official standard that became quite common (in 2006), foreigners in Japan typically were contracted as guest workers for strictly limited terms (e.g. three years) in a given post. Why?

This chapter suggests such standards and policies serve to mark the social oppression of non-Japanese workers. That is, policies regulate foreigners' employment in order to firewall Japanese society from a supposed threat of infiltration. Arguably, the more fierce the pressure Japan faces to integrate its society, then the more rigorously national policies aim to segregate and debase the roles marked for non-Japanese workers. But such causal claims are unnecessary here: actually *the regulation mainly serves as public relations in a xenophobic drama, ritualistically to mark and contain the threat, in order to teach lessons to members of Japanese society that Japaneseness is still strictly and fixedly demarked*. For extensive documentation of these ongoing efforts of Japan's national policies towards foreigners, one should see Arudou (2010a, 2010b): notably, in the past 10 years especially, hoteliers and sports associations have introduced newly constraining policies, as have the courts, ministries and other arms of the national government, towards assuring members of the society that Japan's institutions may not treat foreigners as insiders.

National policies tend to dramatize officialdom's restriction of foreign workers, in order to counter any sense of anarchic, social upheaval. This trend is not new, but the urgency of the drama increased in the 1990s and 2000s. According to many economic prognosticators on Japan's manufacturing economy, it risks decline from a shortage of manual labour, unless it somehow manages to greatly increase the resident foreign work force. (This challenge arises because, while the Japanese population is shrinking and aging, not enough Japanese workers are taking positions characterized by difficult, dirty or dangerous work.) Japan's policy-makers may find they face a stark choice: to lead the Japanese economy towards decline or to lead it towards a huge and rapid expansion of its foreign workforce. Either choice will rock Japanese society's sense of itself. Meanwhile by 2005, an influx of foreigners already was well underway – indeed by that year, relative to 1990, the non-Japanese population had doubled. According to my erstwhile colleagues at Kobe University, Llewelyn and Hirano (2009) (see also Smil, 2007; Onishi, 2008),

> these seemingly inevitable demographic challenges have forced many in the Japanese government to grudgingly accept that a higher immigration intake could be economically beneficial to Japan, although in practice new [pro-immigration] policies have not been forthcoming and a restrictive immigration policy continues to be enforced. (para. 8)

Meanwhile 'Japan's present immigration policy still firmly remains premised on the twin pillars of enforcement and restriction' (para. 9).

Now, let us sketch here the story of the *Nikkei* workers. This category for holders of *Nikkei* visas (including both workers and their families) has been by far Japan's most populous, official, national, new role for resident foreigners. The story of the *Nikkei* programme begins in the 1980s after policy-makers concluded that their efforts failed to increase Japan's workforce by raising the birthrate; the population continued to shrink. If not Japanese workers, who else would work? During the 1990s and 2000s, the Japanese government, in tandem with Toyota and other corporate employers, recruited workers of Japanese descent, from Peru and especially Brazil, until the total population of resident *Nikkei* reached 366,000, all granted permanent residency from their arrival in Japan. If they bet that the *Nikkei*, with their Japanese phenotypes, would blend into Japan, then these policy-makers must have grown sorely disappointed. The *Nikkei* have hardly blended in. Indeed Japanese society has tended to regard them as a particularly unruly category of foreigner. So in 2009, facing a downturn in Japanese manufacturers' demand for the sort of labour they depend largely on *Nikkei* to provide, Japan's top policy-makers moved unambiguously to send the *Nikkei* home. Immigration-averse Japan offered to pay any or all the 366,000 *Nikkei* to leave Japan and never return (see Tabuchi, 2009).

The 2009 stipulation that the departed *Nikkei* never return to Japan is key, because it is scarcely justifiable economically: so it helps show that, though economic pressures may drive recruitment to (or send-off from) Japan, other imperatives shape the use of non-Japanese workers. That is, if a legion of workers became economically extraneous during an economic downturn, national policy-makers did have some justification to rid Japan of some workers if they could, and they could hardly have rid Japan of Japanese workers as easily. Economic efficiency may have mattered here insofar as policy-makers aimed to spare Japan's providers of social services from facing too large a legion of newly unemployed workers and their families. But in order to prepare in case Japan's factories call again soon for more workers than Japan itself provides, efficiency would also dictate that policy allow for the return to Japan of some of these already-trained, partly acculturated workers.

So why did the 2009 policy disfavour the return of departed *Nikkei* workers who had already acculturated by mastering some Japanese language, customs, etc.? Towards answering this question, we will cite the decision in a labour lawsuit brought by Gwen Gallagher, who was a 'native speaker' professor in Japan; but for a moment more, let us continue to try to make sense of the 2009 policy's effort to repatriate the *Nikkei*. This policy reversal, from recruitment to send-off, can tend to puzzle observers who proceed from the assumption that policies must make a consistent form of sense, serving, for example the bottom line of a balance sheet. But such reversals of policy make sense if Japan's national policies towards 'native speakers' are subject to fiercely countervailing impetuses, neither of which dominates for very long.

The *Nikkei* story makes the most sense if one frames it in terms of policy-makers' attempts to minimize any unrest, in a changing world, over slippage in the meaning of Japaneseness. When policy-makers in 1990 faced a strong need for foreign labour in a society fiercely averse to immigration, first they tried to strike a balance with the *Nikkei* programme. But the *Nikkei*'s presence introduced hybridity where supposedly Japaneseness was inviolate. That is, notwithstanding their genotype and phenotype, the *Nikkei* relate to Japanese society as non-Japanese, born and raised abroad in Peruvian and Brazilian families. So how could Japan recruit foreign workers who will remain always clearly marked and segregated as foreigners in the workplace? By 2009, top policy-makers apparently abandoned the recruitment of permanent residents, as a solution to bolstering the workforce. Instead, to strike a balance between xenophobia and a need for foreign labour, policies next have aimed primarily to recruit foreign sojourners into employment contracts bound by strict term limits. According to this new tactic, the society should tolerate efforts to expand Japan's foreign workforce, as long as this workforce, on the whole, is marked as restricted to temporary, segregated low-status roles.

In order to defend Japan's paramount sense of *inclusion*, against threat of that the boundaries of Japaneseness might get blurred, national policy treats foreign workers in accordance with a basic labour-law workaround against social integration within a Japanese workplace: roughly, 'Ensure no chance at inclusion for excluded workers'. That is, according to established legal precedent in Japan, if an employer continuously retains a worker long enough, then regardless of any exclusionary contract, this worker becomes legally a worker inside the company, rather than a worker contingent on a contract and thus easy to dismiss. The simple workaround for a great many employers, particularly employers of foreign workers, is to use 'the revolving door' to ensure churn, so that no worker holds their position for very long, lest a court of law ever rule that *de facto* the employer made the worker an employee inside the company, thus legally difficult to dismiss.

Although many Japanese workers, too, find themselves headed towards such a revolving door, disproportionately this fate is for non-Japanese workers. By some estimates, in 2005, 90% of the non-Japanese workers in Japan were contracted as term-limited workers, rather than employed as members of a workplace. According to Louis Carlet, the Executive President of Zenkoku Ippan Tokyo General Union, the corresponding figure for the entire workforce meanwhile was about 30%. More recent policy more strictly maps foreignness onto the revolving door, with contracts for native speaker jobs.

The foregoing discussion can help explain why Japanese employment of non-Japanese workers features categories such as the native speaker of a non-Japanese language: the role is plainly marked as one for a non-member of Japanese society. Foreignness of the worker is the qualification of the role. According to such schema, there are in Japan no Japanese workers assigned roles as native speakers of foreign languages, because the categories are mutually exclusive.

Meanwhile, the economic justifications for term-limited labour often use biopolitical phrases to frame the proper professional foreigner as a pure and fresh representative of foreignness, as opposed to the stale hybrid who remains more than a few years in Japan. Nowhere are these terms clearer than in regards to labour policies for native speakers, especially since the year 2000.

In 2000, the Sapporo High Court ruled in favor of Asahikawa University, in a lawsuit for wrongful dismissal brought by Professor Gwen Gallagher: as Fox (2001) has documented, the court's ruling held that for a professional foreigner, 'freshness' is necessary for enthusiasm in promoting travel and professorial exchange. So officially, Gallagher's having settled into marriage with a Japanese man in Japan disqualified her to continue serving as a professional foreigner. In this sense, the call for fresh foreigners here is a call for foreigners pure of acculturation to Japan, uncontaminated by the hybridization that results from membership in a Japanese family.

This call expresses a powerful set of polarities that, as a regime of representation in the sphere of work, shape Japaneseness in relation to the native speaker role. First, the teachers enthusiastic about their role in 'professorial exchange' surely are supposed to bring their students to share enthusiasm for travel and exchange: crucially and paradoxically, this exchange is supposed to be between parties previously uncontaminated by exchange. (This is a basic pitfall of multiculturalism, the insistence that each identity group member must maintain their authentic, unhybridized essence in order to represent their identity group properly in exchange with others). The native speaker's pure foreignness functions schematically to keep Japaneseness pure. The basic opposition here is 'purely foreign teachers' versus 'purely Japanese students'. Hybridized foreign teachers risk hybridizing Japaneseness. Moreover, schematically the call for purely foreign teachers strengthens the opposition of 'foreign worker' versus 'Japanese worker'. This polar opposition is most legible in terms of seniority: categorically, the professional foreigner loses value with seniority in Japan as Hall (1998, 2006) and Heimlich (2010) have documented while according to a bedrock tenet of salary in Japan, the Japanese worker gains value with seniority.

In sum, if we ask why rulings and policies favor the revolving door particularly for Japan's native speakers, then as context we should examine the functions of the Gallagher ruling, the termination of the national *gaikokujin kyoushi* position, the *Nikkei* repatriation project and the widespread emphasis on 'native speaker' as a professional role in itself, in terms of what these things all primarily aim to teach Japanese society: that the social rules will firewall Japaneseness from hybridization. Though this interpretation of course is not the only valid one, I submit that no other explanation comes close to explaining as much. Particularly, it is challenging to explain how, given the vast resources Japan commits to the task, it fails to make proportionate advancement towards bringing Japan's students to speak languages other than Japanese. Why do other nations fare considerably better with far less resources? I count myself among those who find Japan's effort here overall runs counter to what may seem its ostensible purpose.

Furthermore, the Gallagher ruling's oft-cited disqualification of the Japan-acculturated native speaker, who supposedly must have lost enthusiasm for travel and exchange, manifests the backlash that channels segregation from an impulse towards integration. That is, the marking of such fresh, requisite enthusiasm functions primarily to counter enthusiasms towards second-language acquisition, often deemed a threat to the purity of Japaneseness. Moreover, such enthusiasm counters the pain of challenging the supposed insurmountable language barrier around the Japanese people. Let us turn next in some detail to a provocative illustration of such dynamic: a 1992 television episode featuring a native speaker as teacher.

Its non-Japanese creator adroitly spoofed English lessons that effectively teach students that the language barrier is insurmountable. Executives at Fuji Television apparently foresaw the episode's appeal to viewers outside Japan, when, after a 13-year hiatus, they decided in 2005 to re-broadcast the episode's series via satellite network. The episode went viral particularly in the United States for its perverse absurdity (a copy of the video had half a million hits on YouTube, it was featured on *The Tonight Show*): its performers incant 'I've got a bad case of diarrhea' while they do a robotic aerobics routine with great enthusiasm.

It starts with a young, seated Japanese woman who clutches her abdomen and speaks in a mix of English, gesture and Japanese to a passing young White man with whom she makes eye contact. In accented but clear English, she says, 'Call an ambulance, please'. The man agrees, then asks her where it hurts. She answers, 'My stomach', but as 'Ma i sutomaku'. Next, as the woman fumbles in Japanese to say more, she adds 'eto . . . eto . . .' ('umm . . . ummm . . .'), and drops eye contact, bending away from him. Suddenly, she exclaims, in Japanese, 'I want to say it correctly but it hurts! It hurts!' When the counter-shot of his face freezes, a disembodied voice-over of an American-accented, older-sounding speaker of English slowly demonstrates pronunciation of 'I've got a bad case . . . of diarrhea', Next comes something completely different from both the scene and the pronunciation demonstration: three young women stand wearing leotards and enthusiastic smiles. They move vigorously in unison, performing rigid calisthenics while staring straight ahead at no one. Over a robotic beat they chant in a strong Japanese accent, using stress unsuited to this phrase: '*I've* got a bad case, *of* diarrhea'.

This televised EFL lesson (which evokes 'radio exercises', or ラジオ体操, *rajio taisou*, long compulsory in many of Japan's schools) satirically celebrates the language barrier's insurmountability. After the foreign passerby fails to recognize that the Japanese woman clutching her abdomen is experiencing pain in her abdomen, she lapses from English into Japanese: the lesson teaches that if one mixes Japanese with English and gesture, the hybrid utterance will cause the emergency conversation literally, nightmarishly to freeze. Next, it teaches that the native speaker teaches as a pristine and disembodied voice from another dimension. The televised lesson comes full circle, as an enthusiastic, highly synchronized, foreigner-free performance comes to substitute for painfully messy interaction between Japanese and non-Japanese people.

The role of professional foreigner here is indeed mainly a teaching role, but hardly one for enabling speakers of different languages to communicate with each other. (At this point, another disclaimer is in order here, to acknowledge that in Japanese entertainment, some professional foreigners maintain social standing much higher than the *Nikkei* labourers. These entertainers are analogous to the native speaker, in some important ways, too, but not as effective subversions of the firewall at work between Japaneseness and foreignness. Rather, their performances serve as licensed release (like a form of carnival – see Stallybrass & White, 1986). Their inclusion teaches this social lesson: after each titillating walk on the wild side, ultimately Japaneseness remains safely firewalled from foreignness.)

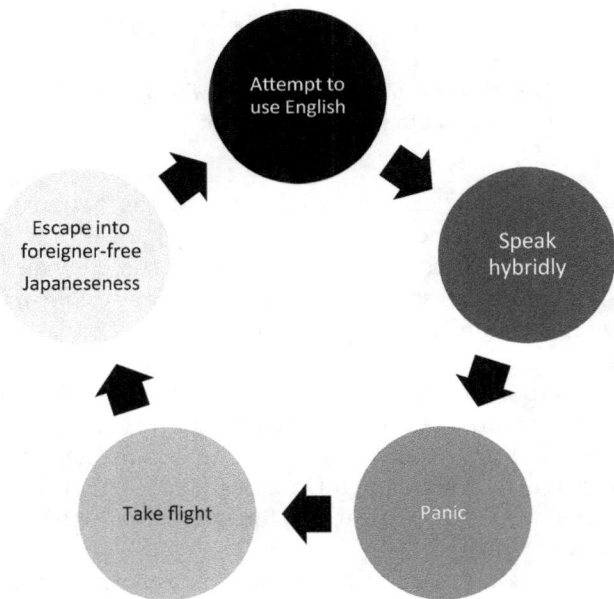

Figure 12.1 The no/EFL eddy, swirling where the pro-communication-with-foreigners current runs adjacent to its opposite current

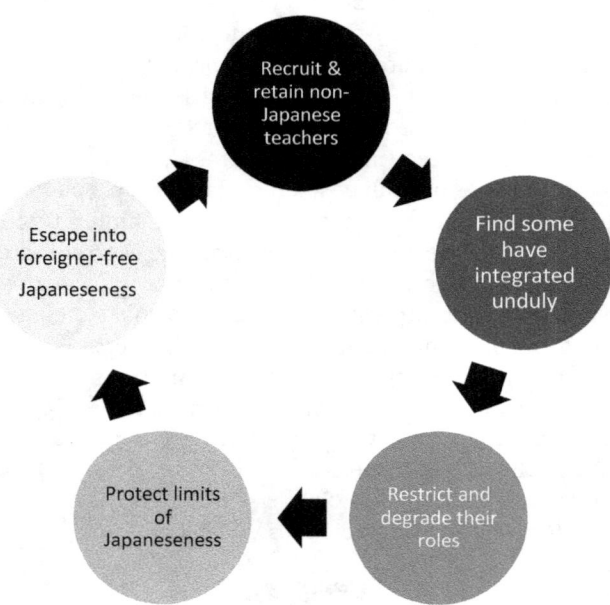

Figure 12.2 Japan's employment-of-foreigners eddy, swirling where the pro-inclusion-of-foreigners current runs adjacent to its opposite current

As Figure 12.1 sketches, the main lesson of the nationalized, native-speaker role is for Japanese society to mark the hermetically pure essence of Japaneseness in contrast to, and relief from, the embodied essence of foreignness. As Figure 12.2 shows, policies aim to keep cycling in new batches of foreign workers in order to keep enabling this rite of social purification of the workplace.

The revolving door then is far more than merely a labour policy: it is moreover the name of the game for marking the insularity of Japaneseness at its threshold. What counts most is the act of cleaning house, to expel the dirt which according to Douglass (1966: 36) is the 'matter out of place' here, the contaminating foreigners and the foreign way they speak.

In any given society featuring pro-integration versus pro-segregation currents, the two currents meet side by side at the figure of the outsiders, because it is they who must be integrated, yet it is also they who must be segregated. And where any counter-currents meet side by side, they tend to form eddies or whirlpools. Their circles, 'the revolving door' for foreign workers, or the approach-then-escape-the-foreigners circuit for Japanese people practising English, are much more apparent than the flows that form them, so when we regard these two figures let us focus on the circles' formation by adjacent counter-currents.

Part 4

Native-Speakerism as a Multi-Faceted and Contemporary Social Phenomenon

13 Scrutinizing the Native Speaker as Referent, Entity and Project

Glenn Toh

Introduction

This chapter seeks to reflect on discourses surrounding the native speaker phenomenon and how this is played out in various discursive spaces in Japan and, in particular, how conversations referencing the native speaker are staged in professional spaces and real-life contestations. The use of the phrase 'native speaker phenomenon' bears some elucidation at the outset, in the sense that 'phenomenon' is often used with the intention of referencing something which draws attention. In Japan, the native speaker features prominently in conversations and narratives on ELT as an often used referent in both corridor and professional exchanges. More than this, the native speaker is both an entity of socio-semiotic significance and a 'project' bearing ideological dimensions within the portals of politicized discourse. Hence, it will be seen that a deeper appreciation of the native speaker phenomenon as such emerges from an understanding of a concatenation of native speaker as referent, semiotic entity and ideologized project. In particular, using frameworks informed by current understandings of discourse, discourse systems and discursive practices (Scollon & Scollon, 2001; van Dijk, 1984, 2001) and how they come to operate within the inner workings of the politics of education (Alderson, 2009), the chapter explores ways in which (1) the native speaker as a construct can, in different instances, be discursively represented, essentialised and 'Othered' in the Japanese situation, and (2) how native speakers as people entering Japan come then to be employed, deployed, typified or otherwise looked upon the way they are.

For the purposes of this discussion, it is vital at the outset to acknowledge the need to distinguish between native speaker as the socio-discursive and socio-semiotic construct that it is and native speakers as the unique individuals (and indeed professionals) encountered in daily life and/or the workplace. It will be noted that much of the discussion will have less to do with native speakers as individuals per se, least of all with the well-meaning individual native speakers who happen, by dint of fate, fancy or foible, to find themselves teaching in Japan, and would almost certainly be a twice removed cousin of the native speaker as rhetorical construct. The latter remains a veritable subject of discursive negotiation in many a social, political or discursive portal in present-day Japan.

Written from the standpoint of someone born and bred in Southeast Asia and whose mother tongue is not English but Cantonese, this chapter seeks to tease out the finer strands of how the native speaker as both seme and construct has acquired the socio-symbolism it now has, to the extent that the subject itself has now even become a focus of discussion in many a book chapter or journal article. The observations in the chapter are borne of the author's experience working in the Tokyo – Yokohama area. As a teacher, program director and tenured applied linguistics professor, the author has had the opportunity to engage in EFL teaching, course planning, materials writing apart from sitting on interview and promotional panels as well as curriculum development committees, while enjoying gainful contact with colleagues in ELT in the course of daily interaction.

Native Speaker as Referent

The native speaker as referent focuses on how the native speaker is easily identified with deictic and referential intent. In other words, when the term 'native speaker' is used, both speaker and listener will more often than not assume shared meanings of what the referent term means in relation to the Japanese situation. In terms of specifics, writers like Honna, Kubota and D'Angelo have vividly characterized Japanese understandings of the native speaker as referent. Kubota (2002b), for example, notes that the native speaker, given a mindset forged and fostered in an environment of ethnic and linguistic homogeneity, is one that tends to be defined by both (foreign) country of origin and race, if not colour. In Japan, the term itself becomes common and convenient, assumed and acceptable, even when it calls to mind the image of the white Caucasian English speaker (Kubota, 2002b; Seargeant, 2009a), reminiscent of what Davies (2003: 7) has to say about how the term itself has been used as 'a useful piece of shorthand'. Davies notes the rough and ready assumptions that can come with the term and observes in this sense that 'the everyday use of the term native speaker can cause offence'.

Thus, what readily comes to mind when someone says something like 'more native speaker teachers are needed in the school system to help improve the standard of English' is essentially the image of a white Caucasian English teacher (D'Angelo, 2008; Kubota, 2002b; Kubota, 2011a; Kubota & McKay, 2009; Seargeant, 2009a) and even more specifically, someone from either the United States or the United Kingdom (Honna, 2008; Honna & Takeshita, 1998). Difficult and imprecise the shared assumptions may be (e.g. varied notions of 'race', 'whiteness' or even 'nativeness'), the following could be said and the utterance would be understood at the level of what Davies (2003: 7) calls 'common sense': 'This letter needs editing. You must find a native speaker to help you' or 'We are very short of native speakers on our staff' or 'We need to source for a few more native speakers of American English to make our programme more attractive'.

Of course, writers in critical applied linguistics and ELT, on their part, make their pitch for more enlightened or at least more progressive views of the native speaker by drawing attention to other native speakers of English who may, albeit, be non-British, non-American or non-white (D'Angelo, 2008; Honna, 2008; Kubota, 2002b) and evidence of such views being taken on board can be found in efforts made to increase the diversity of teachers in terms of culture and nationality (Kubota, 2011a). The point, however, is that referentially speaking, given what Honna and Takeshita (1998) call Anglophilic tendencies in Japanese ELT and given what they have described as a 'proclivity for native-speaker English' that includes a strong measure of 'behavioural acculturation' (Honna & Takeshita, 1998: 118) in the desire among Japanese to 'become like American English speakers' (Honna, 2008: 147), it has proven to be a challenge when it comes to encouraging more enriched conversations around the native speaker, beyond the essentialist stereotypes of accent, race, nationality and colour. Compelling reasons for this are examined in the following section where it is seen how the native speaker takes on iconic status in discourses about English and ELT in Japan.

Native Speaker as Entity

Discussions of ELT in Japan that relate to the hiring of teachers and of target models of English invariably revolve around the native speaker, not so much as a classroom practitioner with a human face, but around what the image of the native speaker has come to represent, very often as an entity upon which a set of standards as well as socio-symbolic and sociocultural values and attributes are abstracted and collaged. It should be noted here that the native speaker as entity is crucial to the current ethos of ELT in Japan, and hardly a sociolinguistic discussion about ELT in Japan will be complete without some treatment of this socio-symbolic aspect of the native speaker. The next section seeks to examine ways the native speaker is represented and then objectivised, as both a commodified tool (Fairclough, 1992) and an allegorised subject in Japanese society, as well as how the native speaker in turn becomes woven into the myths and narratives of Japanese ELT.

The native speaker as entity, hence, in essence, looks at how the native speaker acquires a dimension of mythology in the ELT landscape in Japan. It builds on the 'shared assumptions' relating to native speaker as referent discussed in the previous section, and seeks to focus on the element of myth in the way the human face of the native speaker gives way to a deeper allegorised dimension. For the sake of illustration, one can consider how flight attendants are woven in as an integral part of the mythology of an airline's 'first class' or 'royal class' service and how these are embossed on the persona, not so much of pilots or flight engineers who are responsible for keeping airplanes in the air, but of frontline cabin crew. In similar manner, even as education becomes increasingly commodified (Fairclough, 1992), and the trend is for ELT programmes, be they at private schools or universities, to be 'organised and conceptualised in terms of commodity production, distribution and consumption' (Fairclough, 1992: 207), and as features of marketing become part of the accompanying rhetoric, the native speaker has come to assume a prominent iconic role, be this in advertisements for commercial schools or universities which are facing huge drops in enrolment.

In Japan, such advertisements can be found on suburban tabloids, suburban trains and subway stations, where native speakers are captured and captioned in poster-sized photographs as representations, not just (contortedly) of a quintessential form of English, the mastery of which would promise not only access to proverbial 'globalized' or 'liberated' lifestyles but also access to portals of pre-supposed corporate power. The models featured in such posters are invariably Caucasian, smartly dressed to evoke the likeness of someone from the corporate world. This could explain why many institutions employing native speaker teachers insist that on top of their human face, native speaker teachers need to put on suit and tie, despite the fact that it is in the classroom, where more down-to-earth dressing would prove more practical, that they discharge their duties. Ironically, native speakers teaching pre-school or primary school children can also be found to be similarly attired, this despite the fact that effective classroom practice may not correlate highly with dressing, but would rather involve a range of classroom and group activities where teachers are required to move around different learning stations, making suit and tie or other forms of power dressing quite cumbersome or unnecessary.

To be fair, such practices of imaging, corporate or otherwise, are rife in Japan, which until the time of the bursting of the economic bubble was the Mecca for fashion and retail in East Asia and beyond, as well as a place known to epitomize external refinement and good deportment. Nevertheless, mannequins in big department stores are invariably given markedly Caucasian features, be these in the shapes of noses and/or eyebrows, the size of the eyes or even in the mannequin's 'bone' structure. One would be hard-pressed to find a mannequin of darker hues or oriental build, which are simply not good for attracting attention. Even advertisements for children's wear, or to take it further, babies' clothes, use mannequins of distinctly Caucasian features. Yet, in featuring native speakers as part of glossy university advertisements or language school brochures, however, education finds itself pandering and subservient to a boutique or catwalk mentality in its readiness to be part of an inter-textual network that feeds and fetes the narratives of marketization and commercial retail.

Given all this, Caucasian teachers might also be said to have what might be termed Santa Claus value. Over Christmas season, institutions have Caucasian teachers dress up as Santa Claus to capture the Christmas spirit at community functions, whereas native speaker teachers of Asian or African extract do not quite manage to authenticate such a role. Missionaries in mission outreaches are also favourites as Santa Claus (and numerous other symbolic roles). This is not apart from how Caucasian native speakers get employed part-time as marriage celebrants at Japanese weddings. Displaying the robes of ordained clergy, they are called to perform the solemnization of vows in liturgical English. Celebrated by 'priests' who are neither ordained nor registered, such solemnizations are all of form and little substance, meeting the needs of a clientele wanting an anglophilic tang, in this case, at nuptials. Some wedding boutiques and programme organizers retain a regular pool of native speakers on whom they will call should Japanese couples opt to have their rings and vows exchanged in English.

Understandably, of course, the native speaker as entity may well constitute a way for Japanese society to apprehend and appropriate, and in other instances, cope with the presence of a diversity of people from overseas (not necessarily those who are English speaking at all) living on Japanese soil. An interesting point of relevance here is that among those Caucasians who are from overseas (there would be Caucasians born and bred in Japan as well), there would be those for whom English is *not* mother tongue. They may not speak English at all, and yet will, by dint of appearance, be absorbed within a native speaker persona or stereotype. Such people may well be French, German or Danish but because they are in possession of certain phenotypical features associated with the native speaker as entity, the conclusion is often drawn that they are invariably native speakers of English. The poignancy of this is noted by Seargeant when he highlights the following about the English language: whereas 'the language becomes not so much a tool for international communication, but a living artefact belonging to a foreign culture', native speaker teachers likewise

> become specimens of that foreign culture, their role as instructors of specialised knowledge overshadowed by their status as foreign nationals, so that it is the emblematic presence of a foreign culture in the classroom that is the defining factor for their appointment in schools. (Seargeant, 2009a: 56)

Of course, one may choose for argument's sake to say that Caucasians should have reason enough to be grateful not only for the sort of attention they receive but also for being the likely favourite when it comes to ELT or other jobs. This emerges for attention when comparisons are made with African-Americans (Russell, 1991; Kubota, 2002b) or Asians including Asian-Americans (Sekiguchi, 2002; Kubota, 2011b). African-Americans are, for example, asked about their ability to speak 'standard' English, while Asians can be disadvantaged in terms of salary or be simply viewed negatively by the clientele including parents (Kubota, 2002b, 2011b). Nevertheless, in relation to this discussion, such occurrences serve only to accentuate the depth and particularity of dimension when it comes to native speaker as entity.

Parallels of this can also be drawn with the matter of Miller's (1995) descriptions of the treatment of *gaijin tarento* (foreign stars) on Japanese television. These stars, predominantly (or invariably) white native speakers, are given air time as stand-in (or stood-up) entities for Japan's push towards greater internationalization and greater 'openness' towards matters foreign, but featured primarily because they are to be seen by a Japanese audience as 'phenomena' or curiosities, foreigners speaking Japanese while making grammatical or pronunciation mistakes to be laughed at, 'cute, amusing specimens of the category *henna gaijin* ("weird foreigner")' (Miller, 1995: 197).

Interestingly, however, it could be observed that within such essentialising (both allegorical and symbolic) conceptualizations of native speaker, the native speaker as human personality or even as 'free agent', is accorded, or at least permitted, 'free roaming' status around the ambit of certain accepted roles or interests: that person can be a school teacher or assistant teacher, night school language instructor, university lecturer, tour guide, English speaking au pair, conversation partner, singing teacher, TV talent or entertainer. Thus, it would not be unusual or unacceptable for one and the same person to be employed as university language tutor while moonlighting as a conversation teacher in night school for office workers, and on weekends as an English instructor to pre-school children.

This phenomenon finds a degree of uniqueness in Japan, not least because a confinement within a narrow ballpark of generalist roles can also be very demeaning when set against the ethics and ideals of work dignity. Native speakers sent to state schools are those who find placement as *Assistant* Language Teachers, playing second fiddle to the principal teacher. Other systems like Hong Kong, for example, employ native speakers in schools as full-fledged classroom professionals, not second fiddlers. Expanding beyond this narrow ballpark and assuming roles like creative thinker, conceptualizer or innovator may draw negative responses from colleagues around. As would be true in the case of the ALTs, native speakers are, in general, *not* required to offer suggestions on curriculum or methodology. Indeed, doing so may be viewed as being out of line, precocious or even critical. Similarly, there is relatively speaking a paucity of positions requiring creativity and innovation, academic positions in linguistics or applied linguistics or similar, where native speakers are incentivized to think, theorize or innovate (beyond lip service, of course). In contrast, there are a myriad of advertisements for conversation teachers or language instructors to be employed at all levels, from pre-school to even university.

For a vivid illustration of this, one can turn to Murphey (2004) where a foreign professor's sense of professionalism is put to severe test. Like all full professors in the Japanese university he was working for, this foreign professor, as described in Murphey (2004), was asked to chair the English entrance examination committee for one particular year. As chairperson, Murphey relates how the professor was supposed to oversee construction of test questions. Resolved to make sure that the examinations were fair and valid, the professor set out to measure the index of facility (IF) and index of discrimination (ID) for questions to ensure that they were good questions. Murphey relates the following concerning questions from the year before this professor was asked to take on the chairperson's role:

> Only 36% of the discrete point vocabulary and grammar questions fit[ted] the criteria for good questions (an IF between .30 and .70 and an ID above .30), as did 66% of the reading questions and 75% of the listening questions (on the one in five that had listening each year). (Murphey, 2004: 704)

The professor duly reported this information to the exam administration and, accordingly, recommended that the weighting of the exams be changed in favour of listening questions for the sake of creating better performing questions. Murphey (2004: 705) also retells how the professor pointed out that 'the listening questions ... were distinguishing twice as well as the discrete point vocabulary and grammar questions and somewhat better than the reading section' but at the end of it, his recommendations met with cold response from the powers that be. It was deemed that scrutinizing the quality of questions to set better exams was not part of the job of chairperson. We are subsequently told, in a turnaround of university policy, that it was 'decided that foreigners did not necessarily have to become chair of the entrance exams committee' (Murphey, 2004: 705).

The foreign professor's new ideas were thought to have wandered beyond the ambit of what the Japanese employers were expecting as coming from someone in the chairperson's role. Initially, foreign professors, like *all* professors, were slated to chair entrance examination committees. The interesting point, however, is that once the foreign professor began to make suggestions for change, this practice was reneged upon whereas prior to when the suggestions were made, it was standard practice in that university to oblige full professors to chair entrance exam committees.

Interestingly too, one may note the term 'foreigner' when the native speaker professor was referred to. This brings to mind (as an aside) how the close equation among the Japanese between 'foreigner' and 'white native speaker of English' has been called a 'distorted formula', referring to the perception of *'gaikoku = Amerika = eigo* (English) = *hakujin* (whites)' (Sekiguchi, 2002: 202). The irony of how the collocation of 'foreigner' and 'native speaker' can thus naturalize the native speaker as alienated entity is hard to miss.

Needless to say, decisions like the one described above precipitate both disaffection and dis-identification with what Murphey rightly notes to be 'existing structures' (2004: 707) that somehow also have their way of constituting native speaker as entity, structures that do not quite permit difference and/or diversity, let alone creativity within such a milieu. Rivers (2011a) captures this dilemma in the following:

> For any language teaching practitioner, the unquestioning acceptance of prescribed institutional norms as being irrefutable representations of best practice should be considered as a threat to the integrity of the language teaching profession. It has been documented ... that the teaching of English, especially within foreign language contexts, is as much a political undertaking as it is a linguistic one. (Rivers, 2011a: 103)

Such norms and structures, in this case, ones that impinge upon practices relating to treatment, deployment, stereotyping and, ultimately, containment, of native speakers, do of course find their roots within the inner workings of institutional politics, ideology and power, which is the subject of discussion in the next section.

The Native Speaker as Ideologized Project

The native speaker as ideologized project can be argued as being an ideological exercise in containment and control. Such an observation would point to the existence of practices suggestive of specific orchestrations or designs with regard to the native speaker, a discursive framing of the native speaker wherein operative ideologies are put to work to perpetuate prevailing power relations and structures. One might quickly want to say that such ideologies are at the same time duly resisted through critique and contestation, but it could be argued here that in Japan such resistance is hamstrung by an element of scripted determinism within powerful local discourses relating to English language policy and practice, what Sergeant (2009a: 61) notes to be a 'dominance of ... particular ideologies in the mainstream treatment' of relevant issues surrounding the subject, arguing that 'the ideologies ... at the centre of ... public and institutional discussion of the language ... draw upon ... shared assumptions and generic language' in such a way that any 'generation of knowledge ... is predicated around a few key coordinates'.

Indeed, Sergeant notes that the upshot of the dominance of particular 'coordinated' ideologies is a sort of narrow determinism that in effect causes predicated assumptions to be 'included in the subject' of scrutiny, something strongly symptomatic of operative ideologies at work. For Sergeant, the coordinates and predicated assumptions in question are characterized by forces reminiscent of (1) a cultural insularity that harks back to history, (2) ethnocentricism and (3) an urge to preserve cultural uniqueness. It is here that the native speaker bears further observation, not as referent or entity, but as an ideologized project, in other words, an artefact of the inner workings of ideologies that come to bear both on English language teaching in particular and on the appropriation of the English language in Japan in general. Consequently, an examination of the native speaker as project must look into how the native speaker remains a very important aspect of ideologized and power-laden practices in the teaching of English. Such practices are in turn part of cultural epistemologies through and within which the native speaker as project is enacted or played out in the micro-politics of day-to-day situations in Japanese society in general and within education portals in particular. The native speaker as project, therefore, focuses on various ideological constructions of the native speaker viz-a-viz the sociopolitical and sociocultural landscape of ELT in Japan.

In this connection, the native speaker as project feeds on the sorts of cultural, historical and certainly political demarcations within Japanese society described in Sergeant (2009b) as cultural insularity and preservation. These, too, are invariably linked with wider phenomena to do with the cultural scripting and scriptedness in Japanese society and how, such cultural scripting and scriptedness that Seargeant (2009a) argues is inherently linked to an unresolved ethnocentrism or even xenophobia, the native speaker must, in an ideological sense, necessarily be cast as an alien Other. Murphey's rendition of the positioning of Otherness is albeit soberingly relevant here:

> Those who rarely experience otherness and difference have nothing to contrast their present experience with and tend to believe that their experience is the only right one, the only voice available. Individuals in many communities of practice around the world claim membership in groups perhaps because those are the only groups they know of and can participate in; that is, they have few or no choices, they have few other voices to contrast with their own. This monological kind of ideological becoming seems impoverished and needs a contrasting frame of reference to enable individuals to dis-identify or possibly more deeply identify with it. (Murphey, 2004: 706)

Such an absence of alternative and/or diversity is, of course, embodied deep in a history marked with concerted material actions to shut out anything that invites comparison or contrast with something different that threatens either national uniqueness, the status quo or both, be this, as Seargeant argues, through circumscribed ways of teaching and testing English embodied in grammar-translation methodology and through entrance examination items that test English that is 'picayune, often Victorian and unusually dull' (Stanlaw, 2004: 86), through isolation embodied in the lone island of Dejima where foreigners were confined, or even in present-day Japan where specialized theme parks like the Shakespeare Country Park in Maruyama manage to encapsulate, parody and at the same time shut in and shut out other cultures within circumscribed confines (Seargeant, 2009a). In such instances, one is reminded how ideology and hegemony can ramify society, where societal (in this case Japanese) practices 'both reflect and contribute to the constitution of broader social structures' (Maybin, 2000: 208) and the native speaker then becomes very much part of a sociohistorico-ideological narrative that insularises an established ethos in contrast to one that integrates or embraces diversity and variety in world view.

While Dejima today is no longer the island that it was thanks to reclamation, it remains a veritable metaphor of demarcation, to be seen in the immersion classes taught in English squares, English circles, English villages or many a university's English-only areas. Such demarcations constitute an uncanny modern-day reincarnation of what was once a place where foreigners were confined, the metaphorical overtones of which can only suggest that little has changed since the original Dejima was surrounded by its natural moat. The immersion classes for Japanese learners similarly serve to perpetuate such a metaphor of the watery kind, awash with its rich suggestions of insularity and encapsulation.

To be sure, ideology surrounding the use of English in Japan has been linked to 'notions of national identity, the individual's notion of self and problems of Japan's place in the modern world, and indeed still is' (Stanlaw, 2004: 268). Questions concerning identity, loyalty, solidarity and difference are constantly asked in relation to Japanese people and the English language:

> 'Is a person who uses an exorbitant number of loanwords being modern and cosmopolitan, technical and scientific or merely affected and pretentious? Is a person who uses less English old-fashioned and backward, or perhaps affected and pretentious in a different way?' Similarly, with the widespread use of English loanwords in everyday Japanese communication, heart-searching questions like 'Can Japanese be spoken today without the use of loanwords?' Because of the extent of borrowing, Japanese people face issues everyday in their personal conversations and impersonal encounters with the mass media. (Stanlaw, 2004: 269)

Such dilemmas concomitantly find expression (repercussion) in representations of the native speaker that are attributable to monologic understandings of nation, culture and language (D'Angelo, 2008; Menard-Warwick, 2008), understandings that equate one language with one culture and, unfortunately, with skin pigmentation or hair colour. Hence, Stanlaw (2004) points out that race, culture and language for the Japanese are inexorably linked, resulting in reifications of English and ELT as being tied to larger-than-life white Caucasian personae, very ironically dissimulating an ideology that upholds and perpetuates their foreignness and alienation.

In terms of professional vision, the ideologized native speaker feeds into Goodwin's (1994) discussion of how professional vision, in this case of ELT in Japan, is enacted in and through highlighting, classification, marking out of turf and the articulation of material representations. Goodwin tells how archaeologists and farmers both handle soil as part of their work. However, whereas the farmer views soil samples in terms of fertility and composition, the archaeologist would mark out and highlight different types and layers of soil and examine so marked out sections in terms of what they show about a past long gone. Likewise, Goodwin relates how, by isolating and marking out a sequence of events on video frame by frame, lawyers for the defence in the famous Rodney King case managed to re-contextualize the victim of a police beating (King) as the alleged aggressor. Similarly, selective inscriptions of macro-political conceptualizations of nation, culture, language and identity (Seargeant, 2009a; Stanlaw, 2004) foisted on the native speaker legitimize the marginalization of the native speaker as foreigner and alien. As such, a native speaker's professional qualifications and experience may not be marked out as being of as much value as their ideologically legitimized and reified exoticism. In other words, native speakers are valued not only because they are professionally qualified and accredited but also because of a reified (and rarified) foreignness that commands both interpolated and extrapolated value. The point, therefore, is that ideologies that mark out the native speaker are liable to run at cross-purposes with affirmations of professional standards (Alderson, 2009; Scollon & Scollon, 2001) raising questions of whether the native speaker is ideologically speaking, marked out as being (to use Hallidayan terminology) more of 'token' than 'value'.

A sobering consequence of such Othering is that the native speaker is all too easily bunched in with the foreign in ELT and is summarily called to account for a language for which there is, to face it, (1) scarcely any unified policy for its appropriation based on sociopolitically and sociolinguistically founded principles (Oda, 2007), (2) hardly a clear directive regarding up-to-date pedagogy (Seargeant, 2009a) and (3) still, among local citizenry, a residual whiff of naivete as in 'I love English; I love speaking English to foreigners; I learn English because I love speaking to foreigners' (Kubota & McKay, 2009). In these, the native speaker serves as a compactor of ideological compost resulting from local matters long left unsettled, to be spirited on some hapless Other, even if this Other happens only to be some figment, project or construct.

One last word about ideology is that any discussion concerning ideology can be deemed distasteful, given a culture of denial that a decent profession like ELT could even be so infiltrated. Professional discussions often take place behind a facade of neutrality, where denial of ideology comes under a guise of propriety and objective detachment (Holliday & Aboshiha, 2009). However, not discussing ideology can be equally unhelpful, given the fact that it yields deep insight into the positioning of foreigners and/or native speakers within a strongly ideological ethos.

Conclusions

A dominant motif in the present state of affairs, whether these be where the native speaker comes across principally as referent, entity or project, or indeed a composite of these, is that much of the discussion jettisons concerns about native speakers as unique functioning individuals and/or classroom professionals focusing instead on the native speaker as a phenomenal entity, representing particularized and projected views of English. The sobering thought is that this is uncomplimentary for individual native speakers in general, when native speakers are generically subsumed in iconic, allegorical or even instrumental terminology that can be both alienating and dehumanizing.

In Japan, it appears that the aura and persona of the native speaker remains one powerful construct that thinkers, administrators and policy-makers have to contend with as a matter of conscience and integrity, in light of the fact that much of the discourse thereof militates against efforts to affirm professionalism, not least because professional accreditation and qualifications are liable to be superseded by powerful practices projected on the native speaker, even while the contribution of individual native speakers is often hamstrung by the generalist-repetitive (as opposed to specialist-creative) type of work afforded to them. This is in the way a powerful sub-cultural subterranean counter-current of beliefs exists against which qualification, expertise and valuable experience are silenced and neutered amid powerful superintendent discourses around the native speaker, discourses that also undermine principles relating to equity and social justice.

Unfortunately, problematic as the term may be, its use in everyday and professional parlance is, to be realistic, unlikely to show signs of abatement any time soon. In the immediate term, what, perhaps, the ELT profession needs to do is to raise a degree of awareness through official and public channels – that the term does come with distasteful assumptions that often suggest an imposition of a world view marking out a reductive (and impoverishing) relationship between Self and Other, besides drawing attention to the need for fresh conversations problematizing existing ones and encouraging more inclusive ones. Hopefully, this will have an effect of bringing about greater equity than can be found in present discussions and practices surrounding the teaching of English in Japan.

14 Racialized Native Speakers: Voices of Japanese American English Language Professionals

Ryuko Kubota and Donna Fujimoto

Introduction

***Native speaker is a term frequently found in everyday discourse. While the New Oxford American Dictionary defines the term 'a person who has spoken the language in question from earliest childhood', it is often used in a more restrictive way, conjuring up a very specific racialized image that symbolizes asymmetrical relations of power between those who are viewed as a *bona fide* native speaker and those who are not.

The superiority of the native speaker has been problematized in various scholarly discussions, such as the critique of linguistic imperialism (Phillipson, 1992), native-speakerism (Holliday, 2006), the concept of multi-competence of L2 users (Cook, 2007) and challenges and strengths of non-native speakers as language-teaching professionals (see Moussu & Llurda, 2008). While these discussions mainly focus on issues of language, other voices have drawn our attention to the ways in which racialization and racism influence the lived experiences of the English language professionals of colour (Curtis & Romney, 2006) and how the ideas of race as well as related issues of culture and identity shape various facets of teaching and learning second languages, including curriculum, instruction, teaching materials, peer interactions and teacher education (Kubota & Lin, 2006, 2009).

Issues of race, racialization and racism can be explored by drawing on Critical Race Theory (CRT), which illuminates everyday experiences and perspectives of people of colour through counter-storytelling that reveals their silenced voices. As a qualitative approach, CRT aims to understand situated experiences through interpretive lenses rather than seek scientific generalizability. This chapter focuses on the voices of Japanese American 'native' English-speaking teachers in Japan and provides critical analysis through a lens of CRT. The narratives reveal that native speakerness is a proxy of whiteness, excluding Japanese American native English-speaking teachers. CRT's vision of social transformation further leads us to discuss the importance of dialogues in order to advocate anti-oppression in educational practices. Before introducing some voices of Japanese American teachers, we will briefly introduce the tenets of CRT and its application to language education.

CRT and its Application to Language Education

CRT originates in Critical Legal Studies, which was developed by liberal legal scholars in the 1970s within the civil rights traditions in the United States with an aim to politicize the mainstream approach to legal studies that viewed law as objective, rational, technical and neutral. CRT branched off from Critical Legal Studies in the 1980s by centring race and racism in the inquiry of how the supposedly fair and colour-blind legal system actually favors the racially and economically privileged, thereby perpetuating racial inequalities (Crenshaw et al., 1995).

In the 1990s, CRT was introduced to the field of education as a conceptual tool with a critical lens through which racial inequalities in educational practices such as policies, curriculum, instruction and teacher education are scrutinized (e.g. Ladson-Billings & Tate, 1995). In the field of second-language education, some of the recent publications mentioned earlier incorporate the framework of CRT, which is built upon the following assumptions summarized by Delgado and Stefancic (2001: 7):

(1) racism is so ingrained in social systems in everyday life that colour-blind policies of superficial equality cannot eradicate it;
(2) because racism benefits white elites materially and working-class people psychologically, there is little incentive for people to eliminate it;
(3) 'races are categories that society invents, manipulates, or retires when convenient';
(4) the forms of racialization or racism are socioeconomically influenced and historically evolving;
(5) anti-essentialist understandings of racialized groups by recognizing various kinds of diversity within them is essential;

hidden forms of racism in everyday interactions can be exposed and challenged by counter-storytelling of people of colour (see similar summary offered by Dixson & Rousseau, 2005).

In the field of educational research, CRT underscores the intersectionality between race and other social categories such as gender, class, language, nationality, religion and sexual identity and challenges the colour-blind discourse that privileges objectivity and neutrality while downplaying the real pains and injuries experienced by people of colour (Solórzano & Yosso, 2002). As such, CRT enables professionals to work towards transforming institutional systems, social practices and people's consciousness in order to not only establish racial equality and justice but also eliminate all forms of oppression.

Counter-storytelling constitutes the major methodology of CRT. It is 'a method of telling the stories of those people whose experiences are not often told (e.g. those on the margins of society)' and 'a tool for exposing, analyzing, and challenging the majoritarian stories of racial privilege' (Solorzano & Yosso, 2002: 32). It can be in the form of (auto) biographical narratives juxtaposed with analysis of other published narratives and anti-racist theories or composite narratives (Solórzano & Yosso, 2002). Although it is often criticized as not being objective enough for social science inquiry (Duncan, 2005), it provides powerful cases of untold realities of marginalized groups that have long been excluded from mainstream research. Indeed, *objectivity* often required for scholarly work is in itself the product of Eurocentric colonial white academic culture which has implicitly and systematically suppressed alternative views, expressions and participations of people of colour. These voices thus help us understand human experiences to a greater extent and at the same time problematize taken-for-granted assumptions and practices that perpetuate discriminatory treatments of teachers and researchers of colour, as well as racial prejudices held by students who are themselves people of colour.

It is important to understand that racism exists in different forms (Kubota & Lin, 2009). Racism is often understood only as white-on-black personal prejudice or bigotry. However, it is relational and contextual, involving other racialized groups and many relations of power. Beyond individual racism, racism also manifests itself institutionally as seen in the different levels of funding allocated to different groups of people, the racial composition of teaching staff or representations of racial groups in advertisements. Still, racism exists in an epistemological form, shaping our unconscious beliefs and knowledge about history, literature, academic theories and so on. Part of the reason why racism is difficult to talk about is because it typically invokes only individual racism. There is a realistic fear among many people that talking about racism would position them as racist. However, the existence of other forms of racism clearly indicates that liberal discourses without racist appearance, such as meritocracy, colour-blind equal treatment of all and 'good fit' in research and teaching, do often contribute to perpetuating institutional and epistemological racism (Kubota, 2004).

To apply CRT to second-language teaching, learning and research, we are especially focusing on the intersection of race and language, including the issues of native speakerness. Yet, other social categories such as gender and nationality definitely come into play. In what follows, we present the experiences of Japanese American English teachers working in Japan, followed by the analyses of the incidents.

Voices of Japanese American Teachers

Jonathan's story

> A few years ago I was offered a part-time position at an English conversation school. I was already working full time at a four-year university. A friend of mine came over and said, 'Well, you know you can make some extra cash. If you have a little time, why don't you work for these guys? They're right across the street from your apartment.' So I said, 'Okay, I'll check it out.' I agreed to meet with the administrator and a few days later I was offered the job with a certain hourly amount. By chance I discovered soon afterward that it was only 60% of what the other teacher had been making. I was more highly qualified than the other teacher at that time, and when I confronted ... the person who had talked to me originally who is a white teacher, quote unquote, friend of mine, that worked at my university, he said, 'Well, Jon you know it's the bubble bursting kind of thing' and I wondered what that had to do with it. I found out soon afterward from a concerned confidant who worked there full time that the managers agreed that it would be bad for advertising when it comes to photo shoots. I politely declined the offer. I didn't want to have anything to do with the school (Nosaka, 2007).

This case of race-based wage discrimination clearly indicates that not all native speakers of English are equal. Here, a clear consideration for the pay scale was made in regard to the school's advertising. Jonathan's friend implied that the reason for the difference in salary had more to do with the school's bottom line than anything else, and thus appearance counted. Employers are often influenced by the belief that students want the 'full' experience of being taught by a 'real foreigner' (i.e. white person in this case) and a teacher who 'looks' Japanese would not provide the same qualitative experience. This type of experience is actually quite common for Japanese American teachers of English in Japan. In fact, it is not uncommon for employers to include appearance as one of the criteria for hiring in the first place. Japanese American teachers 'look' Japanese and how this affects students' reaction often becomes a concern for the employer.

If Jonathan had more qualifications than his Caucasian friend, why did that fact alone not take priority over his appearance? This differential treatment could be explained by a persistent ideology that 'blood' above all is what makes a person Japanese (Yoshino, 1992), and thus, Jonathan fell into the category of 'Japanese' and not 'foreigner'. This belief is one of the tenets of *nihonjinron*, an essentialised set of beliefs about the uniqueness of the Japanese people and culture, which became popular after World War II, was taken up by Japanese academics in the 1960s, but has come under intense criticism since then (Befu, 1993, 2001; Kubota, 1998, 1999, 2002b; Miller, 1982). Befu, a leading critic of *nihonjinron*, explains that this set of ideas is based on several flawed assumptions: (a) the Japanese are homogeneous and unique, (b) blood is essential for mutual communication and mutual understanding and (c) geography, race, language and culture are coterminous (Befu, 2001).

These false premises lead some Japanese to unconsciously believe that culture, language and spirit are genetically transmitted. In English language teaching, contrasted to the essentialised 'Japanese' is the 'foreigner' also essentialized as 'white native speakers of English'. Befu (2001: 37) singles out the treatment of the Japanese American English teacher in Japan as a 'blatant expression of reverse racism'. He also writes that the Japanese American English teachers' 'biological background stigmatizes them and diminishes the authority of their credentials as teachers and experts on matters of Western culture and language'. It should also be pointed out that trained Japanese teachers of English are subject to a type of reverse racism within their own country. The Caucasian teacher frequently gets hired while the Japanese national is made invisible.

While Jonathan experienced exclusion from native speakers in a professional context, the following story by Donna Fujimoto, one of the authors of this chapter, reveals exclusion from the ethnic Japanese by Japanese learners.

The children's group: Donna's story

> As a native English-speaking teacher of English, I was teaching young students at a community center, and one day I arrived a bit earlier than usual. Two 7-year-old girls, whom I had been teaching for a year, were already there and they were chatting away in Japanese. They were deep in a very serious discussion ... talking about their teacher's nose. They said something to the effect of 'The teacher is American so her nose is tall, not like ours', and they were touching their noses and indicating a higher bridge than their own. Suddenly I realized that the teacher they were talking about was none other than me! I thought it was quite amusing. Being the teacher, I decided I should set them straight. I entered the conversation and tried to explain to them that although I was American, I was Japanese American, and the only difference between me and other Japanese was that I was born in the United States. I tried to convince them that the shape of my nose was really the same as theirs, and I put my face closer to theirs so they could compare our noses. They did not seem to buy my explanation at all and probably continued to see the bridge of my nose as taller despite my elaborate explanation.

These schoolgirls decided that Donna looked different from them because she was American and spoke English. We argue that their perception reflects shades of *nihonjinron* in a way different from what Jonathan experienced. Why was Donna placed in the same category as a Caucasian teacher? The girls apparently believed that an American was racially different from them, so they used an imagined phenotypical characteristic to differentiate her. Here, we see the conflation of the native speaker with the Caucasian by 7-year-olds.

One result of this differentiation is 'Othering'. The concept of the racial Other at its most basic level is simply positioning oneself in a category that contrasts it with another category the 'us' and 'them'. In a colonial framework, it entails defining and reinforcing one's positive identity by stigmatizing an Other (Bhabha, 1994; Said, 1978). It classifies people according to observable physical characteristics creating distinct groups, whereby the majority (or power) culture distances itself from the different group, rendering the Other as peripheral, marginal and incidental (Pickering, 2001). The dominant group establishes a hierarchical structure which places differential values on members of the groups. The inequities in the power relationship inevitably lead to discrimination both conscious and unconscious, and this unequal treatment has been legitimized by the paradigm.

In some cases, however, the other group is exoticized (Said, 1978) putting its members in an idealized frame, which only serves to hide reality. It is observed in the process of Westernization in Japan in which white people were seen as the idealized Other. With the opening of Japan by the United States in 1853, and the American Occupation after World War II, Japan had an inferiority complex with respect to the West. This spurred efforts to acquire Western know-how quickly, and along with it nationalistic ideas arose accompanied by '… a clear outline of a hierarchy of races in which white people (comprised basically of Europeans and North Americans) were at the top and most Asian and other people were below the Japanese a hierarchy that in part, at least, still seems in place today' (Lie, 2000: 3).

Iwabuchi (1994) argues that the belief system about the unity of 'Japaneseness' is supported and maintained by the fact that not only the Japanese differentiate themselves from an Other but also this Other accepts this differentiation. Western Orientalist discourse on Japan, which views Japan as the inferior Other, has by and large bought into the idea of unique Japaneseness. Miller (1982) writes that Japan's self-exoticization is a 'reverse Orientalism' and claims that the discursively constructed Japaneseness created by this self or reverse Orientalism is made all the more durable because of western Orientalism. The West is Japan's universal point of reference (Sakai, 1988). We now see two-way Othering between Japanese people and Westerners, which is not only based on fixed phenotypical categories but also compounded by language (e.g. English native speaker) and nationality.

The schoolgirls have been clearly influenced by the idea of the uniqueness of the Japanese in their refusal to accept visual proof that their teacher was the same as them. Yoshino (1992: 37) points out that the 'neglect of commonality between Japanese and non-Japanese' is problematic. 'The assumption that uniquely Japanese modes of thinking and behaving are incomprehensible for non-Japanese tends to hinder social communication between Japanese and foreign resident'. For these young Japanese, Donna's being a native English-speaking American meant that there were probably more differences beyond appearance, and despite her teaching them for a year, she would probably remain for them a member of the Other. This instance of Othering brings us to a third story. It is written by Joanne about a conversation at the university.

The English teachers' group: Joanne's story

> One of the white male teachers nonchalantly said, 'Why aren't there any white women part-time teachers at this school?' 'Well, I'm American.' I said. He quickly replied, 'No … not Japanese American.' He continued to

talk about how amazing it was that there were so few white female part-time teachers teaching there .... Although I am a native speaker, I wasn't white so he didn't include me. But why did he have to go on and on about white female teachers. At first I thought I was making a big thing out of nothing, but then it occurred to me that if it were nothing, why was I feeling this pain inside? Why did I feel hurt and insignificant? Was it because he was putting me in the sort of Japanese category because of the colour of my skin? ...

The next time I saw him I reminded him of the white part-time teachers' conversation and told him that I was terribly hurt by his words. I asked why he thought I should be excluded just because I was Japanese American. I am still a native speaker. He said that he was just stating that there were so few white teachers and that he didn't mean anything by it, but that he would apologize if I was offended. After more prompting, he offered further explanation. 'Oh, well ... I wasn't trying to ignore you, but I just didn't know where to place you. You're Japanese because of your roots and you look Japanese. You have ORIENTAL features ...' and I quickly corrected him, 'The word is Asian.' He apologized. Although he obviously wanted to end the conversation, I kept prodding him wanting to dig deeper into what he was thinking.

I was completely floored when he said that I could be Japanese if I wanted to whereas we (meaning white people) can't. 'If you just learn the language you can easily be naturalized Japanese.' I exclaimed that he was not taking into consideration that I was born, raised and educated in the U.S. He failed to take into account my family background and history. I had a feeling he was finally getting the point, but I needed to go further. I pointed out that another teacher who is American of Italian ancestry is never referred to as the Italian American, but I'm always the Japanese American (cited in Fujimoto *et al.*, 2007: 836).

Here, we can see two different perceptions of the Self and Other colliding and causing misunderstanding and hurt feelings. What is especially interesting is that the native English-speaking Japanese American woman claimed membership in the female native English-speaking 'white' teacher group even though she is clearly not white. Her reaction, however, makes sense when we know a little about her background. In a conference presentation in 2005, she explained that she grew up in a predominantly Jewish neighbourhood in the United States, and she said, quite honestly, that she thought she actually *was* white. This is not at all farfetched. When a child from a minority group grows up in a majority racial group, the majority group playmates comprise her main reference group. She becomes socialized into the group learning to act, think and feel the same way as the other members of the group. Years later as an adult, this native English teacher was chatting with her reference group, and she fully expected to be included. She bristled at being referred to as the Japanese American when the white teacher with Italian heritage is never called the Italian American. She resists being Othered because of her perceived race despite her native speakerness and white identity, and she expresses clearly what this action does to people: they feel pain and hurt and are made to feel insignificant.

As for the male colleague, he implicitly conflated native English-speaking teachers with Caucasian, an error all too often made by many Japanese. For him the Other meant the Japanese, and the Self meant white native English speakers. The Other for him also meant native speakers of English who 'look' Japanese, and this is what the Japanese American woman objected to. He tried to qualify his reaction by saying that if she learned the language, she could become a legitimate member of this Other group. Instead of digging himself out of a hole, he was pushing her further away from her reference group and into the Other, yet making it appear that she would be the agent. He was embracing what Miller (1982) calls the modern myth of *nihongo*, that is that the Japanese language is unique, and it is inextricably linked with race and culture. However, racial, cultural and linguistic identities are complex and fluid rather than fixed and static. Referring to the colonial construction of identity in French-speaking Antilles, Fanon (1967) argues that Antillean blacks become white by speaking French. Fanon's following comments resonate with Joanne's identity: 'Subjectively, intellectually, the Antillean conducts himself like a white man. But he is a Negro. That he will learn once he goes to Europe; and when he hears Negroes mentioned he will recognize that the word includes himself as well as Senegalese' (Fanon, 1967: 148).

Whether Joanne's colleague understood her pain or not is not clear. What is clear is that perceptions are powerful, that people are complex and that racial and linguistic self-identities can conflict with perceived or imposed identities in a devastating way.

Discussion

These stories demonstrate complex manifestations of racial exclusion and Othering experienced by Japanese American native English-speaking teachers in Japan. They clearly show how exclusion based on a racial hierarchy of power is entrenched in contemporary Japanese society. At the same time, these individuals' experiences were not influenced solely by race or language in isolation, rather race, language, nationality and other social categories intersect in complex ways in social interactions to shape their experiences.

Yet, what is common across the stories is that their experiences as native speakers were quite different from what white teachers would experience. Despite perceived privileges such as being native English-speaking Americans with professional qualification, they felt marginalized and discriminated against as the Other. It is important to note that positionalities, whether self-chosen or imposed, are not singular; Japanese Americans may position themselves as Americans of Japanese descent or white Americans, whereas they may be positioned as illegitimate native speaker due to their racial background or non-Japanese due to their linguistic background or nationality. In all cases, however, they are positioned as the Other and alienated from the majority white native English-speaking teachers or the majority Japanese people, thereby reinforcing a clear boundary between *us* and *them*. It is also significant that race becomes a proxy for the native speaker.

The stories also demonstrate that the experiences of the Japanese American teachers of English are shaped in social interactions with their colleagues and students. As language professionals committed to social justice, how can we collectively confront oppressive practices?

Toward Situated Engagement in Anti-Oppression

The experiences of Japanese American native English-speaking teachers can leave them with disturbing and painful memories. These feelings are sometimes shared by other native English-speaking teachers in different ways. For example, during a panel discussion entitled 'Racism in ESL and EFL: Constructing action plans' which we presented at a 2007 conference for English language teachers in Japan, one participant shared a horrible case of an Irish assistant English teacher working for public schools in Japan. She was told that she must teach using an American accent and was eventually removed from teaching. This story demonstrates that discrimination against native speakers (and any other people) can occur on the basis of not only race but also accents and other social categories. What should we do to challenge racial and linguistic discrimination and all forms of oppression?

When facing oppressive practices, it is necessary to raise our voice as long as the situation is safe enough to do so. Joanne in our story directly confronted her colleague. People in the majority group are often not aware of hidden injuries experienced by non-mainstream people. Thus, exposing minority views and feelings to the majority group is essential for raising awareness. However, in what way can we address racism? At the aforementioned panel discussion, one white female participant expressed how she was annoyed by comments made by her Japanese colleagues such as 'More blond teachers should be hired' or 'It's too bad that she (a job candidate) is Japanese American'.

She found these comments to be explicitly racist but wondered whether she should have pointed it out by saying 'That's racist'. We suggested that we should probably not use the term 'racist' but engage in a conversation in a sensitive and strategic manner.

In contrast, one white male native English-speaking university-level teacher mentioned that he had used the word *jinshu sabetsu* (racial discrimination) to address problems and this strategy turned out to be effective. However, it is necessary to be aware that one's gendered, racialized and linguistic positionality in a particular context influences the effects of our utterances. People of colour are vulnerable in a situation like this and are likely to be perceived as the 'angry Asian woman' (Lin *et al.*, 2006) or the 'angry Black man' (Hayes & Juarez, 2009), whereas white people advocating for people of colour are viewed as a good white person or 'colonizers who refuse' the colonial system for the cause of the colonized (Collins, 1998: 130; Lin *et al.*, 2006: 59). Yet when white liberals advocate for people of colour, those advocating often benefit more than those being advocated for, thereby preserving their own privilege and power (Collins, 1998; Hayes & Juarez, 2009; Lin *et al.*, 2006). However, this does not imply that white native English-speaking colleagues, or any dominant racialized group in a particular context, should not challenge racism; rather, it is necessary to reflect on the role of white privilege in advocating for the racially marginalized, consider potential consequences of advocacy and attempt to take an ethical course of action consistent with an anti-racist vision.

In conclusion, race is a crucial category to consider in understanding how '(non)native speakerness' shapes people's beliefs and educational practices.

Simultaneously, it is important to understand the complex intersectionality of race and other social categories and to engage in situated ethics of anti-oppression in second-language education.

15 Native-Speakerism through English-Only Policies: Teachers, Students and the Changing Face of Japan

Jennifer Yphantides

Introduction

Two common assumptions of many language teachers and learners alike are that the native speakers of a given language are its rightful users and that native speakers have exclusive ownership of 'their' language (Cook, 1999). On a regular basis, advertisements for native speaker teachers are found on recruitment websites and in newspapers, students declare their primary language learning goal is speaking like a native and samples of native speech are collected for corpuses which are used to shed light on 'natural' language use. However, despite the assumptions that native speakers are the only legitimate users of a language and are therefore the best teachers of that language, the construct of the native speaker has been problematized in the literature and its boundaries are being constantly negotiated and redrawn (Canagarajah, 1999a; Cook, 1999; Kachru, 1986; Kubota, 2002b; Pennycook, 1994; Phillipson, 1992). In addition, the academic discourse surrounding the native speaker is not only theoretical. Practical applications that have the potential of making a significant pedagogical impact are gradually manifesting themselves in the Japanese English language classroom (Noguchi & Fotos, 2001). The purpose of this chapter is to extend this discussion by exploring the connection between native-speakerism and the pervasive yet fundamentally flawed English-only policies found within Japanese educational contexts. Focus will then be shifted to teacher and student attitudes towards English-only policies, the potential pedagogical and social impacts of relaxing such policies and the possible creation of a less prescriptive atmosphere for learning.

Native Speakers: Packaging, Power and Powerlessness

Glancing at advertisements aimed at recruiting new teachers to come to Japan to work in English conversation schools or as ALTs in the Japanese public school system, one striking aspect prospective applicants may notice is that often the only requirements are to be a native speaker of English and possess an undergraduate degree (to satisfy the minimum visa requirements) in any field to qualify for a job (see, for example, the following websites: www.eltnews.com/jobs, www.jobsinjapan.com and www.ohayosensei.com). However, while it may appear on the surface as if these are the only qualifications one needs, the necessity of having to provide a photograph with a job application hints that a certain physical image is also required. For example, on the website for Sagan Speak, a third-party dispatch company based in Tokyo, job applicants are required to supply the company with 'a color photograph wearing formal clothes and a smiling, happy face' (www.saganspeak.com/recruit, para.13).

In this way, companies can weed out applicants whose skin color, age or facial features are deemed unmarketable without having to invite them for an interview. Once a teacher has secured employment within this select band of native speakers who fit with the image demanded by dominant social representations (see Rivers, 2011e), he or she is often photographed for promotional material advertising the school. Quite often, next to their photographs, the teachers' country of origin is listed (see, for example, www.englishvillage.com) solidifying the linear linkage between nation and language, one that is so actively embraced within the Japanese context. While there may be legitimate justification for this kind of publicity, particularly given the demographic situation in Japan and the difficulty of recruiting students in a flooded educational marketplace, it represents a blatant oversimplification of a given teacher's background and a convenient cover for their possibly inconvenient multilingual, multicultural or multinational identities which bring shades of grey to an otherwise black and white situation. While some teachers may not take offense to this rigid system of classification, the practice can cause the perpetuation of the 'us and them' mentality by casting teachers not as individuals but as monolingual and monocultural entities. In addition, in these photographs, the native speaker, particularly the native speaker of European extraction, is cast as the idealized speaker of the language and, more often than not, as the expert and purveyor of Western cultural values (Seargeant, 2009a). Again, while some teachers may not take offense to this and some may even find a certain measure of power and prestige in these practices, the photographs and accompanying national flags and labels feed into stereotypes of what a 'good' English teacher should look like. As Rivers (2010b: 109) argues, such images 'immediately bind teachers to student representations of a particular nation and create linguistic, cultural, behavioral, and attitudinal expectations and assumptions based upon an assumed linearity between the nation, the individual, and the language spoken'. It is as if the teacher, working consciously or unconsciously in cooperation with the Japanese company, exists as a gatekeeper providing paid access to a fantasy-laden world of English language and culture.

Within this frame, the native speaker can be considered as an entity in possession of some degree of power in Japanese society. However, this is only part of the native speaker reality. While native speakers may often be revered as linguistic and cultural experts, they are at the same time set apart from the society in which they live in a variety of ways. First, their native speaker status and socially assigned identities often depend upon strict separation from their Japanese co-workers. This distinction can be manifested in office assignments, segregated staff meetings and even segregated departments at the university level (see Rivers, Chapter 5). Second, in a society that has historically defined itself as homogeneous (one nation, one language and one culture), bilingual and multilingual identities can be perceived as a threat (Train, 2003). For example, people who do not look like Japanese are often regarded with surprise if they speak Japanese proficiently and occasionally resort to speaking English so that their interlocutors feel more at ease (Siegal, 1995).

However, despite this apparent difficulty some people may have in registering that a non-Japanese looking person may speak Japanese proficiently, or indeed that a Japanese person can be proficient in English, some Japanese regard English as a language of prestige and Japanese speakers of English tend to be associated with positive images such as 'cool', 'international' and 'smart' (Yamamoto, 2001: 39). On the other hand, Kobayashi (2011) reports the opposite and describes how Japanese who are proficient in English often hide their skills to avoid exclusion or resentment in the workplace. Either way, for these individuals, the preferred route to bilingualism is usually that of the elite bilingual, or the person who was a monolingual Japanese speaker, learned English as an adult and can now pass for a native speaker of English. This elite bilingual is held in contrast to the less idealized folk bilingual who has learned English at home from a foreign parent as a heritage language (Yamamoto, 2001). It is this separation of native English speakers from the rest of Japanese society as a whole and the reverence afforded to elite bilinguals which feeds into and off English-only policies that are common in the Japanese education context.

English-Only as Best Practice: Deconstructing the Myth

Of course, English-only policies are not exclusive to Japan. Cook (2001) identifies their roots in the 'Great Reform' of the late 19th century and the assumptions commonplace at the time: that speech is easier than writing, explicit grammar discussion should be avoided, and the focus of study was to be on whole language rather than on parts. Embedded in these assumptions was a backlash against the Grammar-Translation method which led to strict limitations on or complete bans on the students' L1. In today's classrooms, the ban on the first language is often based on additional assumptions including the idea that L2 is acquired in the same way as L1, that languages are compartmentalized separately in the brain and that maximum exposure to the target language yields the best results (Cook, 2001).

Despite these common assumptions, much work has been done in the field in recent years to overturn the status quo (see, for example, Anton & DiCamilla, 1998; Brooks & Donato, 1994; Nation, 2003; Swain & Lapkin, 2000). While these studies focus primarily on the cognitive benefits of limited use of the L1 in the second or foreign language classroom, other work has looked at the ideological side of English-only. Auerbach (1993) argues that these kinds of exclusive language policies are not only pedagogically suspect but also rooted in a particular ideological perspective. Auerbach puts forth the ideas that language policies create unequal social and economic relationships, unequal divisions of power and resources, and can be interpreted as a post-colonial strategy to maintain cultural and economic hegemony. For example, drawing on the classroom language policy descriptions used by native English-speaking teachers working within an English-only university environment, Rivers (2011a: 106) highlights how

> In addition to promoting monolingual norms to multilingual students, the symbolic power assigned to each language places one language (English) in the position of being 'normal' and 'valued' and the other language (Japanese) in the position of being 'abnormal' and 'devalued'; thus, the status quo of a paradoxical system of inequality and exclusion is maintained.

However, from within the isolated confines of Japanese education, these arguments often fall on deaf ears for two reasons. First, a majority of students and their parents (who normally fund their children's English language education) believe that the most expedient route to fluent and accurate English is an English-only class with a native speaker (Klevberg, 2000). In addition, arguments of unequal economic power distribution and post-colonialism would likely be met with firm denial because common social discourse dictates that Japan was never actually colonized and many Japanese state that they learn English in order to improve their economic prospects or are interested in becoming a more international person (Rivers, 2012; Taguchi et al., 2009).

Perhaps, the creation of a more international self along the lines of Dörnyei's (2005) 'ideal L2 self' begins with associations with monolingual native English speakers who are often represented as young, white, attractive and successful in their business attire. While this is the essentialized image being sold to English language students in Japan, there are other stereotypical beliefs about language learning and teaching that serve to underpin the image. One such belief is that English-only policies are essential to good communication and vital in order to prepare for travel abroad or experience with the imagined monolingual foreign people in Japan, and therefore the students should get as much practice as possible with the so-called 'authentic' native speakers in the classroom (Weschler, 1997). Second, as Klevberg (2000) notes, there is intense institutional pressure to submit to English-only policies because the majority of students, influenced by principles established within the domain of conversational English, expect their teachers not to use any Japanese, an act which is seen as having a contaminating effect on interactions. While schools often justify their English-only policies by stating that Japan is an EFL context and students are thus limited in the time they can feasibly spend speaking English, they also claim that it is difficult to find a sufficient number of native speakers of English who are proficient enough in Japanese to be able to use the students' L1 in the classroom (Klevberg, 2000).

While English-only policies have become a useful marketing tool for institutions that sell a certain image and a certain kind of communication class to their clients, it is not that only the schools that are responsible for reinforcing the policies. As mentioned, English-only is also an expectation of numerous students, and teachers themselves often believe that English-only is the fastest way to improved communication skills in the Japanese context (see McMillan & Rivers, 2011). For example, Critchley (1999) has noted that there are very few studies coming from the Japanese context about the use of the L1 in the English language classroom, primarily because such research contradicts popularly held notions about the communicative approach and can be considered a challenge to institutional policies. Despite this, Critchley's (1999: 10) study investigated the use of L1 (Japanese) in the English language classroom. The researcher came to the conclusion that the students in Japan are well aware of 'the dangers of overuse of the L1'. While this study does shed some light on teachers and students' attitudes towards the use of Japanese, it seems to suggest that the use of L1 is, in fact, considered 'dangerous' to rapid progress and should be strictly limited, if used at all.

Another action research-based study on the use of Japanese in the English language classroom indicates a similar slant in disapproval of L1. Schmidt (1995) reports that many teachers in Japan admit to using some Japanese in their classes (or allowing their students to do so) despite the English-only policy in place in their institutions. Teachers provided some examples of how they use L1, including getting students to brainstorm ideas before speaking and writing, simple word-to-word translation, and to build positive rapport with students. Schmidt (1995: 29) opines that these functions are linguistic, practical and affective in nature. Yet, at the same time, the study concluded by suggesting ways to limit the use of L1, insisting that it is possible to 'slowly wean students from L1 dependence' and by stating that 'teachers need to set an example for students' (Schmidt, 1995: 30).

Klevberg's (2000) study also reveals that teachers (both Japanese and non-Japanese) use a certain measure of Japanese in their English language classes to achieve a variety of goals. Teachers reported using the students' L1 to establish rapport, to translate difficult vocabulary, to explain grammar points and to generally help younger or less proficient learners. However, despite using Japanese to accomplish these goals successfully, teachers admit that they feel guilty or ashamed about their use of the students' L1 because they felt they were being lazy and could have accomplished these goals by using English-only were they skilful enough. Somewhat ironically, these same negative feelings were reported by Rivers (2011b: 42) as being present in students who could not live up to the expectations of 100% target language use demanded by an English-only policy 'a bi-product of this unrealistic demand is a negative impact upon the learner's psychological and emotional well-being through the promotion of feelings of guilt, disappointment, resignation, and indifference'.

Other research conducted by Burden (2000) on Japanese students' feelings about the use of their L1 in the English language classroom seems to demonstrate that there is some type of misunderstanding between students and teachers. Burden's (2000) findings indicate that while students expect English to be used in the EFL classroom, they do report that being able to use some Japanese in the class and knowing that the teacher can use Japanese has some benefits. First, the students complained that they felt nervous beginning a new English class with people they had not met before and the use of limited Japanese helped them to feel more at ease with their classmates and with the teacher. Second, students appreciated that they were able to use their first language for basic translation of a difficult word or phrase. They reported that translation was more efficient than trying to define a word using English-only. Embodying a sense of hope for future change, more recent research indicates that although many institutions still maintain English-only policies, teachers are able to be flexible with their implementation. McMillan and Rivers (2011: 251) showed that teachers believed that selective use of Japanese 'could enhance L2 learning in various ways within a communicative framework'. In this study, teachers reported using the students' L1 (not only Japanese but also other languages in different teaching contexts) in order to accomplish a variety of goals including translation, contrastive analysis and showing appreciation for the students' language and culture. However, certain comments from teachers demonstrated the uncovering of a far more complex situation than the simple debate for the use or ban of L1. For example, one teacher commented that not all students in the EFL class shared the same first language, including in the Japanese context. Another teacher mentioned that the affective side of a student being able to use L1 with another student, or with the teacher, does not always help the student to feel more comfortable. This teacher said that students reported they felt more confident with her because she did not know their L1 and, as a result, they knew they had to communicate in L2. In this situation, being sure of what language to use, and indeed being forced to use it to communicate, provided the students with increased confidence that they could successfully use L2 for real purposes.

Relaxing English-Only: Costs and Benefits

Perhaps, one of the most obvious costs of relaxing English-only policies would be the loss of a powerful marketing tool. Since students often expect English-only, despite the benefits they recognize from the use of L1, it will likely be difficult to sell them on another idea regardless of the potential educational benefits. In addition, the majority of teachers, particularly those who have less training or less experience, often believe that best practice includes enforcing an L2-only policy. Their thinking on the issue, and their practice, would need to undergo significant adjustment. However, these costs may be easy to cope with compared to some possibly less obvious ones in the Japanese context. As was previously mentioned, Japan, like other nations, is constructed by and for its people primarily as a monolith. Within this framework, bilingualism and biculturalism are often considered to be unwelcome challenges to the status quo and actually serve in undermining national and individual identity. Just as native speaker teachers are separated from their Japanese colleagues, so must languages and cultures be separated, and indeed constantly contrasted in order to uphold traditional constructs of the self and the other. While learning English may be considered by some students as a problematic but necessary pathway to more lucrative job prospects or an opportunity to develop a more international self, native English speaker teachers speaking Japanese act as a threat to the attainment of these goals by blurring the lines of national identity and national language.

While such heavy costs may seem daunting, the benefits of relaxing English-only policies are numerous enough to merit serious official consideration. First, it is likely worthwhile to further probe students' feelings about their own use of L1 and teachers' use of L1 in the English language classroom. Although, as previously discussed, most students mainly expect English in the EFL classroom and are sold on English-only policies, the few studies that have been done in the Japanese context indicate that both students and teachers appreciate some flexibility in responding to the specific needs of their students in a particular class. Second, while teachers and students' feelings, representing the affective side of learning, are important, of equal importance are the cognitive benefits of L1 as support for the acquisition of another language.

These cognitive benefits are well-documented. For example, Swain and Lapkin (2000) report that students who were allowed to use their L1 in order to scaffold tasks, maintain inter-subjectivity and internalize cognitively demanding tasks fared better on assignments than did students who did not have the opportunity to use L1. In terms of vocabulary acquisition, Nation (2003) reports that bilingual word cards are more effective than translation from L2 to L2. Anton and DiCamilla's (1998) study indicates that students who use L1 for meta-linguistic functions and for mediating and scaffolding tasks produce superior writing than students who use L2 exclusively. Finally, Brooks and Donato (1994) concluded from their research that meta-talk (defined as talk about the task amongst learners) helps mediate cognitive difficulties students have when negotiating meaning and determining how to proceed with a task. They report that because the learning of a foreign language is such a complex cognitive and affective process, it is most effective for students to be in control of the pace and mode of their learning. A limited number of studies coming from within the Japanese context also look at the affective benefits of L1 use in the classroom (Klevberg, 2000; McMillan & Rivers, 2011; Rivers, 2011a, 2011b, 2011c; Schmidt, 1995; Weschler, 1997). The conclusion one could draw from this is that Japanese students may need more reassurance and support in the classroom and might not feel as confident as EFL students in other regions combining and blurring the deeply entrenched boundaries of their cultural and linguistic identities.

Organizations such as TESOL support bilingual education and rally against English-only policies in the United States. The Japan Association of Language Teachers (JALT) does not have an official position on bilingual education, but a special interest group exists within the organization that encourages bilingual and bicultural education in Japan. As the studies previously cited in this chapter show, many teachers use some Japanese with their classes, despite feeling some measure of guilt or wrong doing. However, since so much research demonstrates the benefits of L1 support, it is surprising that teachers do not speak out against English-only policies. Perhaps, some teachers feel that having a policy in place allows them more control because they have some official point of reference for what should be happening in the class for the majority of time. Fairclough (cited in Auerbach, 1993) suggests that there are two reasons for the maintenance of an official policy. The first is coercion and the second is consent. While some teachers may feel forced into accepting English-only because of heavy institutional pressure, others might consent to it because they unconsciously support English-only as best practice because they have not fully investigated the assumptions behind their practice. One reason for this may be that they enjoy, perhaps even unconsciously, their position of quasi-power as a native speaker in the Japanese context. Regardless of the individual teacher's situation, however, Auerbach (1994) stresses the importance of being aware of the ideological roots of English-only policies, even if we no longer (consciously) identify with them today.

The Changing Face of EFL, the Changing Face of Japan

Although there are numerous cognitive and affective reasons for relaxing English-only policies, the fact that Japan is becoming a more diverse country is probably the most significant factor to consider when rethinking classroom language policy. EFL classrooms in Japan have seen some major changes over the past 30 years. For example, a significant number of students have had the experience of living abroad for long periods of time and then returning to the Japanese context (the so-called 'returnees'), and an ever-growing number of other students come from mixed race backgrounds (Noguchi, 2001). The linguistic presence of these students in the English language classroom puts into question the construct of the native speaker and their social presence presents a challenge to what is often conceptualized as a monocultural society. As Kanno (2001) emphasizes, however, the students who are 'returnees' or who come from mixed backgrounds build their social identity within the learning context and not in isolation. This is not commonly a positive experience. Perhaps with more support from teachers and administration, these students would not be exposed to the discrimination they often complain of experiencing at the hands of their peers.

In recent years, the issue of the changing face of Japan has been a challenge to traditional modes of EFL classroom operation. In their book on bilingualism, Noguchi and Fotos (2001) call for the creation of a new paradigm in Japanese schools that is more inclusive and which better reflects the linguistic and cultural realities of the students. However, despite the presence of more linguistically, culturally and racially diverse students, the predominant English-only policy seems to serve in assimilating students to the homogeneous construct, casting all students as EFL students and the teacher as the monolingual native English speaker. One problem in coping with this gradually growing diversity is that teachers are under pressure to follow prescriptive policy and do not have training to deal with language minority students (Seibert Vaipae, 2001).

As Katz (1995) notes, native speaker students can offer valuable linguistic and cultural insights to other students in the class. However, if native or near-native students are forced to use English-only, they run the risk of being cast as essentialized objects of cultural and linguistic perfection that their peers need to emulate. Within the Japanese context, this is problematic for two reasons. First, returnee, heritage or native English-speaking students may face bullying from classmates for being 'different'. Rather than emphasizing their 'difference' and separating them further from their classmates, a more relaxed language policy could offer the possibilities of easing the homogeneous myth and encouraging a more multilingual and multicultural environment which is more inclusive and more representative of the changing demographic situation, particularly in the bigger cities.

Second, English-only can deny students access to and expression of their pluralistic backgrounds. Although institutions are responsible for putting in place language policies, teachers are in a position to interpret the policies. It is a constant challenge to balance institutional demands with creating a sense of belonging and community in the classroom (Blyth, 1995). One possible way of doing so is to construct a context for meaningful discourse by taking advantage (rather than denying) students' rich personal, cultural and linguistic backgrounds (Bialystock & Hakuta, 1994). As Houghton (2009) suggests, identifying student diversity from within the student body itself may provide educators with a key to bringing diversity to the surface and grappling with it in the public platform of the classroom. It may be time for teachers to start reconsidering their interpretation of English-only, not only in light of the cognitive and affective benefits but also in light of the needs of a rapidly changing student body.

Part 5

Native-Speakerism from Socio-Historical Viewpoints

16 Changing Perceptions? A Variationist Sociolinguistic Perspective on Native Speaker Ideologies and Standard English in Japan

Robert M. McKenzie

Introduction

Japan is historically categorized within the expanding circle of Kachru's influential World Englishes model (1985) and thus, English in Japan is considered to serve a restricted range of functions, has not gained the status of an official language, does not function as a *lingua franca* within the country and is taught, albeit extensively, as a foreign language in the education system. In contrast to (native) inner-circle varieties, regarded as 'norm-providing', and outer-circle varieties, often described as 'norm-developing', English in the expanding circle tends to be classified as 'norm-dependent', in that educators, policy-makers and the users of English themselves generally look to native speakers from the inner circle for linguistic norms of use (Jenkins, 2009; McKenzie, 2010).

In Japan, the varieties historically selected to serve as pedagogical models in English language classrooms were initially (pre-World War II) Received Pronunciation (RP) and later (post-1945) General American (GA) (i.e. standard/mainstream US English) (McKenzie, 2008a). As a consequence of the long-standing policy of the recruitment of native speakers, at all levels of the Japanese educational system, to teach English as the major foreign language, perceptions amongst Japanese users of English of the superiority of inner-circle norms of English speech have perhaps become institutionalized, the implication of which being that native speakers of

English hold sole ownership of the language. Nevertheless, in the wake of the unprecedented global spread of English, well-documented in recent years by sociolinguists, and the subsequent growth of English for international communication in Japan (e.g. Hino, 2009) and elsewhere, it may be the case that attitude changes are underway regarding perceptions of (speakers of) native and non-native varieties of English (McKenzie, 2008b).

The purpose of this chapter is to provide a critical analysis of research conducted amongst Japanese nationals regarding their social evaluations of (speakers of) *specific* varieties of native and non-native English speech, i.e. focusing precisely upon those language attitude studies in Japan which take into account the substantial social and regional variation within English speech and the resultant lexical, phonetic and morphosyntactic diversity which exists between different forms of the language. It is hoped that the information gained will help build up a more thorough picture of the current, changing sociolinguistic position of English and its varieties in Japan. Moreover, the conclusions drawn will also offer a deeper insight into the direction of any attitude changes towards English language variation occurring amongst the Japanese population, the implications of which have the potential to aid educators, policy-makers and researchers involved in the learning and teaching of the English language in Japan, and elsewhere in the expanding circle.

Defining the Native Speaker and the Non-Native Speaker

Although the World Englishes model is influential and widely employed, it presents fundamental problems (see, for instance, Bruthiaux, 2003; McKenzie, 2010). One such issue relates to the priority the model assigns to the differentiation between native speakers (i.e. from the inner circle) and non-native speakers of English (i.e. from the outer and expanding circles). It has proved somewhat controversial for academics to provide precise definitions of what constitutes a 'native speaker' and a 'non-native speaker' of a given language. The labelling of an individual as a native speaker or, more especially, as a non-native speaker of a given language has also proved controversial. For instance, McKenzie (2010) has criticized the categorization of speakers as native or non-native as overly reliant upon genetic inheritance and/or geography. To illustrate the difficulties involved, McKenzie (2010) discusses the cases of Quebec, where many individuals acquire English and French simultaneously, and of India, as one example of an increasing number of multilingual nations, where it can be extremely problematic to identify which is a speaker's L1, L2 or L3. A further illustration of the problem associated with defining individuals as native speakers or non-native speakers is provided by Trudgill (2008: 83) who discusses whether Henry Kissinger, born in Germany but following migration to the United States at the age of 12 subsequently developing 'native-like proficiency' in English (with the exception of phonetics and phonology), should be categorized as a native or non-native speaker of the language. For a more detailed discussion of controversies surrounding defining native and non-native speakers, see Davies (2003) and Jenkins (2000).

Nevertheless, despite the difficulties outlined above, for the purposes of this chapter, it is worthwhile to offer working definitions, however generalized they may seem, of both terms. There is, for instance, a widespread acceptance of the definition of a *native speaker*, offered by Richards *et al.* (1992) as an individual who acquires the language in early childhood (i.e. up to approximately eight years of age). Native speakers of the language in question thus have sole ownership of a particular *habitus* – that is to say, dispositions acquired during the early childhood which, although not determined by explicit rules, generate relatively consistent attitudes, preferences, behavioural norms and practices (Bourdieu, 1991). Similar notions regarding human dispositions are well-established in Western philosophy; for instance, in the writings of the early 18th-Century English philosopher Thomas Hobbes, whose first philosophical proposition refers to the durability of human beings' appetites and aversions (Hobbes, 1951). Language, of course, is a central component of the human disposition. In contrast, a *non-native speaker* can be thought of as an individual who learns the language after early childhood as a second and/or foreign language (Singh *et al.*, 1995). The reader should bear in mind, however, that the labelling of an individual as a native speaker or a non-native speaker is not necessarily an issue of *either-or* but rather a matter of *more-or-less* (Trudgill, 2008) and, for this reason, as Figure 16.1 illustrates, it is perhaps appropriate to place the constructs of the native speaker and the non-native speaker at opposite ends of a linguistic continuum; thus allowing for the speech of certain individuals to be more native than others.

Native_____**Non-Native**

Figure 16.1 The native speaker/non-native speaker linguistic continuum

Native Speaker Attitudes Towards Varieties of English

The vast majority of research investigating attitudes towards English language variation that has been conducted from the 1960s onwards involved measuring the perceptions of *native* speakers of the language. Although notions of what constitutes standard English speech varies from area to area, and between speech communities (McKenzie, 2010), it has been detailed extensively that speakers of those varieties deemed 'standard' amongst a particular population of native speakers tend to be judged highly in terms of status (also operationalized as competence/correctness). Speakers of these varieties tend to be rated positively on traits such as intelligence, wealth and education. This appears to be the case whether those making the evaluations are speakers of standard or non-standard varieties of English. In contrast, forms of English categorized as non-standard tend to be evaluated more favourably in terms of solidarity (also operationalized as social attractiveness/pleasantness). As such, speakers of non-standard English varieties tend to be judged positively on traits such as honesty, sociability and trustworthiness. A great deal of consistency in studies involving native speakers has been demonstrated in the distinctions made between perceptions of standard and non-standard varieties of English and in a wide range of inner-circle countries such as Australia (Bradley & Bradley, 2001), England (Coupland & Bishop, 2007), Scotland (McKenzie, 1996) and the United States (Labov, 2006).

Milroy (1999) believes that the consistency found in research examining native speaker attitudes towards English language variation can be attributed to the existence of a 'standard language ideology', where amongst a specific population (of native speakers) in a given area, a specific form of English satisfies 'notions of correctness' and hence, is recognized as 'the standard'. It is scarcely necessary to say that a specific spoken variety of a given language is not inherently superior to other forms of speech. Rather, certain varieties are afforded the status of a standard precisely because their *speakers* are perceived as having high status (Milroy, 2001). Thus, individuals' attitudes towards languages and language varieties are better viewed as a reflection of the level of prestige associated with particular speech communities, and that listening to a speech variety acts as a stimulus or trigger which evokes attitudes about the speech community in question (for a more detailed description, see Edwards, 1999; McKenzie, 2010).

Japanese Attitudes Towards Varieties of English in Japan

The earlier language attitude studies in Japan, conducted from the 1970s onwards, tended to concentrate on perceptions of the English language conceived as a *single entity*, and thus, as detailed above, researchers generally failed to investigate Japanese nationals' evaluations of the wide social and geographical diversity which exists within English. For this reason, the majority of such studies tended not to employ samples of English speech for the purposes of evaluation. While space constraints here do not allow for a detailed discussion of the results of studies investigating Japanese perceptions of English as a single entity, research has tended to indicate that Japanese informants are mostly favourable towards English and its use in Japan and that the language, as a whole, enjoys a relatively high degree of prestige in the country, despite some reservations regarding the potential effect of the spread of English on the Japanese language. Examples of studies which have concentrated solely on the attitudes of Japanese nationals towards the English language as a whole include attitudes towards English in television advertising (Haarmann, 1986, 1989), attitudes towards learning English (Chihara & Oller, 1978), attitudes and motivation for learning English (Benson, 1991), gender and attitudes towards English (Kobayashi, 2002) and language ideology and attitudes towards English (Seargeant, 2009a).

It is only relatively recently, however, that research measuring the attitudes of learners towards specific native and non-native varieties of English has been conducted. This is perhaps surprising considering the importance of attitudes towards language variation in the building of sociolinguistic theory (e.g. Garrett, 2010). Positive learner attitudes towards variation in the target language are also considered, to some extent, to enhance levels of proficiency (Ellis, 2008). Moreover, the findings from studies investigating learner evaluations of specific varieties of English are likely to be of value to educators and policy-makers involved in the teaching and learning of English because the results can indicate which variety/varieties students prefer to serve as linguistic targets in the English language classroom. The findings may also be of use to the learners themselves since any classroom discussion generated about discussions of language attitudes can help raise awareness of the range both of potential target varieties of English and of the possible sociolinguistic implications of choosing specific linguistic model(s).

In Japan itself, Matsuura *et al.* (1994) conducted one of the earliest studies, investigating the attitudes of 92 Japanese university students towards seven outer-circle speech varieties and an unspecified form of American speech. The results indicated that the informants' evaluated the American variety of English more positively in terms of status than any of the outer-circle speech varieties. It was also found that informants who perceived English to be a global language tended to be more tolerant of outer-circle forms of English. In a follow-up study, Chiba *et al.* (1995) measured the perceptions of 169 Japanese university students of varieties of English from the inner circle (unspecified UK and US speech), the outer circle (Hong Kong, Malaysia and Sri Lanka) and the expanding circle (Japan). Again, the informants were found to be more favourable towards the native, inner-circle varieties of English than the non-native, outer- and expanding-circle forms of English. Furthermore, it was demonstrated that informants who were most positive towards spoken varieties of UK and US English tended to be less tolerant of the outer-circle and expanding-circle speech.

McKenzie (2003) investigated the attitudes of 32 Japanese university students towards Scottish Standard English (SSE) and non-standard Glasgow vernacular (GV). Statistical analysis indicated that the informants were broadly favourable towards both standard and non-standard forms of Scottish English speech. In a follow-up study, McKenzie (2004) again examined perceptions of SSE and GV among Japanese undergraduates studying either in Scotland or in Japan. While attitudes towards both speech varieties were again generally positive, informants expressed a clear preference for Scottish Standard English speech. Place of residence and gender were not found to account for differences in the informants' evaluations.

Cargile *et al.* (2006) measured the attitudes of 113 Japanese university students towards mainstream US English speech (MUSE) and African-American vernacular English speech (AAVE). Principal Components Analysis of the data revealed two distinct evaluation dimensions: status and (social) attractiveness. Although no significant differences were found between the informants' evaluations of the two US speech varieties in terms of attractiveness, the students rated the MUSE speech significantly more positively than the AAVE speech in terms of status.

Moloney (2009) conducted a series of studies measuring Japanese university students' perceptions of two Australian varieties of English: (general) standard Australian English and (broad) non-standard Australian English. The results of the first part of the study demonstrated that the students tended to judge the standard Australian speech more positively than the non-standard Australian speech. The findings of a follow-up study also indicated that students, listening to a series of speech samples, generally had difficulty in identifying forms of Australian English when compared to varieties of UK and US speech.

A recent in-depth study investigating the attitudes of 558 Japanese undergraduates and postgraduates both towards varieties of standard as opposed to non-standard varieties of English speech and towards native as opposed to non-native varieties of English speech was conducted by McKenzie (2008a, 2010). Four native (inner-circle) varieties of English speech were recorded for the purposes of evaluation: Scottish Standard English (SSE), (non-standard) Glasgow vernacular (GV), mainstream US English (MUSE) and (non-mainstream/non-standard) Southern US English (SUSE). Two recordings of two non-native (expanding-circle) speakers of Japanese English were also utilized: moderately accented Japanese English (MJE); and heavily-accented Japanese English (HJE) (and passim). Principal components analysis of the informants' ratings revealed the existence of distinct evaluative dimensions of status and solidarity. Further inferential statistical analysis demonstrated that, in terms of status, the Japanese students' ratings fell into a tripartite hierarchy with standard and non-standard US English speech most positively evaluated, followed by the Scottish English varieties, with the Japanese-accented speech the least preferred. In contrast, in terms of solidarity, the informants' ratings for the heavily accented Japanese English speech were significantly more favourable than for the other five varieties. McKenzie (2008a) concluded that this finding indicates that the Japanese informants perceive a high degree of solidarity with the HJE speaker and implies that the HJE speech is itself a salient marker of in-group identity amongst Japanese users of English. The moderately accented Japanese English speech was rated significantly less favourably, suggesting a categorization of the MJE speaker as out-group, and hence, the degree of accentedness affects solidarity ratings to the extent that the more 'Japanese' a speaker is considered to sound, the more favourable ratings are likely to be. Gender, level of previous exposure to English, self-perceived proficiency in English and attitude towards variation within the Japanese language were all found to play a significant role in determining the attitudes of the informants, pointing to social differentiation in attitudes towards forms of English within the Japanese population generally.

Moreover, the results of a separate 'variety recognition question' indicated that the informants were generally able to categorize the six speakers correctly as either native or non-native (for a more detailed description, see McKenzie, 2008c, 2010). Multivariate analysis of variance (MANOVA) indicated that the Japanese students judged the status of the *native* speakers significantly more positively when their provenance was identified correctly (i.e. as the United Kingdom or the United States). McKenzie concluded that the significantly more favourable ratings for the correctly identified varieties of inner-circle English speech implies that the informants tend to look towards both standard and non-standard varieties of native English speech for correctness and points to the construction of a *native* speaker ideology, as opposed to a *standard* language ideology (see above), amongst English language users in Japan more generally.

Changing Perceptions in a Changing Japan? Implications for the Sociolinguistic Role of English

The studies detailed above, concentrating specifically on Japanese nationals' social evaluations of English language variation, represent a substantial contribution to language attitude research involving non-native speakers of English in general and to the investigation of the sociolinguistics of English in Japan in particular. In terms of the latter, a number of themes emerge from the results of these studies, with important implications for English language policy and the learning of the language in Japan.

First, Japanese nationals appear to be very positive towards the English language generally and tend to rate standard varieties of US and, to a lesser extent, UK English highly in terms of prestige. Attitudes towards non-standard forms of inner-circle English also tend to be favourable. Second, there is some evidence that Japanese nationals express solidarity with 'authentic' forms of Japanese English speech, most likely as a salient linguistic marker of in-group identity and thus, it is possible to speculate that specific linguistic features of Japanese English may, to some extent, be undergoing a process of enregisterment amongst Japanese users of English in the country. Such evidence suggests that an identifiable form of Japanese English may be one potential pedagogical model to be employed in English language classrooms in Japan (see below). Third, the consistent finding in prior studies that Japanese nationals are especially positive towards varieties of inner-circle English, together with evidence that they tend to categorize speakers of English, at least in the initial stages of the identification process, as either native or non-native, points to the existence of 'a native speaker ideology' and implies that Japanese users of English tend to look towards inner-circle English for 'notions of correctness' (see also McKenzie, 2010). Fourth, the findings obtained in previous attitude studies have demonstrated that social differentiation within the Japanese population can account for variations in evaluations of specific forms of English speech – compelling evidence that different sections of the population in Japan hold different perceptions of varieties of spoken English and these studies offer valuable information regarding the direction of any attitude change amongst Japanese nationals towards native and non-native English speech.

However, the role of English in Japan is becoming increasingly important. Greater numbers of Japanese are being exposed, and for longer and longer periods of time, to English within formal education settings. For instance, many students now begin learning English at grade three in elementary school (i.e. between 8 and 9 years of age), whereas previously the vast majority of Japanese children started studying the language when they attended junior high school (i.e. aged 12 – 13).

It is increasingly likely that Japanese students will be exposed to non-standard inner-circle, outer-circle and expanding-circle Englishes. The JET Programme, for instance, established by the Japanese government in 1987 as a means of recruiting young overseas university graduates, historically from the inner-circle of English use, to participate as assistant language teachers in high schools in Japan, has expanded greatly in recent years and led to a greater number of non-Japanese nationals communicating in English with Japanese schoolchildren. The official figures for 2010 – 2011 demonstrate that out of a total of 3974 ALTs, 2310 were AETs from the United States, 390 from the United Kingdom, 232 from Australia, 193 from New Zealand, 457 from Canada and 107 from the Republic of Ireland (CLAIR, 2010b). It is clear from the list above the recruitment of these participants from the inner-circle represents a wide regional and social diversity of English speech and, as a result, Japanese high school students learning English, as a group, are likely to be exposed to a wide range of standard and non-standard forms of native English speech. It may well be that such exposure will result in a greater awareness of the social and geographical diversity between and within inner-circle forms of English. Interestingly, since 2000, nationals from the outer circle have also been eligible to participate as AETs. Statistics from 2010 – 2011 indicate that 55 participants were from Jamaica, 49 from Singapore, 25 from Trinidad and Tobago, 17 from India, 8 from Barbados and 1 each from Kenya, Antigua and Barbuda. Although the number of AETs from the outer-circle remains comparatively small, the total grows each year and provides Japanese high school students with increased opportunities for greater exposure to, and to develop increased awareness of, outer-circle varieties of English.

By providing additional opportunities for English language practice and with the objective of attracting more Japanese students, a growing number of universities in Japan have begun teaching undergraduate and/or postgraduate courses in English. Despite a great deal of heated debate surrounding the potential economic, social and political benefits of internationalizing Japanese higher education (e.g. Goodman, 2010; Yonezawa, 2010), another aim for universities in Japan of increasing the amount of courses taught in English is to recruit a greater number of overseas students. Indeed, the policy has a degree of governmental support, as demonstrated by the decision made by MEXT (2009d, 2010a) to select 30 high-ranking Japanese universities to function as 'core institutions' for the education of international students, with the specific aim of enrolling 300,000 overseas students in Japanese higher education by 2020. In order to cater to these international students, a major expansion of the number of degrees that can be awarded based on participation in 'English-only classes' is being planned. The Japanese government is also in the process of establishing offices for the recruitment of these international students in seven countries: Tunisia, Egypt, Germany, Russia, India, Uzbekistan and Vietnam. It is notable from the above list that the intention is to establish offices in countries which are all traditionally categorized within the outer and expanding circles of English use and hence, despite undertaking their degrees solely in English, the vast majority of overseas students recruited will presumably be non-native speakers of English, thus providing Japanese students with more opportunities to be exposed to a range of English speech.

Outwith the public educational system, private language schools hire overseas teachers of English, historically from the inner circle but more recently also from the outer circle, to teach *eikaiwa* (English conversation), a popular activity amongst Japanese nationals of all ages. Seargeant (2009a) notes that foreign language schools represent a lucrative 670 billion yen industry, created upon a successful narrative of the aspirational benefits of (predominantly) English language education for the Japanese population, and there is no doubt that the existence of these institutions offer more opportunities for Japanese nationals to interact with native speakers and, increasingly, non-native speakers of English.

Much of the research investigating the attitudes toward varieties of English amongst non-native speakers of English more generally has focused upon the preferred linguistic model for learning/teaching the language in particular contexts. In the specific case of Japan, as stated above, a UK standard variety of English (RP) and, later, a US standard variety of English (GA) were historically chosen as appropriate teaching models in English language classrooms. However, for different reasons and at different times, researchers have proposed a number of 'de-Anglo-Americanized' pedagogical models for classrooms in Japan with the aim of enabling Japanese students to be able to express 'Japanese values' rather than 'native speaker values' in English (Hino, 2009: 107). In the 1970s, two models were proposed: Kunihiro's *eigo no datsu-eikaba* (de-Anglo-Americanization of English) and Suzuki's *Englic* (for an overview, see Hino, 2009). Unfortunately, no detailed descriptions of their linguistic features have ever been provided. More recently, the Department of World Englishes at Chukyo University in Nagoya has suggested a target variety for students to attain based upon 'educated Japanese which possesses international intelligibility' (Yoshikawa, 2005: 352). Hino (2009: 109) has also proposed 'a production model of Japanese English for international communication ... capable of expressing Japanese values and also be internationally intelligible'. It is worth noting that Hino is much more specific regarding some of the linguistic, sociolinguistic and paralinguistic features of the model for Japanese students.

The findings from the attitude studies detailed above demonstrate that the evaluations of Japanese nationals towards social and regional variation within English speech tend to be complex. Moreover, given the changing sociolinguistic role of the English language in Japan, where young Japanese are likely to gain greater exposure than previously to a range of standard and non-standard varieties of inner-circle English speech as well as to spoken English from the outer and expanding circles, it seems somewhat counter-productive for students if researchers, policy-makers and educators attempt to impose a single variety, or indeed, a restricted number of varieties of English to serve as linguistic models in English language classrooms in Japan. A similar view is taken by Saraceni (2009), who advocates that academics should not be tempted to take upon themselves the responsibility of pedagogical norm-providers, no matter how well-intentioned they may be or, indeed, how sociolinguistically and culturally appropriate the proposed models may seem. Furthermore, since there is evidence that exposing learners to a particular variety increases comprehension of that variety (Major *et al.*, 2005), it would also be beneficial for learners of English in Japan (and elsewhere) to familiarize themselves with a wide a range of varieties of English speech from the inner, outer and expanding circles of English use, both inside and outwith the classroom. It may also be worthwhile to raise sociolinguistic awareness amongst both students and teachers of English through discussion about variation within English (and within other languages) (see also McKenzie, 2010).

It is, however, important to remember that learners themselves are active agents and, hence, will actively select which English model(s) to speak and whether, and to what extent, to give priority, when making such a choice, to the perceived status or to the perceived potential to articulate the identity of their local speech community when choosing a particular variety (McKenzie, 2008a). It may well be the case, for instance, that the majority of Japanese users of English continue to adhere to the previously pervasive 'native speaker ideology', demonstrated by much of the prior attitude research into English in Japan. It is perhaps surprising, however, that users of English in the expanding circle and outer circle have not been consulted more frequently regarding their preferred linguistic models (Kirkpatrick, 2006).

For the reason detailed above, it would be profitable to conduct further attitudinal research focusing specifically upon Japanese nationals' social evaluations of English language variation. In particular, there is a requirement of conducting longitudinal studies amongst subsections of the Japanese population investigating attitudes towards other forms of native and non-native English speech. In addition to building up a more detailed account of Japanese users' attitudes towards social and regional variation in English (and hence to refine the methodology of the investigation of the issues involved in Japan and elsewhere in the expanding circle), the findings from such studies are also likely to provide valuable information regarding the direction of any attitude change occurring within the country.

Any changes in attitude are likely to be a reflection of the shifting relationship between English and Japanese, and are thus likely to be of considerable value to sociolinguists interested in the role of both languages in Japan. Given that linguistically Japan is undergoing both a loss of diversity (in terms of Japanese) and a new diversification (in terms of the increased presence of other languages) (Heinrich & Galan, 2011), sociolinguistic information regarding the direction of language attitude change amongst the population seems especially relevant. The findings of future attitude studies are also likely to have further theoretical, methodological and pedagogical implications for researchers, policy-makers and educators interested in the sociolinguistics of English in Japan.

17 Ideologies of Nativism and Linguistic Globalization

Philip Seargeant

Introduction

The question I address in this chapter is what value the concept of the 'native speaker' has in today's world, a world in which processes of globalization are reshaping traditional social structures, where language practices are intimately involved with these shifts in the nature of social organization and where notions of cultural identity are likewise complicated by the changing patterns of community and communication by which people live. To explore this question, I will analyse the various facets that constitute the concept of the native speaker, examine certain key domains in which these different facets flourish and contrast traditional notions of the concept, traditional in so far as they provide the ideological foundations for social practice in the Japanese education system (which operates as a broad context for the book as a whole) with examples from the lived experience of a 'native speaker English teacher' working within this context.

The chapter begins with two key contentions. The first is that the concept of the native speaker, while partially shaped by physiological and psycholinguistic facts about human development, is also a product of cultural beliefs about the nature of language. In other words, it is an ideological construct, and as such, is time and place specific and is engaged in complex relations with wider networks of cultural belief. The second contention concerns the era in which we live, and the influence that globalization is having upon this moment in history. Central to the way that globalization processes are producing new forms of social organization are the increased possibilities for mobility (both geographical and social) that now exist, and the development of new, non-traditional forms of community (Blommaert, 2010). A key consequence of these changing social frameworks is their effect on notions of identity. The move from a predominantly local-based group identification to a more dispersed, global network of affiliations has problematizing implications for many traditional identity categories, including that of the native speaker.

Working on the basis of these two contentions, that is given the fact that the concept of the native speaker is in part ideological construct and that the social and linguistic practices of broad sectors of the world's population are undergoing extensive and rapid change, the question arises as to whether traditional notions of the native speaker are still valid. Do they continue to have analytic value as descriptors of the sociolinguistic realities in which most people live? And if not, do they serve some other cultural or political purpose? To address these questions, I will begin with an analysis of how the concept of the native speaker operates as an ideological construct, before going on to consider the relationship between its traditional ideological aspect and the actual experience of English speakers in a globalized world as these are manifest in the case of the foreign language teacher working in Japan.

Twin Perspectives on the Native Speaker

Psycholinguistic determinants on language acquisition

Throughout the often dramatic changes that the *eikaiwa* (private language school) industry has experienced in recent years, *The Japan Times* cites a report suggesting that revenue in the sector dropped dramatically from ¥17.2 billion in February 2006 to less than a third of that, ¥5.7 billion, in 2010 (Smart, 2010), traditional conceptions of the native speaker appear to persist in the teaching profession in Japan. Advertisements for ELT instructors both in the private *eikaiwa* sector and in higher education institutions still regularly include personal specifications which list native speaker status as essential; and in many cases, this is the primary, if not only, criterion needed for eligibility for such jobs.[1]

The concept of the native speaker that is used in these contexts is in great part a product of Romantic ideologies of language and its relationship with cultural identity. That is to say, it is composed of two presuppositions: (1) the psycholinguistic determinants of proficiency in a particular language and (2) the identity between a specific language and the people who speak that language. These two elements together constitute the category of the native speaker as it operates as an indicator of the type of attributes that are sought for English teachers, and these two elements have long been fundamental to an understanding of what the category of native speaker means for knowledge of a language.

After saying that this concept is predominantly a product of the Romantic era in Europe, and of ideas that flourished during that period concerning the identity of nation, culture and language (ideas most often associated with the 18th-century German philosopher Johann von Herder's contention that a language displays the genius of a people), these two strands (the psycholinguistic and the cultural) can, in fact, be discerned in conceptualizations of language which date from much earlier than this. The works of Shakespeare, for example, contain two references to the idea of language nativism, each representing one of these key elements. The first is made by Thomas Mowbray, Duke of Norfolk, in *Richard II* (Act 1, Scene 3, ll: 159 – 173). On the occasion of his banishment abroad following his quarrel with Bolingbroke, Mowbray laments:

> The language I have learn'd these forty years,
> My native English, now I must forego:
> And now my tongue's use is to me no more
> Than an unstrung viol or a harp,
> ...
> I am too old to fawn upon a nurse,
> Too far in years to be a pupil now:
> What is thy sentence then but speechless death,
> Which robs my tongue from breathing native breath?

In this formulation, one's native language is equated with the very ability to communicate. As the language one learns from birth, it is the means of existing in the social world, of communicating with and understanding those around you. For Shakespeare's Mowbray, to be banished to a non-English speaking territory is to be condemned to social isolation for the suggestion is that at his stage of life, acquiring in another language the same communicative abilities he has in his native tongue is a cognitive impossibility.

This is a conception founded primarily on the psycholinguistic determinants of language acquisition, and the fact that acquisition in infancy is of a qualitatively different nature from that which can occur post-puberty. The learning process is, for most people, much harder later in life, and leads to a form of the new language which has some level of influence from the first language and to a less instinctive feel for the way the language is spoken in a particular speech community. In Mowbray's formulation, the psycholinguistic determinants which lead to a different type of acquisition and language socialization in infancy as compared to adulthood are considered so stark that exile from his native speech community is akin to social death.

Social perspectives on the meaning of the native speaker

The second Shakespearean reference to the idea of a native language comes in *Henry V* (Act V, Scene 1, ll: 75 – 79), where Gower, an English captain in Henry's army, chastises Pistol, one of the common soldiers, for mocking the Welsh Fluellen.

> You thought, because he could not speak English in the native garb, he could not therefore handle an English cudgel. You find it otherwise; and henceforth let a Welsh correction teach you a good English condition.

The use of the concept here is in a context which elides language with national identity. Although nationalist ideologies were not consolidated until almost two centuries later, an emergent concept of the nation is already developing at this time, and in passages such as this we can see examples of an early association between linguistic resources and national identity (see Seargeant, 2009b, for discussion). Native speaker status (as indicated by accent) is seen as an index not simply either of being able to communicate competently in a particular language or of being a member of a community who share that language, but rather as having certain cultural values. The concept of the 'non-native' speaker is then used conversely to *exclude* people from membership of this community and the values it holds. So Pistol perceives Fluellen as not properly English because of his non-native accent: and not being a native speaker is perceived as not having an English identity and thus not being committed to the English national project (in this case, fighting on the English side against the French). In this formulation, it is not linguistic or communicative competence that is salient, but instead linguistic nativism as a *politico-cultural* quality.

Critiquing the Concept of the Native Speaker

These two vignettes are founded, then, upon two fundamental aspects of the concept of the native speaker that often underpin its use in various forms of social practice. In summary, the concept is one which reflects a broadly conceived phenomenological reality: that children are almost invariably brought up speaking one or more languages which they acquire in a manner markedly different from that by which people learn languages later in life, and that for a great number of people, languages learnt later in life (i.e. after puberty) will not be spoken with the same instinctive fluency and will usually have the trace of the first language in accent, and maybe syntactical structure, in the way they are spoken. In addition, though, the strong bond between language and cultural identity that is made in many societies that was evident in the Renaissance (Seargeant, 2009b), and developed into a dominant political ideology in the Romantic era (Anderson, 2006), means that the imprint of childhood language practices becomes part of the way a person's identity is perceived. As such, the concept of the native speaker includes not simply proficiency in a language but also associations with a body of cultural knowledge, and possibly cultural values, which in turn are seen as defining features for membership of a particular (national) community.

Standard concepts of the native speaker such as the above formulation, which have been influential both in linguistics and in educational practice, have been critiqued from various standpoints in the past few decades (e.g. Cook, 1999; Davies, 2003; Paikeday, 1985; Rampton, 1990), and the issue has become a key site of debate for broader discussions about the status of English in the world. One line of critique is that in the context of the global spread of English, the demographics of world-wide English users mean that more people now learn the language as a second or additional rather than first language, and thus the status of the native speaker as exemplar of correct or desirable usage should be reconsidered. While it may be the case that '[a]s a rule, native speakers are viewed around the world as the genuine article, the authentic embodiment of the standard language' (Kramsch, 1998: 16), as the number of non-native English speakers continues to rise and the language is used more and more for *lingua franca* purposes in encounters which include no native speakers at all, notions of what counts as 'authentic' English usage need to be revised. In other words, in *lingua franca* scenarios, what may count as 'authentic' usage for the native speaker might well be inappropriate or unnecessary for the non-native. And given this de-centring of the native speaker from its position of influence in language education politics, its significance as a theoretical concept in the study of language use is reduced.

Another line of criticism pursues the issue of who should (or can) count as a native speaker. Davies (2004: 436), for example, asks whether a second language learner can ever become a native speaker of a target language. He suggests that this line of questioning reduces to whether acquiring a language in early childhood is a necessary prerequisite to native speaker status (as is usually the assumption), and that this in turn leads to another question of what it is that the child actually acquires in learning a first language. He concludes by suggesting that '[t]he problem is that we cannot fully and absolutely distinguish non-native speakers from native speakers except by autobiography' (Davies, 2004: 438). That is to say, in the final instance, attributing native speaker status to someone relies on knowledge of their linguistic background rather than being a property of the way they actually use the language. Again, therefore, deconstructing elements at the core of the concept diminishes the authority associated with the native speaker within language studies and language education.

Ideologies of Nativism

One result of the above critiques is to highlight the way that the category of native speaker has permeable and shifting boundaries. This is in great part due to its being a social construct, and thus one whose meaning is to an extent at least determined by the way the concept is used in particular contexts by particular communities. In other words, while broad trends in human behaviour (physiological and psycholinguistic determinants on language acquisition) provide the basis for the concept, it then becomes refined by the language-ideological beliefs of the groups or communities using it. People use the term according to their different understandings of the role of language in society and the particular analytical or political ends they have. The concept can thus be seen as a tool, employed to assist both in language research and theorizing (i.e. in academic contexts) and in processes of social organization (e.g. in language education policies, as discussed later in the chapter). As such, when analysing its meaning, it is never possible to get to the 'truth' of what a native speaker actually is because the concept is always part phenomenological fact, part the social and cultural interpretation of this fact within specific contexts. Debates over the concept then arise from how the phenomenological facts are or could be used in programmes of social organization, and debates of this sort are always, in the final instance, political; they are about one person's (or faction's) view of how society should be organized versus that of another.

The context of education and specifically language education is one in which the status of being a native speaker takes on a particular social significance, and is thus one in which the issues surrounding the concept are brought into tangible relief. A person may ordinarily conduct their life without giving any great consideration to whether they have the status of a native or non-native speaker, yet when they are placed within the institutionalized context which regulates (language) educational practices, this issue can suddenly become a salient identity marker. In the Japanese context, for example, the concept of native speaker and the binary divide between native and non-native speaker is an a *priori* category regularly applied in gate-keeping processes for the profession. It is often the case that native speaker teachers are promoted both in the curriculum and in schools' publicity as exemplars of a foreign culture, and that their roles as educators, as experts with specialized knowledge of a topic, is of less apparent importance than their symbolic status as foreign nationals (Breckenridge & Erling, 2011;

Haque & Morgan, 2009). In contexts such as these, then, the concept of the native speaker is being used as part of local debates about cultural identity (Seargeant, 2009a), and its meaning is shaped as much by its use in this type of social practice as by the physiological and psycholinguistic determinants on language acquisition which underpin its origins. Thus, the use of the category enacts ideologies of language and culture, ideologies which in this instance rely in great part on modernist views of identity, that is those based on stable membership of a linguistic community, which is conceived as being co-extensive with a politically circumscribed community (here, a nation state) which speaks a discrete national language such as 'English' or 'Japanese' (Pennycook, 2010).

The problem that arises, though, is that in a world marked by increased mobility and non-traditional community alignments (Giddens, 1999), this framework fails to reflect the sociolinguistic realities and cultural identity politics of a great number of people. Thus, the category as it is applied in contexts such as language education institutions in Japan can be in direct conflict with the experiences of those who live and work within these contexts.

The Native Speaker in the Era of Globalization

Before moving to an illustrative example of how the lived experience of an individual complexifies aspects of the traditional conception of the native speaker, it is first worth analysing in greater detail how the effects of globalization problematize the assumptions about society upon which this traditional conception is based. Central to this 'traditional' concept are specific assumptions about (1) the nature of the speech community and (2) the developmental circumstances of the speaker. For both these elements, a stable and non-complex situation is supposed. With respect to the speech community, this means monolingualism and orientation towards a universal standard. In other words, the community is supposed all to speak (as their L1) the same variety, and to speak that variety alone. Yet, as Mesthrie (2010: 595) notes, 'The monolingual British or North American native speaker is a recent arrival upon the world's linguistic stage'. From its very inception, English was used as part of a multilingual repertoire by those communities who spoke it (Beal, 2011); and with the global spread of English and its present-day multiplex existence as a family of world Englishes, again the norm (i.e. the overwhelming tendency) is for it to function as part of a multilingual repertoire, rather than be the sole code used by an individual. The ideology of monolingualism informing the concept of the native speaker is thus historically specific to societies where ideas of linguistic homogeneity have been promoted, usually as part of the nation-building process. And we may suppose that it persists in the Japanese context as a form of transference from embedded beliefs about the linguistic homogeneity that Japan itself possesses (Maher & Yashiro, 1995).

Assumptions about the developmental circumstances of the speaker again suppose a stable and homogeneous language community. Specifically, these assumptions suppose a language community in which the parents or caregivers speak the same variety as the child's peer group, as it is the norms spoken by this peer group which have the greatest influence on the variety learnt by the child (Mesthrie, 2010). In communities in which there is a marked disparity between the linguistic usage of the peer group and that of the family, the concept of the 'mother tongue' and by extension the 'native speaker' is complexified. And again, processes of globalization particularly those relating to patterns of migration mean that in societies around the world today, complexity is most often the norm rather than the exception.

In summary, then, conceptualizing linguistic practices in terms of singular native 'languages' fails to take into account the varied repertoires of (pluri)lingual and semiotic competences people have at their disposal due to socialization in linguistically heterogeneous environments. And such everyday complexity is in conflict with the presuppositions about language and language development which form the nucleus of the native speaker concept.

An Illustrative Example

How, then, is this conflict manifest in the case of English language teachers in Japan whose linguistic and cultural profiles do not fall neatly within the native/non-native speaker dichotomy? To illustrate the issues discussed above, this section now reports on the biographical experiences and personal and professional reflections of an English language teacher whose profile does not conform in a strict sense to this traditional concept of the native speaker. The data is the result of an interview conducted with the informant via both email and recorded audio, which examined the relationship between biography and language affiliation, between language and cultural identity and between employment opportunities and linguistic/cultural profile. Specific details of the informant's biography (including her name and places of employment) have been anonymized. As a reflective commentary on her own situation, the data offers a picture of how perceptions relating to notions of the native speaker affect the experiences of an individual. In other words, the data specifically considers beliefs about the concept of the native speaker as these are viewed by (and affect) someone working within the education sector in Japan.

The interview subject is a Canadian citizen whose parents both emigrated from South Asia. She was born and raised in Ottawa, and considers English to be her native language. Her early biography, however, means that other language influences were also present and, indeed, multilingualism at a national, familial and personal level was there by default in the context in which she was raised. Canada is an officially bilingual country, and though Ottawa is English-dominant, one of her earliest influences was the French she learnt from her Francophone babysitters. Her parents switched between Bengali (which they would consider as their mother tongue), English and a number of other languages (thus, the home environment was very much a multilingual one), and while the informant herself speaks and understands Bengali, she considers it at the level of a 'home language' within her repertoire, and is unable to understand formal registers of the language. For this reason, she does not consider herself a native speaker of Bengali. For her, English is her mother tongue, despite the fact that this was neither one of the first languages of her parents nor even the first language of those who acted as caregivers during infancy. In summary, then, although the concept of the native speaker is one she feels has some validity and she offers a definition of it as the language in which one is most 'communicatively comfortable' her own personal language history is one of multiplex linguistic influences, and marked by heterogeneity rather than homogeneity.

The informant worked in Japan for two periods of time: the first in the 1990s (when she was part of the JET Programme, and also taught private classes) and then again in the early 2000s. Her experiences match those that suggest that being a native speaker is a key criterion for getting hired as an English teacher in Japan. During her time in the country, she taught at universities, colleges, community centres, cram schools and, while on the JET Programme, elementary and middle schools, and in each case she was hired on the basis of being a native speaker. The concept, as she understood it to be applied in these contexts, meant someone from a native speaker country (e.g. the United States, Canada and the United Kingdom), and when she returned to Japan for the second stint, she noticed that employers were also distinguishing between different types of native speaker much more frequently: with the American accent being the most sought after. The concept as she encountered was also one inflected by race, and she felt that her being of South-Asian descent often resulted in a disconnect between what the interviewers imagined on the basis of her written application and what they saw when she turned up for an interview. The interviews themselves invariably included explicit questions about where she was born, and required her to bring in her passport as proof of this. When she returned for the second stint, she had advanced qualifications (she held a master's degree and was studying for a doctorate) which, she feels, were seen as a 'bonus' to her native speaker status. Throughout both periods of time, gaining employment was never a problem, which she puts down to a mixture of being a native speaker with a north American accent, and having professional and advanced academic qualifications.

While she herself, therefore, did not experience negative prejudice in the job market around the concept of the native speaker, she witnessed it in the case of others. In one school, she had an English teacher colleague from the Philippines who was assigned less prestigious jobs (e.g. teaching in factories) than she herself was given (e.g. teaching classes at large multinational companies), and she is of the belief that this was due to the difference in prestige of their respective English repertoires. She also relates the story of a friend from Trinidad who had a high-level education in language studies, yet did not fit the ideal of the native speaker that employers were working to. When the informant was offered a job which, for various reasons, she could not take herself, she suggested instead this friend. He was told, however, that he was not eligible because they were looking specifically for a native speaker. When he explained that English was his native language, and showed his passport to prove place of birth, he was told that they needed a 'real' native speaker. This friend is of Indo-Trinidadian descent, so is similar in appearance to the informant, and speaks with a soft Trinidadian accent. Yet, within the category system being applied by this employer, being from Canada counted as being *more* of a native speaker than being from the Anglophone Caribbean.

Along with hierarchies of accent and country of origin, the informant also felt that the category is complicated by issues of race and ethnicity. In another instance, when she and her colleagues on the JET Programme were looking for private part-time tutoring jobs, those who were African-American often felt that they were denied work when they showed up in person for interviews. Her colleague from Canada who is of Japanese descent, on the other hand, experienced prejudice in the form of criticism about her limited Japanese-language skills, but was highly sought after as a teacher because it was supposed that, owing to her ethnic background, she would understand Japanese cultural practices better than other foreign teachers. In instances such as these, therefore, the notion of the native speaker is part of a wider complex of ideologies concerning culture and ethnicity, which are often informed more by stereotype than experience.

Conclusions

The experiences attested to by this informant point to a continuing high profile for the concept of the native speaker in Japan, where it operates as part of the apparatus of social organization in the education sector (being, for example, cited as a rationale for decisions over the hiring of staff, while also existing as an aspirational ideal for learners or their parents). Yet the category, as it is applied, is often a crude and one-dimensional template when compared to the actuality of the linguistic profile of someone such as this informant, whose multilingual background shows a complex interplay of languages, domains, affiliations and identity concerns.

The consequences of the erasure of this complexity by the binary equation of native or non-native English speaker are various. For this informant, the way the category was applied did not prove negatively prejudicial in the job market and, due to a combination of possession of a North American accent and advanced qualifications, she never had difficulty gaining employment. For friends and colleagues with similar 'non-traditional' backgrounds, however, the situation was often different, and the lack of flexibility in this formulation of the native speaker worked on occasions to exclude them from employment opportunities. This exclusion had a complexity of its own, though, as it was not presented simply as a question of the applicants' status as a native speaker, but with them being what she describes as the 'wrong type' of native speaker, that is not coming from one of the paradigmatically central Anglophone countries, or it was to do with preconceived ideas about ethnicity, cultural identity and language affiliations.

What is clear from the various strands of this example is that the concept, as it is used in all the contexts described, is very much a social construct. While it may be founded on certain physiological or psycholinguistic facts, its actual application in social practice relies equally on ideologies about the nature of language, the nature of culture and the relationship between language and culture ideologies which are context specific and part of a wider network of beliefs about political and cultural identity in Japan (Seargeant, 2009a). These ideologies of nativism are an inheritance of a cultural and political mainstream centred on the primacy of the nation state, and while such beliefs were always idealizations (i.e. they never matched exactly the lived experiences of individuals living in even the most homogeneous of communities), the nature of modern-day society, where community affiliations are more dispersed and mobility is often a frequent element of an individual's biography, means that these traditional concepts are ever less appropriate for many people across the globe.

There is, then, a conflict between the category of the native speaker as it is promoted in the Japanese education sector and the sociolinguistic realities and cultural identity politics of many of those to whom it is applied. Yet it is not possible to say simply that this traditional concept is flawed and that it needs to be revised to take account of the actuality of the language practices of people living in the era of globalization. This would be to suppose it is primarily a scientific category that its meaning can and should be equated with known facts about the relationship between language acquisition and competence and to mistake its social function. As part of social construct, as partly shaped by its use and function as a tool in processes of social organization, the meaning it has here is a reflection of wider ideologies about the relationship between language and cultural identity which operate in Japanese society. In this context, therefore, questions about the value of the concept of the native speaker are predominantly not linguistic but political, and engaging with them becomes an issue of negotiating the cultural politics of the globalized era.

Note

(1) For example, selected advertisements from the Jobs in Japan website (http://www.jobsinjapan.com; accessed 23 October 2010) included the following:

XXX ENGLISH SCHOOL recruits Native English Speakers teaching conversational/business English to children/adults at student's home, teacher's home, a cafe, or companies in OSAKA, NAGOYA, FUKUOKA, and HYOGO on weekdays or weekends. 3,000 – 5,000 yen/hour plus transportation. Teaching days & time are negotiable..

XXX seeks Native English teachers 2 min. from XXX station. 1-week business English intensive; November 8 to 12, 9 am – 6pm. 3,000 yen per hour + transportation. Working visa required..

Advertisements for university or junior college positions included examples such as the following personal specifications (http://jrecin.jst.go.jp/; accessed 23 October 2010):

(1) Native speaker of English;
(2) Minimum of a master's degree in the humanities or social sciences;
(3) Extensive experience in teaching English as a second or foreign language OR successful completion of a TESOL program with teaching experience;
(4) The first-class certificate of Japanese Language Proficiency Test, OR sufficient command of Japanese in order to carry out administrative duties.

18 The Native Speaker Language Teacher: Through Time and Space

Martine Derivry-Plard

Introduction

The purpose of the chapter is to enlarge the notion of the native speaking English teacher to a broader one: the native speaker language teacher. Following Bourdieu's theoretical framework, the point is to demonstrate that the linguistic field of Foreign Language (FL) teaching has been structured along a binary opposition between native and non-native teachers of FLs. This so-called linguistic divide is above all a social construct, which can be found through time and space within different linguistic and educational contexts. Examples are presented to support the argument, with English teachers in France and their views on nativeness, based on PhD research (Derivry-Plard, 2003), with international students' perceptions of their French native and non-native teachers (Derivry-Plard, 2008) and with demand for native speaker language teachers (Derivry-Plard, 2011: 183 – 185).

The 'Native Speaker' as a Social Construct

Though the notion of 'native speaker' is no longer relevant for linguists (Davies, 1994; Paikeday, 1985; Singh, 1998) and for researchers in language teaching and learning (Braine, 1999; Zarate et al., 2011), the 'native teacher' as a social representation is nonetheless a very powerful image (Clark & Paran, 2007). Therefore, this notion has to be discussed with regard to the particular position that language teachers have within the global context of education and language markets. In fact, language teachers as mediators of languages and cultures depend on the symbolic and economic values of languages which are linked to diverse social and international hierarchies and to different linguistic markets (Alao et al., 2008; Calvet, 2002; Derivry-Plard,

2003). However, FL teachers as mediators of languages and cultures have a historically and socially specific position, based on a go-between role, to relate at least two languages and two cultures. They are situated at varied degrees on an international scale, traditionally relating only 'two nations'. These FL teachers consequently depend on the symbolic hierarchies or social prestige given to languages and cultures. Thus, the specific position of English language teachers is the first point to consider when analysing the language teaching field. Demand for English teachers world wide keeps growing along with English used as a *lingua franca*, with more than 2 billion English learners (Graddol, 2006). English is usually the first FL taught throughout the world, as in Japan and France. Therefore, perceptions of FL teachers being 'native' or 'non-native' speakers of the language taught will be dealt with regarding English, French and Japanese.

FL Teachers and the Language Teaching Field

The dominant sense of legitimacy is nowadays to the benefit of the 'native teacher'. The dichotomy 'native/non-native' has a long history (Derivry-Plard, 2003; Howatt, 2004; Lasagabaster & Sierra, 2002; Medgyes, 1994; Moussu & Llurda, 2008) and has been well documented for EFL teachers (Borg, 2006) either in English-speaking countries or in other countries like France and Japan. This pattern seems nonetheless to function for all languages taught as FL. Throughout time and space, native speaker teachers of foreign languages have not always been in high demand, as demand is linked to the dominant diplomatic and economic powers of the time (e.g. Chinese in Asia with the spread of Chinese characters in ancient times, French in 18th-century Europe and English in the 21st-century global world).

For centuries, in Western Europe, there has been a slow shaping of formalized language teaching based on Latin language transmission, meaning that foreign languages were often taught as dead languages because Latin and Ancient Greek worked as core teaching models within schools and universities. In the 15th and 16th centuries, vernacular language uses progressively took over Latin, and their teaching developed both for commerce and for cultural and educational purposes. A kind of 'warfare' between native and non-native masters was reported even as far back as the 16th century for the teaching of French in England, as French was the dominant language for cultural exchanges and diplomacy at the time. Remarkably, the first ever French grammar treatise was written by an Englishman, John Palsgrave in 1530, as another example of the dominance of French at the time. With the arrival of French Huguenots in England (after Louis XIV's Revocation of the Edict of Nantes in 1685), newly opened schools boasted that they offered French taught with 'true' French masters, and 'A good pronunciation was one of Holyband's chief aims (...) and his main justification for charging high fees as a native-speaking teacher' (Howatt, 2004: 28). Strikingly, the same arguments of 'the good accent' and 'the right language' of the 'native' teacher were expressed in the precise terms that we find nowadays, some 400 years later.

With the institutionalization of teaching in 19th-century Europe, where more or less all European countries created free and compulsory primary education for all, and with the development of secondary education for the flourishing bourgeoisie, foreign language teaching progressively occupied two distinct spaces, that of secondary education and that of the private language schools like Berlitz. Along with these changes, the terms of 'language masters, governesses, private tutors' were to be replaced by 'language professors and teachers' (Fernandez Fraile, 2005). The institutionalization of educational systems in 19th-century Europe entailed the steady institutionalization of FL teaching, and language teachers were recruited following strict standardized procedures. Being a native of the country was an undeclared prerequisite (only nationals could instruct within the schooling system). On the other hand, language schools were not submitted to the strict procedures of the state and could employ native speaker teachers. When European educational systems emerged under the powerful supervision of the nation states (Thiesse, 1999), two distinct foreign language teaching spaces were established: institutional and non-institutional. Non-native teachers were recruited in state-controlled educational institutions, whereas native teachers were more likely to be found in language schools or non-institutional education. For years, there were no exchanges between these two foreign language spaces in Europe, following a staunch partition imposed by the states. However, two professional legitimacies developed at the same time, taking into consideration the different positions of the language teachers:

- The professional legitimacy of non-native teachers in institutional spaces was based on the assumption that they were the best teachers as they went through the same learning process as their pupils, so they would be better able to explain the target language to learners sharing the same 'mother tongue'. This is the legitimacy of the FL teacher as a learning model.
- The professional legitimacy of native teachers in non-institutional spaces was based on the opposite assumption that they were the best teachers because they taught their own 'mother tongue' and that they knew more about it. This is the legitimacy of the FL teachers as a language – culture model.

These two FL teaching legitimacies functioned within each teaching space and were not challenged for years. However, these two spaces have been steadily eroded with the breakthrough of economic globalization and the marketing of educational systems world wide. This overall political trend accounts for increasing tensions between native and non-native FL teachers as strict educational boundaries between institutional and non-institutional educations have collapsed. There is now a reshuffling of perceptions within a renewed space of FL teaching, where a globalizing market of language teachers enforces fierce competitive opportunities. Developing a professional legitimacy on the basis of teaching expertise and qualifications inscribed in plurilingual and pluricultural repertoires (Zarate *et al.*, 2011), whatever be the gender, race, religion or native language, should help counter-balance the excessive limitations of marketing attitudes towards language teachers. This consideration of 'native speaker' is particularly important in Japan, as native English speaker teachers are in high demand but are at the same time relegated to part-time contracts, to a status of assistants, and are denied credit for proper teaching competence and expertise. This situation could be compared with that of the English speaker teachers in state secondary schools in France, where access to the profession has been made more difficult for them than for locals.

Today, even though non-native FL teachers outnumber native FL teachers world wide, the model of the 'ideal monolingual native speaker' is extremely powerful within societies, whereas communication in all languages is expanding at the same time through internet and IT. Denying the complexities of reality, the symbolic monolingual model still functions as a very powerful doxa or ideology of native-speakerism, which imbibes beliefs and representations according to very rigid perceptions and schemata.

A Dominant Position for English and for English Language Teachers

The prevailing situation of English has a direct impact on the ever-increasing demand for English teachers, and growth in the number of English as a Foreign Language (EFL) teachers plays an important part in the current guidelines and agendas for language research and language learning and teaching within the teaching field of foreign and second languages. In other words, research in English language teaching/learning and pedagogical practice has varying repercussions on research in other languages and on 'best practices' for teaching and learning other languages (Alao *et al.*, 2008; Byram & Risager, 1999). Research in language acquisition, the designing of curricula and syllabuses as well as language kits, textbooks for learners and teachers, teacher training programmes, 'good' practice and 'good' testing and assessment of the 'centre' (i.e. the English speaking world) are being dispatched throughout the peripheries (English speaking and non English speaking) following their more or less traditional link to the centre (Kachru, 1985). This global and somewhat ethnocentric perception of English as the international language has been criticized and labelled as linguistic imperialism (Phillipson, 1992, 2003). The linguistic policies promoting English have been carefully managed by the different English-speaking nations of the 20th century, and their combined efforts have increased their effectiveness. The economics of English language teaching operates at all levels of schooling from pre-school to university in Japan, France or other countries. In particular, all subjects and disciplines are further analysed in their lexis, stylistics, narratives and specific discourses, increasing editorial policies to a limitless market: English for business, English for marketing, English for specific purposes, English for academic purposes, English for medical studies, English for computing, English for the internet and so on. Thus, the hegemonic position of English entails an interest in all dimensions of the English language as there is a wider and more diverse public for English. For instance, you may easily find an English language textbook in commercial English for German speakers of level A1 of the Common European Framework of Reference (CEFR), but it is unlikely to find a Polish textbook in commercial Polish aimed at level A1 (CEFR) for Croatian speakers, as Polish does not concern a lot of people and Croatian even fewer. So, the 'interest' in English cross-nationally sustains thriving educational and editorial markets that diffuse Anglo-American values pervading the language textbooks (Canagarajah, 1999b; Cook, 1999). These textbooks are based on principles that are sometimes ethnocentric when dealing with language functions, communicative repertoires and strategies, learning and teaching cultures, language assessment and testing, and they disseminate other cultural references and models in a very insidious way (Bourdieu & Wacquant, 1998). In materials design, assessment criteria or background knowledge often go unquestioned, although they are both culturally constructed (Bourdieu, 1991; Clément et al., 2006; Derivry-Plard, 2005).

Methodology on Native/Non-Native Speaker Teachers of FLs

The following data was collected avoiding common methodological weaknesses in teacher research (Moussu & Llurda, 2008). In fact, teaching situations and contexts and all socio-professional variables (among them social and educational background, linguistic and cultural trajectories and itineraries) of teachers have to be taken into account with great care so as to question the category 'native/non-native' teachers. Otherwise, two supposedly homogeneous groups are usually dealt with, thus transmitting the dichotomy which is under investigation. Finding two similar groups in which the researcher will be able to 'isolate' the variable is part of the sociological task. The data presented was based on such a comparison for English language teachers in France: teachers had the same socio-professional features and professional *habitus* (Bourdieu's term) but differ with their socializations. Among the 38 English teachers interviewed, 19 were native speakers of English. However, their professional features were identical: they taught the same syllabus for the HND (Higher National Diploma) and had the same teaching responsibilities and work contracts. They participated equally in the exam boards. They all had the same French qualifications and the same average experience in teaching English in France and in teaching HND students, who also had the same kind of school achievements and social features.

Very often, surveys are based on the postulate of the researcher (usually complementary competences between the two profiles of teachers), but all the socio-professional variables have not been controlled for, and the results are not necessarily valid: observed discourse differences between 'native/non-native' teachers cannot always be attributed to the fact that they are 'native' or not. Factors such as being experienced or pre-service teachers in the local setting, teaching similar or different classes (conversation vs. grammar), having the same qualifications or not (PhDs vs. TESOL certificates), qualifications obtained in the same country or not, could be of higher significance than being 'native' or 'non-native' (Derivry-Plard, 2003). Moreover, some surveys about 'native/non-native' teachers do not question the fact that sometimes 'native speaker teachers' are monolingual and are compared with their 'non-native speaker colleagues' who are always by definition bilingual (Kramsch, 1997).

Other chapters presented in this book that adopted qualitative research methodology show that discourses on native/non-native speaker teachers are linked to different positions such as structural inequalities in work contracts in Japan between foreigners and locals, qualified Japanese language teachers and less qualified foreign language teachers, men and women, white and non-white people, and the different levels of the Japanese educational system. All these factors contribute to our understanding of how native English speaker teachers in Japan face a social double bind: being praised and idealized as representative of the language and culture and being denied, at the same time, any recognition of real teaching expertise for Japanese learners. It seems that the Japanese context highlights the extreme social contradictions imposed on language teachers through a schizophrenic kind of representation of the native speaker and the language teacher (Medgyes, 1983). In this context, the native English speaker teacher is included as a native speaker and excluded as a true teacher. Conversely, the non-native English speaker teacher is included as a teacher (a 'true' teacher) and excluded *de facto* as a near-native English speaker teacher. Therefore, not 'truly' native and not 'truly' teacher are equally essentialist and racist attitudes at work categorizing what is 'pure' or what is not.

FL Teachers and Beliefs about the 'Native Speaker' within the Language Teaching Field

We have seen that social demand through job offers is for the 'native speaker teacher' of English, French or Japanese. We have also seen that language teachers have to deal with these common representations when they have to find a job, and usually mention that they are 'native speakers' of the language when posting an advertisement (Japanese teachers, in our case study). If they are 'non-native speakers', they will emphasize the fact that they have lived in the country of the target language for years and that 'surprisingly' they can be more effective: *I've lived for a very long time in Japan and I can initiate to this very beautiful language. A non-Japanese teacher can paradoxically be more effective to begin with*. These arguments can also be observed with English or French teachers (Derivry-Plard, 2008). In order to find positions language teachers have to take market preferences into account (Braine, 1999; Clark & Paran, 2007).

Language learners prefer 'native speaker language teachers'

Two surveys were based on similar questionnaires. Learners of English and learners of French were asked how they perceived their language teachers based on experiences of having been taught the target language by both native and non-native speaker teachers in 1997 and 2007, respectively (Derivry-Plard, 2003, 2008). A majority of respondents declared they would rather have a 'native' speaker as a teacher. It is significant that both types of learners used the same words to qualify their choices, the first group was learning English and the second group was learning French, even though a decade had passed between the two surveys (Derivry-Plard, 2008). The categories of perception found through a content analysis were similar. Learners used the same arguments and words for expressing their preferences irrespective of the language taught: 'native' teachers were entrusted with very positive values as they were considered to have a greater linguistic competence than their non-native counterparts. Some 80% of the text examined through a thematic content analysis mentioned that greater linguistic competence, expressed in the terms used by the respondents, meant that 'native teachers' had no 'accent', a 'better pronunciation', 'more words, phrases and idioms' and 'no grammar mistakes'. Then, 20% of the remaining text was about greater cultural competence. These learners' representations mirrored to a certain extent traditional views on language learning, basically perceived as linguistic learning above all. The notion of cultural competence which accounts for less of all the discourse was also expressed with naive statements such as 'they own the English culture', 'love their countries', 'master the English culture', 'they know France better' and 'understand French culture' (Derivry-Plard, 2008: 281 – 291).

Language teachers think it an advantage to be a 'native speaker language teacher'

Investigating English language teachers in France, the same broad schema of perceptions of native/non-native speaker teachers was also at work, even though the language used was complex. A thematic content analysis applied to all semi-directive interviews (Derivry-Plard, 2003) showed that the theme of the native English speaker teacher predominated. However, native English-speaking teachers spoke more about the native English teacher than their French colleagues did. This result focusing on the theme of the native teacher seems to confirm that even for language teachers, the native speaker teacher is considered more legitimate as a teacher, being the dominant reference from which teachers develop their professional discourses. In all the responses came the theme of the non-native teachers, and then a very small proportion of all text dealt with the ideas that native and non-native teachers have complementary roles or that both types of teachers are, in fact, exactly the same professionals. In other words, the professional discourse of these English teachers worked on binary oppositions with value judgements more than on relational perspectives. Moreover, positive judgements came first when native teachers spoke about native teachers, and when non-native teachers spoke about themselves. However, non-native teachers were more critical and severe about themselves than the native teachers were. The data revealed strong oppositions between teachers, expressing in a very significant way the 'little warfare' (Price, 2000: 8) traditionally mentioned between foreign language teachers in France. When analysing these value judgements, the same categories expressed by learners are at work: non-native teachers are extremely critical about the teaching competencies of their native colleagues:

... some had not the project of teaching English ... I have seen native English-speaking teachers who did not do the job ... but, it is just because they are not teachers, they turned up in a classroom ... they delivered what they could, they thought that speaking English for two hours is enough! ... but this is not having a conversation, speaking about this or that for an hour ? ... And some do not know French enough, which is a problem ... Some do not teach! (Derivry-Plard, 2003: 336).

With the above extract, we can see that native English speaker teachers were perceived more as native speakers than as teachers. The natural link they have with the language even hampers their teaching competence. This essentialist perception categorizes the native speaker by a natural link to the language implying a natural approach to language teaching. As for native English-speaking teachers, their main criticisms were about the insufficient linguistic competence of non-native English speaker teachers (either for spoken or for written English), which was sometimes visible in schoolbooks designed by non-native English teachers:

... well, it's second language, it's second-hand! ... in this schoolbook written by French, there are a few mistakes ... they make mistakes, with English vowels, their accent is not as good .... Sometimes, her accent was awful and there were English teachers I could barely understand ... She made so many mistakes ... and some pupils were as good as she was in English! .... She could not give a precise meaning of a word with all the connotations ... even if the dictionary gives that meaning, it has no longer that meaning ... at a certain point, a non native teacher will be embarrassed, this is for sure because, at one point, he/she will apply a grammar rule that we no longer use ... they will never get all the shades of meaning ... (Derivry-Plard, 2003: 340).

Thus, non-native teachers were critical about the teaching competence of their English colleagues whereas the English colleagues were critical about the linguistic and cultural competence of their French colleagues. However, the fact that all teachers interviewed dwelt more on the theme of the native English speaker teacher confirmed the idea of greater linguistic competence for the native English speaker, complying with the explicit categories imposed by society and the market. A non-native English speaker teacher summarized that greater legitimacy of the native English-speaking teacher in the following terms: 'The ideal is an English teacher who has a pedagogic sensibility and who is native!' (Derivry-Plard, 2003: 354).

FL Teachers and Social Beliefs about the 'Native Speaker Language Teacher'

Within this geopolitical context where language teaching seems to become global rather than international, with English as the driving force of language teaching, how can we characterize the field of FL and the specific position of teachers? To what extent are teachers included or excluded within the field of language teaching? First, one has to question the goal of language teachers. Are they facilitators for dialogues between different peoples? Do they help mutual understanding by fostering mediating attitudes? Or, are they still defined as 'ambassadors' of the language they teach, passing on cultural patterns and values of the country where the language is spoken and thus contributing to language warfare (Calvet, 1999)? These questions raise another perspective when the teacher is also a 'native speaker' of the language taught, a cultural representative of the language whose loyalties to the language and home culture are at stake. In that sense, the native speaker language teacher seems included within the culture and language whereas the non-native speaker language teacher seems excluded as a linguistic and cultural outsider. But this is far too simple an assertion, as plainly speaking, a language and a culture do not make the teacher, just as a language and a culture do not make the individual. On the other hand, the term 'native speaker' does point to a problematic social dimension of an affiliation to a language. Within each linguistic market, the stakes are high, depending on the symbolic capital of each variety of language.

Examples of social beliefs through job offers and tuition advertisements

The French language from Quebec or from Senegal does not stand on the same linguistic footing as the French from France. Equally, the English language from India or Kenya does not benefit from the same social prestige as British English. The power struggle to own the legitimate language is deeply rooted in a social dimension and has strong political and economic implications. So, a teacher from Quebec will probably confront problems in teaching French to foreigners in France and even more so to French people in France. Likewise, a teacher from India would probably meet the same obstacles in teaching English in England or in the United States. We may question the reason for such a situation as both teachers are native speakers, the former of French and the latter of English. Similarly, a teacher of English who is a French native speaker might experience the same difficulty when teaching English to foreigners in England or English to British people. In the same way, a teacher of French, whose native tongue is Japanese, might encounter similar impediments when teaching French in France to foreigners or to French people. These examples highlight a range of social hierarchies both within 'native speaker' communities and within the ranks of 'native/non-native speakers', based on the apparent affiliation to a language. What is at stake is part and parcel of social order, which is linked to social hierarchies within and between linguistic markets on the international language market. Representations of language teachers expressed by society as a whole continue to convey a very positive idealized view of the 'native teacher'. Job advertisements were gathered over a three-month period for an unpublished study conducted in 2009 – 2010. Comparing ads for teaching English, French and Japanese on three different influential websites in France will illustrate these views of the market:

- Job offers for teachers of English (from Société des Anglicistes de l'Enseignement Superieur, SAES, the most well-known list and association of English teachers in France, September 2009):
  - The English department of the Institut Catholique de Paris .... Candidates should be anglophone with a knowledge of phonetics. ... There is no doctoral requirement for lab colleagues. (Advertisement in English)
  - University of Paris 8 is looking for a Language Assistant for the academic year.... English mother tongue – The teacher will mainly be in charge of listening and speaking classes as well as ESP classes. (Advertisement in French)
- Job offers for teachers of French written in French (in France, from le français dans le monde, FDLM, the most well-known list and association of French as a FL, summer 2009):
  - Language Centre: 3 French teachers ... in the Language Centre in Burgundy.
    Requisites: good sense of humour, French as a mother tongue, fluent English, being in charge, well-organised, good relationship with learners. Experience is a must.
  - Preparatory training for foreign student: University of Maine (....) Requisites for application: a FFL degree or strong experience in teaching FL, francophone (French mother tongue) and the applicant has been living in France for many years, has attended higher education ... in France...

- Tuition advertisements offered by teachers of Japanese, written in French (in France, from a well-known freelance teachers website: http://www.kelprof.com, summer 2010):
  - Japanese tuition in Toulon: The Japanese language is my mother tongue, I have a good experience as a SENSEI (teacher) and I have been living in France for 5 years. … Yasuko
  - Hello, Japanese mother tongue teacher offers Japanese tuitions: grammar, vocabulary and conversation all levels, in Paris…

Society and markets prefer 'native speaker language teachers'

For English and French teachers, more than 60% of job offers over the time analysed of the case study were for native speaker teachers. For Japanese teachers, it was an internet list where teachers posted their own offers, and in that context more than 60% of the job offers came from non-native speaker teachers. Here, Japanese teachers' ads reflect supply as compared to English and French teachers' ads reflecting demand. In both cases, 'native speakerism' (Holliday, 2006) is at work.

This very simple calculation shows a stark imbalance on the FL teacher market, as demand is higher for native speaker teachers than for non-native speaker teachers, who find it more difficult to get a job on the free market. However, recruitment procedures are different at universities or in secondary state schooling, explaining how non-native speaker teachers may still enjoy some employment protection in France at secondary level. Analysing either these job or tuition ads, the 'native speaker' is confused with a 'native teacher'. Furthermore, irrespective of the language taught, English, French or Japanese, the social demand is for 'native' teachers. Analysing these advertisements, it is clear that the 'native speaker' is associated with the 'native teacher' as if there were an affiliation or obvious link between the native speaker of a language and the teacher of that language. Similar examples of the confusion can be found in the press, the political sphere or even the language teaching field (Derivry-Plard, 2008). One may wonder about this ideology of 'native-speakerism', which seems stronger nowadays as it participates in an even broader global ideology where human relationships are ethnicized casting aside traditional social power struggles (Michaels, 2006). In fact, insisting on being a 'native speaker' is a way of labelling the individual whose identity is reduced to one 'essential' dimension, which is a process of stigmatism and racism. This process is usually obscured within the generous and positive values of the language teaching field, promoting acceptance of diversity of languages and cultures (Kubota, 2002a, 2006; Zarate *et al.*, 2011).

From Exclusion to Inclusion: Deconstructing 'Native Speakerism' and Constructing Professional Language Teachers

Deconstructing the ideology of 'native-speakerism' provides a conceptual framework for professional language teachers facing a more global and conflicting kind of world. Shifting from a monolingual paradigm to a multilingual one (Widdowson, 2000) entails an even more critical perspective on the social conditions of the international circulation of ideas (Bourdieu & Wacquant, 1998; Zarate & Liddicoat, 2009), in which language teachers are *de facto* key actors and participants. Therefore, language teachers as professionals have to get rid of such essentialist, reductive images of identities, in order to think of their professional language teaching field as a truly intercultural communicative space where binary oppositions like native/non-native, exclusion/inclusion should be overcome. This is a prerequisite for establishing the conditions of a multilingual field of language learning and teaching where individual trajectories and itineraries of teachers and learners alike as mobile social actors are to be considered first and foremost (Fenoulhet & Ros i Solé, 2011; Miller *et al.*, 2009).

Acknowledgement

Special thanks to Rhoda McGraw, Lecturer at ENPC, France, for her insightful comments on this chapter.

References

Aboshiha, P. (2008) Identity and dilemma: the 'native speaker' English language teacher in a globalizing world. Unpublished PhD thesis, Canterbury Christ Church University, UK.

Acker, S. (1980) Women, the other academics. *British Journal of Sociology of Education* 1 (1), 81–91.

Acker, S. (1994) *Gendered Education: Sociological Reflections on Women, Teaching and Feminism*. Buckingham: Open University Press.

Acker, J. (2009) From glass ceiling to inequality regimes. *Sociologie du Travail* 51, 199–217.

Alao, G., Argaud, E., Derivry-Plard, M. and Leclerq, H. (eds) (2008) *'Grandes' et 'petites' langues, pour une didactique du plurilinguisme et du pluriculturalisme*. Berne, Peter Lang,

Alderson, J.C. (2009a) Setting the scene. In J.C. Alderson (ed.) *The Politics of Language Education: Individuals and Institutions* (pp. 8–44). Bristol: Multilingual Matters.

Alderson, J.C. (2009b) The micropolitics of research and publication. In J.C. Alderson (ed.) *The Politics of Language Education: Individuals and Institutions* (pp. 222–236). Bristol: Multilingual Matters.

Ali, S. (2009) Teaching English as an international language (EIL) in the Gulf Corporation Council (GCC) countries: The brown man's burden. In F. Sharifian (ed.) *English as an International Language: Perspectives and Pedagogical Issues* (pp. 34–57). Bristol: Multilingual Matters.

Allsi (2007, March) *Allsi Newsletter*. Online document: http://www.allsi.org/allsinews1.pdf.

Allsi (n.d.) *About Allsi*. Online document: http://www.allsi.org/allsinews1.pdf.

Altbach, P.G. (2004) The past and future of Asian universities: Twenty-first century challenges. In A.G. Philip and T. Umakoshi (eds) *Asian Universities: Historical Perspectives and Contemporary Challenges* (pp. 13–32). Baltimore: Johns Hopkins University Press.

Altbach, P.G. (2005) Globalization and university: Myths and realities in an unequal world. In National Education Association (ed.) *The NEA 2005 Almanac of Higher Education* (pp. 63–74). Washington DC: National Education Association.

Amin, N. (1997) Race and the identity of the nonnative ESL teacher. *TESOL Quarterly* 31 (3), 580–583.

Anton, M. and DiCamilla, F.J. (1998) Socio-cognitive functions of L1 collaborative interaction in the L2 classroom. *Canadian Modern Language Review* 54 (3), 314–335.

Appleby, R. (2010a, September) An acceptable masculinity: White men talk about heterosexual relationships in Japan. Paper presented at IGALA conference. Tsuda College (Kodaira Campus), Tokyo, Japan.

Appleby, R. (2010b) *ELT, Gender and International Development*. Bristol: Multilingual Matters.

Arudou, D. (2009) *Blacklist of Japanese Universities*. Online document: http://www.debito.org/kitakyushudata.html.

Arudou, D. (2010a, 6 July) Japan's hostile hosteling industry. *The Japan Times*. Online document: http://search.japantimes.co.jp/cgi-bin/fl20100706ad.html.

Arudou, D. (2010b, 2 March) Sumo body deserves *mawashi wedgie* for racist wrestler ruling. *The Japan Times*. Online document: http://search.japantimes.co.jp/cgi-bin/fl20100302ad.html.

Asahi Shimbun (2010, 4 August) *ALT 'Nan' yamazumi* [Problems piling up with ALT]. Morning Edition, 2.
Auerbach, E. (1993) Re-examining English only in the ESL classroom. *TESOL Quarterly* 27 (1), 9–32.
Auerbach, E. (1994) Comments on Elsa Auerbach's 'Re-examining English only in the ESL classroom': The author responds. *TESOL Quarterly* 28 (1), 157–161.
Bandura, A. (1997) *Self-efficacy: The Exercise of Control.* New York: W.H. Freeman & Company.
Barratt, L. and Kontra, E.H. (2000) Native-English-speaking teachers in cultures other than their own. *TESOL Journal* 9 (3), 19–23.
Baumeister, R.F. (2005) *The Cultural Animal: Human Nature, Meaning, and Social Life.* Oxford: Oxford University Press.
Baumeister, R.F. and Leary, M.R. (1995) The need to belong: Desire for interpersonal attachments as a fundamental human motivation. *Psychological Bulletin* 117 (3), 497–529.
Baumeister, R.F., Brewer, L.E., Tice, D.M. and Twenge, J.M. (2007) Thwarting the need to belong: Understanding the interpersonal and inner effects of social exclusion. *Social and Personality Psychology Compass* 1 (1), 506–520.
Baumeister, R.F., DeWall, N.C., Ciarocco, N.J. and Twenge, J.M. (2005) Social exclusion impairs self-regulation. *Journal of Personality and Social Psychology* 88 (4), 589–604.
Beauchamp, E.R. and Vardaman, J.M. Jr. (1994) *Japanese Education Since 1945: A Documentary Study.* New York: M. E. Sharpe.
Beal, J. (2011) A national language. In P. Seargeant and J. Swann (eds) *English in the World Today: History, Diversity, Change.* Abingdon: Routledge.
Beck, U. and Sznaider, N. (2006) Unpacking cosmopolitanism for the social sciences: A research agenda. *British Journal of Sociology* 57 (1), 1–23.
Befu, H. (ed.) (1993) *Cultural Nationalism in East Asia: Representation and Identity.* Berkeley, CA: Institute of East Asian Studies, University of California.
Befu, H. (2001) *Hegemony of Homogeneity: An Anthropological Analysis of Nihonjinron.* Melbourne: Trans Pacific Press.
Benesse, Kyouiku Kihatsu Senta (2006) *Dai 1 kai shougakko Eigo ni kansuru kihon chousa (kyouiku chousa), sokuho ban* [First Basic survey of elementary school English (education survey)]. Tokyo: Benesse Corporation.
Benson, M.J. (1991) Attitudes and motivation towards English: A survey of Japanese freshmen. *RELC Journal* 22 (1), 34–48.
Benson, J., Masae, Y. and Debroux, P. (2007) The prospect for gender diversity in Japanese employment. *The International Journal of Human Resource Management* 18 (5), 890–907.
Berger, P. and Luckmann, T. (1979) *The Social Construction of Reality.* Harmondsworth: Penguin.
Bhabha, H. (1994) *The Location of Culture.* London: Routledge.
Bigelow, G. (2005, 1 May) Let there be markets: The evangelical roots of economics. *Harper's Magazine.* Online document: http://harpers.org/archive/2005/05/0080538.
Bialystock, E. and Hakuta, K. (1994) *In Other Words: The Science and Psychology of SLA.* New York: Basic Books.
Blackburn, R.M., Browne, J., Brooks, B. and Jarman, J. (2002) Explaining gender segregation. *British Journal of Sociology* 53 (4), 513–536.
Blitz, B. (1999) The resistant guild: Institutional protectionism and freedom of movement in the Italian university system. *South European Politics and Society* 4 (1), 27–47.

Blitz, B. (2010) Fractured lives and grim expectations: Freedom of movement and the downgrading of status in the Italian university system. *Bulletin of Italian Politics* 2 (2), 123–140.

Blommaert, J. (2010) *The Sociolinguistics of Globalization*. Cambridge: Cambridge University Press.

Blyth, C. (1995) Redefining the boundaries of language use: The foreign language class as a multilingual speech community. In C. Kramsch (ed.) *Redefining the Boundaries of Language Study* (pp. 145–183). Boston: Heinle and Heinle.

Borg, S. (2006) The distinctive characteristics of foreign language teachers. *Language Teaching Research* 10 (1), 3–31.

Bourdieu, P. (1991) *Language and Symbolic Power*. Harvard: Harvard University Press.

Bourdieu, P. and Wacquant, L. (1998) Sur les ruses de la raison impérialiste [The Cunning of Imperialist Reason]. *Actes de la Recherche en Sciences Sociales* 121/122, 109–118.

Bradley, D. and Bradley, M. (2001) Changing attitudes to Australian English. In D. Blair and P. Collins (eds) *English in Australia* (pp. 271–286). Amsterdam: John Benjamins.

Braine, G. (ed.) (1999) *Non-Native Educators in English Language Teaching*. Mahwah, NJ: Lawrence Erlbaum Associates.

Breckenridge, Y.M. (2010) Professional identity and the 'native speaker': An investigation of essentializing discourses in TESOL. Unpublished PhD thesis, University of Alberta, Canada.

Breckenridge, Y. and Erling, E.J. (2011) The native speaker English teacher and the politics of globalization in Japan. In P. Seargeant (ed.) *English in Japan in the Era of Globalization* (pp. 80–100). Hounslow: Palgrave Macmillan.

Breen, M.P. and Candlin, C.N. (1980) The essentials of a communicative curriculum in language teaching. *Applied Linguistics* I (2), 89–112.

Brender, A. (2001, 23 March) Foreign lecturers bear the brunt of budget pain at Japanese universities. *The Chronicle of Higher Education*. Online document: http://chronicle.com/article/Foreign-Lecturers-Bear-the/16509.

Brooks, F.B. and Donato, R. (1994) Vygotskyan approaches to understanding foreign language learning: Discourse and communicative tasks. *Hispania* 77 (2), 262–274.

Brown, G. (1989) Sitting on a rocket: An interview with Professor Gillian Brown. *ELT Journal* 43 (3), 167–172.

Brown, R. (2000) *Group Processes: Dynamics Within and Between Groups*. Oxford: Blackwell.

Bruthiaux, P. (2003) Squaring the circles: Issues in modelling English worldwide. *International Journal of Applied Linguistics* 13 (2), 159–174.

Bueno, E.P. and Caesar, T. (2003) *I Wouldn't Want Anybody to Know: Native English Teaching in Japan*. Tokyo: JPGS Press.

Burden, P. (2000) The use of the students' mother tongue in monolingual English conversation classes at Japanese universities. *The Language Teacher* 24 (16), 5–10.

Byram, M. (2008) *From Foreign Language Education to Education for Intercultural Citizenship*. Clevedon: Multilingual Matters.

Byram, M. and Risager, K. (1999) *Language Teachers, Politics and Cultures*. Clevedon: Multilingual Matters.

Calvet, L.-J. (1999) *La guerre des langues et les politiques linguistiques* [Language Warfare and Linguistic Policies]. Paris: Hachette/Pluriel.

Calvet, L.-J. (2002) *Le marché aux langues: les effets linguistiques de la mondialisation* [Language Market: the Linguistic Impact of Globlisation]. Paris: Plon.

Canagarajah, A.S. (1999a) Interrogating the 'native speaker fallacy': Non-linguistic roots, nonpedagogical results. In G. Braine (ed.) *Non-Native Educators in English Language Teaching* (pp. 77–92). Mahwah, NJ: Lawrence Erlbaum Associates.

Canagarajah, A.S. (1999b) *Resisting Linguistic Imperialism*. Oxford: Oxford University Press.

Cargile, A.C., Takai, J. and Rodriguez, J.I. (2006) Attitudes toward African-American vernacular English: A US export to Japan? *Journal of Multilingual and Multicultural Development* 27 (6), 443–456.

Carli, L. (2001) Gender and social influence. *Journal of Social Issues* 57 (4), 725–741.

Carroll, L. (1871) *Chapter VI: Humpty Dumpty. Through the Looking Glass*. Online document: http://gopher.elib.com:8070/0/Library/Fulcrum/lglass16.txt.

Casanave, C.P. and Schecter, S. (eds) (1997) *On Becoming a Language Educator: Personal Essays on Professional Development*. Mahwah, NJ: Lawrence Erlbaum Associates.

CESCR (1976) *International Covenant on Social, Economic and Cultural Rights*. Online document: http://www2.ohchr.org/english/law/cescr.htm.

Charles, M. and Grusky, D.B. (2004) *Occupational Ghettos: The Worldwide Segregation of Women and Men*. Stanford: Stanford University Press.

Cheng, X. (2000) Asian students' reticence revisited. *System* 28 (3), 435–446.

Chiba, R., Matsuura, H. and Yamamoto, A. (1995) Japanese attitudes toward English accents. *World Englishes* 14 (1), 77–86.

Chihara, T. and Oller, J.W. (1978) Attitudes and attained proficiency in EFL: A sociolinguistic study of adult Japanese speakers. *Language Learning* 28 (1), 55–68.

Chung, E.A. (2010) *Immigration and Citizenship in Japan*. Cambridge: Cambridge University Press.

Clark, R. and Gieve, S.N. (2006) On the discursive construction of 'the Chinese Learner'. *Language, Culture and Curriculum* 19 (1), 54–73.

Clark, E. and Paran, A. (2007) The employability of non-native-speaker teachers of EFL: A UK survey. *System* 35 (4), 407–430.

Cleary, F. (1998) Strike at the Prefectural University of Kumamoto: A personal view. *PALE Journal of Professional Issues* 4 (3). Online document: http://www.debito.org/PALE/.

Cleary, F. (1999) Taking it to the top: The Union visits Monbusho. *PALE Journal of Professional Issues* 5 (1). Online document: http://www.debito.org/PALE/.

Cleary, F. (2010, 27 December) Interview.

Clément, F., Escoda, M.R., Schultheis, F. and Berclaz, M. (eds) (2006) *L'inconscient académique* [The Unconscious Academic]. Genève/ Zurich, Seismo.

Clemente, A. and Higgins, M. (2008) *Performing English as a postcolonial accent: ethnographic narratives from México*. Tufnell Press, UK.

Collins, P.H. (1998) *Fighting Words: Black Women and the Search for Justice*. Minneapolis: University of Minnesota Press.

Cook, C. and Waters, M. (1998) The impact of organizational form on gendered labor markets in engineering and law. *The Sociological Review* 46 (2), 314–339.

Cook, H. (2006) Joint construction of folk beliefs by JFL learners and Japanese host families. In M. DuFon and E. Churchill (eds) *Language Learners in Study Abroad Contexts* (pp. 120–150). Clevedon: Multilingual Matters.

Cook, V. (1999) Going beyond the native speaker in language teaching. *TESOL Quarterly* 33 (2), 185–209.

Cook, V. (2001) Using the first language in the classroom. *Canadian Modern Language Review* 57 (3), 402–423.

Coupland, N. and Bishop, H. (2007) Ideologised values for British accents. *Journal of Sociolinguistics* 11 (1), 74–93.

CLAIR (2009a) The goals of the JET Programme. Online document: http://www.jetprogramme.org/e/introduction/goals.html.

CLAIR (2009b) JET Programme FAQs. Online document http://www.jetprogramme.org/e/faq/faq02elig.html#2-1.

CLAIR (2010a) Welcome to the JET Programme. Online document: http://www.jetprogramme.org/e/introduction/index.html.

CLAIR (2010b) JET Programme participant numbers. Online document: http//jetprogramme.org/e/introduction/statistics.html.

Creaser, F. (2012) Harassment prevention policies at a Japanese university. *The Journal and Proceedings of the Gender Awareness in Language Education (GALE) Special Interest Group of the Japan Association for Language Teaching* 5, 22–37.

Crenshaw, K. (1989) Demarginalizing the intersection of race and sex: A black feminist critique of antidiscrimination doctrine, feminist theory, and antiracist politics. *University of Chicago Legal Forum 1989*, 139–167.

Crenshaw, K. (1992) Whose story is it anyway? Feminist and anti-racist appropriations of Anita Hill. In T. Morrison (ed.) *Race-ing Justice, En-gendering Power: Essays on Anita Hill, Clarence Thomas, and the Construction of Social Reality* (pp. 402–441). New York: Pantheon.

Crenshaw, K., Gotanda, N., Peller, G. and Thomas, K. (1995) Introduction. In K. Crenshaw, N. Gotanda, G. Peller and K. Thomas (eds) *Critical Race Theory: The Key Writings that Formed the Movement* (pp. xiii–xxxii). New York: The New Press.

Critchley, M. (1999) Bilingual support in English language classes in Japan: A survey of students' opinions on L1 use by their foreign language teachers. *The Language Teacher* 23 (9), 10–13.

Crompton, R. (2006) *Women and Work in Modern Britain*. Oxford: Oxford University Press.

Crooks, A. (2001) Professional development and the JET program: Insights and solutions based on the Sendai City program. *JALT Journal* 23 (1), 31–46.

Crystal, D. (1997) *English as a Global Language*. Cambridge: Cambridge University Press.

Curtis, A. and Romney, M. (eds) (2006) *Color, Race, and English Language Teaching: Shades of Meaning*. Mahwah, NJ: Lawrence Erlbaum Associates.

Cabinet Office of Japan (2009, May) *White Paper on Gender Equality: Outline*. Online \ document: http://www.gender.go.jp/whitepaper/ewp2009.pdf.

D'Angelo, J. (2008) The Japan context and the expanding cricle: A Kachruvian response to Debbie Ho. *Asian Englishes* 11 (2), 64–74.

Davies, A. (1994) Native speaker. In R.E. Asher (ed.) *The Encyclopedia of Language and Linguistics* 5 (pp. 2719–2725). New York: Pergamon Press.

Davies, A. (2003) *The Native Speaker: Myth and Reality*. Clevedon: Multilingual Matters.

Davies, A. (2004) The native speaker in applied linguistics. In A. Davies and C. Elder (eds) *The Handbook of Applied Linguistics* (pp. 431–450). London: Blackwell.

De Beauvoir, S. (1963) *La Pensée de Droite, Aujord'hui* [Right-wing Thought Today]. El Pensamiento politico de la Derecha. Buenos Aires.

Deacon, B. (2003) Priceless peer-mentor observation. In J. Egbert (ed.) *Professional Development in Language Education Series (Vol. 1): Becoming Contributing Professionals* (pp. 81–88). Alexandria, VA: TESOL.

Decision of the European Ombudsman on complaint 161/99/IJH against the European Commission (2000, 13 September). Online document: http://www.ombudsman.europa.eu/cases/decision.faces/en/1160/html.

Delanty, G. (2008) Dilemmas of secularism: Europe, religion and the problem of pluralism. In G. Delanty, R. Wodak and P. Jones (eds) *Identity, Belonging and Migration* (pp. 78–97). Liverpool: Liverpool University Press.

Delanty, G., Wodak, R. and Jones, P. (2008) Introduction: migration, discrimination and belonging in Europe. In G. Delanty, R. Wodak and P. Jones (eds) *Identity, Belonging and Migration* (pp. 1–20). Liverpool: Liverpool University Press.

Delgado, R. and Stefancic, J. (2001) *Critical Race Theory: An Introduction.* New York: New York University Press.

Derivry-Plard, M. (2003) Les enseignants d'anglais « natifs » et « non- natifs ». Concurrence ou complémentarité de deux légitimités ["Native" and "Non-Native" speaking English teachers. Competitive or complementary legitimacies]. PhD Dissertation, Paris 3 Sorbonne Nouvelle. Online document: http://www.anrtheses.com.fr/.

Derivry-Plard, M. (2005) 'Native' and 'non-native' teachers: how to compare their results? *Research News* 15, 62–65.

Derivry-Plard, M. (2008) Students' representations on native speaker teachers of FL. In M. Pawlak (ed.) *Investigating English Language Learning and Teaching* (pp. 281–293). Poznan: Faculty of Pedagogy and Fine Arts in Kalisz, Adam Mickiewicz University.

Derivry-Plard, M. (2011) Native and non-native teachers: two types of professional competing on the language market. In G. Zarate, D. Lévy and C. Kramsch (eds) *Handbook of Multilingualism and Multiculturalism* (pp. 183–185). Paris: E.A.C.

DiPardo, A. and Potter, C. (2003) Beyond cognition: A Vygotskian perspective on emotionality and teachers' professional lives. In A. Kozulin, B. Gindis, V. S. Ageyev and S. M. Miller (eds) *Vygotsky's Educational Theory in Cultural Context* (pp. 317–345). Cambridge: Cambridge University Press.

Dixson, A.D. and Rousseau, C.K. (2005) And we are still not saved: Critical race theory in education ten years later. *Race, Ethnicity and Education* 8 (1), 7–27.

Dörnyei, Z. (2005) *The Psychology of the Language Learner: Individual Differences in Second Language Acquisition.* Mahwah, NJ: Lawrence Erlbaum Associates.

Dörnyei, Z. (2007) *Research Methods in Applied Linguistics.* Oxford: Oxford University Press.

Douglas, M. (1966) *Purity and Danger: An Analysis of Concepts of Pollution and Taboo.* London: Routledge and Keegan Paul.

Douglass, M. and Roberts, G. (2000) *Japan and Global Migration: Foreign Worker and the Advent of a Multicultural Society.* Honolulu: University of Hawai'i Press.

Duff, P. (2008) *Case Study Research in Applied Linguistics.* New York: Routledge.

Duncan, G.A. (2005) Critical race ethnography in education: Narrative, inequality and the problem of epistemology. *Race, Ethnicity and Education* 8 (1), 93–114.

ECJ (1993, 2 August) Case (C-259/91).
ECJ (1997, March 20th) Case (C-90/96).
ECJ (2001a, 26 June) Case (C-212/99).
ECJ (2001b, 11 December) Case (T-191/99).
ECJ (2006a, 1 June) Opinion of Advocate General, Case (C-371/04).
ECJ (2006b, 18 July) Case (C-119/04).

Edwards, J. (1999) Refining our understanding of language attitudes. *Journal of Language and Social Psychology* 18 (1), 101–110.

Ellis, R. (2008) *The Study of Second Language Acquisition.* Oxford: Oxford University Press.

Elwood, J. and MacLean, G. (2009) ICT usage and student perceptions in Cambodia and Japan. *International Journal of Emerging Technologies and Society* 7 (2), 65–82.

Erikawa, H. (2008) *Nihonjin wa Eigo o dou manande kitaka: Eigo kyouiku no shakaibunkashi* [How Japanese have learnt English: The cultural history of English education]. Tokyo: Kenkyusha.

Erikawa, H. (2011) *Juken Eigo no Nihojin: Nyushi mondai to sankousho kara miru Eigo gakushuushi* [Japanese and examination English: The history of English learning seen from the perspective of examination tests and reference books]. Tokyo: Kenkyusha.

European Parliament (1995, 13 July) Human Rights. Online document: http://www.europarl.europa.eu/omk/omnsapir.so/pv2?PRG=CALDOC&FILE=9507 13&LANGUE=EN&TPV=DEF&LASTCHAP=12&SDOCTA=9&TXTLST=8&Ty pe_Doc=RESOL&POS=1.

Fairclough, N. (1992) *Discourse and Social Change*. Cambridge: Polity Press.

Falout, J. (2010) Strategies for teacher motivation. *The Language Teacher* 34 (6), 27–32.

Falout, J., Murphey, T., Elwood, J. and Hood, M. (2008) Learner voices: Reflections on secondary education. In K. Bradford Watts, T. Muller and M. Swanson (eds) *JALT2007 Conference Proceedings* (pp. 231–243). Tokyo: JALT.

Falout, J., Murphey, T. and Stillwell, C. (2012) Avoiding burnout by lighting fires: Three contexts of change. In C. Coombe, L. England, and J. Schmidt (eds) *Reigniting, Retooling and Retiring in English Language Teaching* (pp. 9–22). Ann Arbor, MI: University of Michigan Press.

Felstead, A. (n.d.) Vocational qualifications: Gender barriers to the certification of work-related skills. *CLMS Working Paper 9*. University of Leicester: Centre for Labour Market Studies. Online document: http://www.clms.le.ac.uk/publications/workingpapers/working_paper9.pdf.

Felstead, A. and Gallie, D. (2002) For better or worse? Nonstandard jobs and high involvement work systems. *SKOPE Research Paper* No. 29 Spring. Oxford and Warwick Universities, UK. Online document: http://www.skope.ox.ac.uk/sites/default/files/SKOPEWP29.pdf.

Felstead, A., Gallie, D., Green, F. and Zhou, Y. (2007) *Skills at Work, 1986 to 2006*. Universities of Oxford and Cardiff: ESRC Centre on Skills, Knowledge and Organisational Performance. Online document: http://www.cardiff.ac.uk/socsi/.../alanfelstead/SkillsatWork-1986to2006.pdf.

Fenoulhet, J. and Ros i Solé, C. (2011) Mobility and localisation in language learning. *Intercultural Studies and Foreign Language Learning* 5. Bern: Peter Lang.

Fernandez Fraile, E. (2005) Du maître de langues au professeur: Parcours sémantique d'une evolution sociale et professionnelle [From master of languages to professor: The semantic course of a social and professional evolution]. *SIHFLES* 33/34, 110–120.

Finkel, E.J. and Baumeister, R.F. (2010) Attraction and rejection. In R.F. Baumeister and E.J. Finkel (eds) *Advanced Social Psychology: The State of the Science* (pp. 419–459). Oxford: Oxford University Press.

Fiyouzat, R. (2003) Eat this Amsterdam! Persisting in Japan. In E.P Bueno and T. Caesar (eds) *I wouldn't want anybody to know: Native English teaching in Japan* (pp. 40–58). Tokyo: JPGS Press.

Fox, M.H. (2001, 1 January) Update on Gwen Gallagher Case: Working papers – language educators and labor law. *The Language Teacher Magazine* (25). Online document: http://www.debito.org/HELPSpring2001.html#chronicle.

Freire, P. (1970) *Pedagogy of the Oppressed*. London: Penguin Books.

Freire, P. (2000) *Pedagogy of the Oppressed* [30th Anniversary Edition]. London: Continuum.

French, H. (1999, 15 November) 'Japanese Only' policy takes body blow in court. *The New York Times*. Online document: http://www.nytimes.com/1999/11/15/world/japanese-only-policy-takes-body-blow-in-court.html.
Fujimoto, D., Kusaka, L. and Sakayori, S. (2007) A sense of community through Nikkei identity. In K. Bradford-Watts (ed.) *JALT 2006 Conference Proceedings* (pp. 827–839). Tokyo: JALT.
Funabashi, Y. (2000) *Aete eigo kôyôgo ron*. [Theory of English as the Official Language]. Tokyo: Bungei Shunjuu.
Funamori, M. (2008) 'Daigaku no kokusaika (saiko)' series, No.3, 'daigakuuneino kokusaika' o kangaeru. [The internationalization of higher education (a reconsideration) series, No. 3. The internationalization of university management]. *IDE*, 8–9, 62–68.
Garrett, P. (2010) *Attitudes to Language*. Cambridge: Cambridge University Press.
General Union (2009) City seizes bank account to pay health insurance premiums. Online document: http://www.generalunion.org/News/576.
Gender Equality Bureau (2009) White paper on gender equality. Online document: http://www.gender.go.jp/english_contents/white_paper_index.html.
Gender Equality Bureau (2010) The active participation of women and revitalization of economy and society (From the 'White Paper on Gender Equality 2010' Summary). Online document: http://www.gender.go.jp/english_contents/white_paper_index.html.
Giddens, A. (1999) *Runaway World: How Globalization is Reshaping Our Lives*. London: Profile.
Goodman, R. (2010) The rapid redrawing of boundaries in Japanese higher education. *Japan Forum* 22 (1–2), 65–87.
Goodwin, C. (1994) Professional vision. *American Anthropologist* 96, 606–633.
Gopinathan, S., Ho Wah Kam, A. Pakir, V. Saravanan (eds) 2004. *Language, Society and Education in Singapore: Issues and Trends* (Language and Linguistics). Singapore: Marshall Cavendish.
Gorsuch, G. (2000) EFL educational policies and educational cultures: Influences on teachers' approval of communicative activities. *TESOL Quarterly* 34 (4), 675–710.
Gorsuch, G. (2002) Assistant foreign language teachers in Japanese high schools: Focus on the hosting of Japanese teachers. *JALT Journal* 24 (1), 5–32.
Graddol, D. (2006) *English Next*. Plymouth: British Council.
Gramsci, A. (1975) *Letters from Prison [Lettere dal carcere]*. London: Jonathan Cape.
Grant, R. and Lee, I. (2009) The ideal English speaker: A juxtaposition of globalization and language policy in South Korea and racialized language attitudes in the United States. In R. Kubota and A. Lin (eds) *Race, Culture, and Identities in Second Language Education: Exploring Critically Engaged Practice* (pp. 44–63). New York: Routledge.
Green, V. (2001) *Race on the Line: Gender, Labor, and Technology in the Bell System, 1880–1980*. Durham: Duke University Press.
Grimshaw, T. (2010) Styling the occidental other: Interculturality in Chinese university performances. *Language and Intercultural Communication* 10 (3), 243–258.
Guba, E.G. and Lincoln, Y.S. (2005) Paradigmatic controversies, contradictions, and emerging confluences. In N.K. Denzin and Y.S. Lincoln (eds) *Handbook of Qualitative Research* (pp. 191–215). Thousand Oaks: Sage.
Gudykunst, W. and Hammer, M. (1988) Strangers and hosts: An extension of UR theory. In Y.Y. Kim and W. Gudykunst (eds) *Cross-Cultural Adaptation* (pp. 106–139). Beverly Hills, CA: Sage.
Guilherme, M. (2002) *Critical Citizens for an Intercultural World: Foreign Language Education as Cultural Politics*. Clevedon: Multilingual Matters.

Guilherme, M. (2007) English as a global language and education for cosmopolitan citizenship. *Language and Intercultural Communication* 7 (1), 72–90.

Haarmann, H. (1986) *Language in Ethnicity*. Berlin: Mouton de Gruyter.

Haarmann, H. (1989) *Symbolic Values of Foreign Language Use: From the Japanese Case to a General Sociolinguistic Perspective*. Berlin: Mouton de Gruyter.

Haberland, H. (2011) Ownership and maintenance of a language in transnational use: Should we leave our lingua franca alone? *Journal of Pragmatics* 43, 937–949.

Habhab-Rave, S. (2008) Workplace learning in communities of practice: How do schoolteachers learn? In C. Kimble, P. Hildreth and I. Bourdon (eds) *Communities of Practice: Creating Learning Environments for Educators* (Vol. 1) (pp. 213–231). Charlotte, NC: Information Age Publishing.

Hagos, M. (2011) Recognizing and defeating the oppressor within and without. Online document:http://www.lovefreedomorquestionwhoyouare.com/wp-content/uploads/2011/11/Recognizing-and-Defeating-the-Oppressor-Within-and-Without.pdf.

Hall, I. (1998) *Cartels of the Mind: Japans Intellectual Closed Shop*. New York: W.W. Norton & Company.

Hall, I. (2006) Communities or cartels of the mind. In JALT 2006: 32nd Annual International Conference on Language Teaching and Learning. Kokura, Japan. Online document: http://www.debito.org/ivanhallPALE110306.htm.

Hall, S. (1991a) Old and new identities, old and new ethnicities. In A.D. King (ed.) *Culture, Globalization and the World-System* (pp. 40–68). New York: Palgrave.

Hall, S. (1991b) The local and the global: Globalization and ethnicity. In A.D. King (ed.) *Culture, Globalization and the World-System* (pp. 19–39). New York: Palgrave.

Hall, S. (1996) The West and the rest: Discourse and power. In S. Hall and D. Held (eds) *Modernity: An Introduction to Modern Societies* (pp. 184–228). Oxford: Blackwell.

Hamilton, D.L. and Neville Uhles, A. (2000) Stereotypes. In A.E. Kazdin (ed.) *Encyclopedia of Psychology* 7 (pp. 466–470). Oxford: Oxford University Press.

Hannerz, U. (1991) Scenarios of peripheral cultures. In A.D. King (ed.) *Culture, Globalization and the World-System* (pp. 107–128). New York: Palgrave.

Haque, E. and Morgan, B. (2009) Un/Marked pedagogies: A dialogue on race in EFL and ESL settings. In R. Kubota and A. Lin (eds) *Race, Culture, and Identities in Second Language Education*. New York: Routledge.

Hashimoto, K. (2011) Compulsory 'foreign language activities' in Japanese primary schools. *Current Issues in Language Planning* 12 (2), 167–184.

Haslanger, S. (2009) Exploring race in life, in speech, and in philosophy: Comments on Joshua Glasgow's 'A theory of race'. *Symposia on Gender, Race and Philosophy* 5 (2). Online document: http://web.mit.edu/sgrp/2009/no2/Haslanger1009.pdf.

Hatori, R. (2005) A policy on language education in Japan: Beyond nationalism and linguicism. *Second Language Studies* 23 (2), 45–69.

Hausmann, R., Tyson, L. and Zahidi, S. (2010). The global gender gap report 2010. World Economic Forum. Geneva, Switzerland. Online document: http://www.weforum.org/reports/global-gender-gap-report-2010?ol=1.

Hayes, C. (1927) Contributions of Herder to the doctrine of nationalism. *The American Historical Review* 32 (4), 719–736.

Hayes, C. and Juarez, B.G. (2009) You showed your Whiteness: You don't get a 'good' White people's medal. *International Journal of Qualitative Studies in Education* 22 (6), 729–744.

Heimlich, E. (2010) Towards De-centering: Challenges in theorizing international American studies. In J.F. Duarte *et al.* (eds) *Trans/American, Trans/Oceanic, Trans/lation: Issues in International American Studies*. Newcastle upon Tyne: Cambridge Scholars Publishing.
Heinrich, P. and Galan, C. (2011) Modern and late modern perspectives on language life in Japan. In P. Heinrich and C. Galan (eds) *Language Life in Japan* (pp. 1–13). London: Routledge.
Herrington, M., Baig, R., Dye, V., Hughes, J., Kendall, A. and Lacey, C. *et al.* (2008) Space, resistance, and identities: University-based teacher-educators developing a community of practice. In C. Kimble, P. Hildreth and I. Bourdon (eds) *Communities of Practice: Creating Learning Environments for Educators* (Vol. 1; pp. 191–211). Charlotte, NC: Information Age Publishing.
Hino, N. (2009) The teaching of English as an international language in Japan: An answer to the dilemma of indigenous values and global needs in the expanding circle. *AILA Review* 22, 103–119.
Hirahata, N. (2008) The new role of native Japanese speaking teachers in Asia: From the view point of nativeness and Japaneseness. *Japanese-Language Education Around the Globe* 18, 1–19.
Hobbes, T. (1951) *Leviathan*. Harmondsworth, Middlesex: Penguin.
Hofstede, G. (1983) The cultural relativity of organizational practices and theories. *Journal of International Business Studies* 14 (2), 75–89.
Hofstede, G. (1991) *Cultures and Organizations: Software of the Mind*. London: Harper-Collins.
Hofstede, G. (2001) *Culture's Consequences: Comparing Values, Behaviors, Institutions and Organisations Across Nations*. Thousand Oaks, CA: Sage.
Holliday, A. (2005a) *The Struggle to Teach English as an International Language*. Oxford: Oxford University Press.
Holliday, A. (2005b) How is it possible to write? *Journal of Language, Identity and Education* 4 (4), 304–309.
Holliday, A. (2006) Native-speakerism. *ELT Journal* 60 (4), 385–387.
Holliday, A. (2008) Standards of English and politics of inclusion. *Language Teaching* 41 (1), 119–130.
Holliday, A. and Aboshiha, P.A. (2009) The denial of ideology in perceptions of 'nonnative speaker' teachers. *TESOL Quarterly* 43 (4), 669–689.
Holliday, A. (2011) *Intercultural Communication and Ideology*. London: Sage.
Holliday, A., Hyde, M. and Kullman, J. (2004) *Intercultural Communication*. London: Routledge.
Honna, N. (2008) *English as Multicultural Language in Asian Contexts: Issues and Ideas*. Tokyo: Kuroshio.
Honna, N. and Takeshita, Y. (1998) On Japan's propensity for native speaker English. *Asian Englishes* 1 (1), 117–137.
Horio, T. (1988) *Educational Thought and Ideology in Modern Japan: State Authority and Intellectual Freedom*. Tokyo: The University of Tokyo Press.
Houghton, S. (2002). Gaikokujindewanai gaikokujinkyoshi? [Foreign lecturers who are not foreign] All current foreign lecturers are foreign. Where are the non-foreign foreign lecturers? *Forum: Journal of the University of Kitakyushu Union* 23, 54–31.
Houghton, S. and van Dresser, S. (2002) *Japan: Foreign Nationals and the Japanese Pension System*. Online document: http://www.debito.org/karakikan.htm.
Houghton, S. (2008, December) *The Development of Intercultural Communicative Competence: A Challenge for Both Foreign Language Teachers and Students*. Paper presented at the

International Conference on Cultural and Linguistic Practices in the International University (CALPIU '08), Roskilde University, Denmark. Online document: http://imw.ruc.dk//calpiu/calpiu/History/calpiu08/conference-calpiu08/power%20point%20slides/Houghton.pptm/view.

Houghton, S. (2009) Within-self diversity: Implications for ELT materials design. Proceedings of the SoLLs.INTEC.09 Conference: Language and Culture – Creating and Fostering Global Communities 2009, 469–492. Online document: http://pkukmweb.ukm.my/~solls09/Proceeding/PDF/StephanieHoughton.pdf.

Houghton, S. (2012) *Intercultural Dialogue in Practice: Managing Value Judgment through Foreign Language Education.* Bristol: Multilingual Matters.

Houghton, S. and Yamada, E. (2012) *Developing Criticality in Practice through Foreign Language Education.* Frankfurt Am Mein: Peter Lang.

Howatt, A. (2004) *A History of English Language Teaching.* Oxford: Oxford University Press.

Ibarra, H. (1992) Homophily and differential returns: Sex differences in network structure and access in an advertising firm. *Administrative Science Quarterly* 37 (3), 422–447.

ICERD (1969) *International Convention on the Elimination of all Forms of Racial Discrimination.* Online document: http://www2.ohchr.org/english/law/cerd.htm.

International Labour Organization, United Nations (2007) Gender issues in Education and training: A case of unequal access. Online document: http://www.ilo.org/public/english/dialogue/sector/sectors/educat/emp-gender.htm.

Jenkins, J. (2000) *The Phonology of English as an International Language: New Models, New Norms, New Goals.* Oxford: Oxford University Press.

Jenkins, J. (2009) *World Englishes.* London: Routledge.

Johnston, B. (1997) Do EFL teachers have careers? *TESOL Quarterly* 31 (4), 681–712.

Johnston, B. (1999) The expatriate teacher as postmodern paladin. *Research in the Teaching of English* 34 (2), 255–280.

JPRI (1996) Foreign teachers in Japanese universities: An update. *JPRI Working Paper* 24. Online document: http://www.jpri.org/publications/workingpapers/wp24.html

Just Response (2003, 26 August) *Roman Catholic principles of corruption in Italy: An interview with Domenico Pacitti.* Online document: http://www.justresponse.net/explaining_corruption.html.

Kabel, A. (2009) Native-speakerism, stereotyping and the collusion of applied linguistics. *System* 37 (1), 12–22.

Kachru, B. (1985) Standards, codification and sociolinguistic realism in English. In R. Quirk and H. Widdowson (eds) *English in the World: Teaching and Learning the Languages and Cultures* (pp. 11–30). Cambridge: Cambridge University Press.

Kachru, B. (1986) *The Alchemy of English: The Spread, Functions and Models of Non-Native Englishes.* Oxford: Pergamon.

Kachru, B. (1992) *The Other Tongue: English Across Cultures.* Illinois: Board of Trustees of the University of Illinois.

Kachru, B. and Nelson C.L. (1996) World Englishes. In S. McKay and N. Hornberger (eds) *Sociolinguistics and Language Teaching.* Cambridge: Cambridge University Press.

Kanno, Y. (2005) *Negotiating Bilingual and Bicultural Identities: Japanese Returnees Betwixt Two Worlds.* Mahwah, NJ: Lawrence Erlbaum Associates.

Kanter, R.M. (1977) *Men and Women of the Corporation.* New York: Basic Books.

Katayama, T., Saiga, T. and Ueno, H. (2008, 23 December) Eigo jugyô yureru genba [English class unsettle classrooms]. *Asahi Shimbun.* Morning Edition, 34.

Katz, S. (2003) Near native speakers in the FL classroom: The case of Haitian immigrant students. In C. Blyth (ed.) *The Sociolinguistics of Foreign Language Classrooms: Contributions of Native, Near Native and Non-Native Speakers* (pp. 131–152). Boston: Heinle.

Kawai, Y. (2007) Japanese nationalism and the global spread of English: An analysis of Japanese government and public discourses on English. *Language and Intercultural Communication* 7 (1), 37–55.

Kelsky, K. (1999) Gender, modernity, and eroticized internationalism in Japan. *Cultural Anthropology* 14 (2), 229–255.

Kelsky, K. (2001) *Women on the Verge: Japanese Women, Western Dreams*. Durham, NC: Duke University Press.

Kim, M.S. (2005) Culture-based conversational constraints theory. In W.B. Gudykunst (ed.) *Theorizing about Intercultural Communication* (pp. 93–117). Thousand Oaks: Sage.

Kinjo, K. (1995) Legal challenges to the status quo. In K. Fujimura-Fanselow and A. Kameda (eds) *Japanese Women: New Feminist Perspectives on the Past, Present, and Future* (pp. 353–363). New York: Feminist Press at the City University of New York.

Kirk, D. (2001) Limited-term appointments and their effect on curriculum development. The language teacher online. Online document: http://www.jalt-publications.org/old_tlt/articles/2001/02/kirk.

Kirkpatrick, A. (2006) Which model of English: native speaker, nativised or lingua franca? In R. Rubdy and M. Saraceni (eds) *English in the World* (pp. 71–83). London: Continuum.

Klevberg, R. (2000) The role of translation in Japanese young learner classrooms. *The Language Teacher* 20 (10), 1–6.

Klitzman, S. and Stellman J.M. (1989) The impact of the physical environment on the psychological well-being of office workers. *Social Science & Medicine* 29 (6), 733–742.

KNS (1993, 30 December) *Kumamoto Kenritsu Daigaku' ni shinsetsu no 'Sougou Kanri Gakubu*. [Prefectural University of Kumamoto establishes new 'Faculty of Administration'].

KNS (1997, 22 October) *Gaikokujin sabetsu no, Kenritsu Daigaku no kyoushi, joukin motome roudou kumiai kessei*. ['No' to discrimination against foreigners, PUK teachers form union to demand regularization].

KNS (1998, 18 June) *Gaikokujin kyoushi ga sutoraiki, Kenritsudai, taiguu kaizen motome 24 ka kara*. [PUK Foreign teachers to strike on the 24th, calling for improved terms of employment].

KNS (1998, 25 June) *'Hijoukin koyou wa kokuseki sabetsu', gaikokujin kyoushi rousou ga suto, Kenritsu Daigaku*. ['Part-time employment is nationality discrimination', foreign teachers' union strikes against PUK].

KNS (1998, 1 October) *'Hijoukin keiyaku koushin sezu', taiguu kaizen youkyu no gaikokujin kyoushi, Kenritsudai gakuchou*. [President of PUK will not renew part-time contracts of foreign teachers calling for better employment terms].

KNS (1999a, 19 February) *Gaikokujin kyoushi koyou mondai, Monbushou, jijou choushu e, Kumamoto Kenritsu Daigaku*. [Ministry of Education to question PUK about employment of foreign staff].

KNS (1999b, 19 February) *Koukai Eigo kouza zenki wa 'kyuukou', tantou kyoushi kakuho dekizu*. [First semester of extension English classes to be cancelled, unable to find teachers].

KNS (1999, 25 February) *Sennin koushi to mitomezu, Kenritsudai gaikokujin kyoushi mondai de, Monbushou.* [Ministry of Education does not recognize PUK claim that foreign teachers are sennin].
KNS (1999, 26 February) *Kenritsudai, koyou hoken kakezu, gaikokujin hijoukin koushi 3 nin ni.* [PUK did not enroll 3 foreign part-time teachers in employment insurance].
KNS (1999, 2 May) *Chouryuu: Nihon no kokusaika ni mondai teiki, Kenritsu Daigaku to gaikokujin kyoushi no wakai, Teshima Takashi Gakuchou ni kiku.* [Tide of the times: Questions raised about Japan's internationalization, settlement agreement between PUK and foreign teachers: Interview with President Teshima].
KNS (1999, 2 May) *Chouryuu: Nihon no kokusaika ni mondai teiki, Kenritsu Daigaku to gaikokujin kyoushi no wakai, okureta 'kyousei' e no taiou.* [Tide of the times: Questions raised about Japan's internationalization, settlement agreement between PUK and foreign teachers, steps toward 'coexistence' too late].
KNS (1999, 16 November) *Nyuu Yooku Taimuzu ga Kumamoto Kenritsudai mondai o shouhou, 'gaikokuji kyoushi o sabetsu koyoui.* [New York Times publishes detailed article on PUK issue, 'Discriminatory employment of foreign teachers'].
KNS (2002, 2 February) *'Sabetsuteki koyou' teppai o: Kenritsu Daigaku nado ni gaikokujin kyouinra ga shomei teishutsu.* ['End discriminatory employment!' Foreign teachers and supporters deliver petition signatures to PUK].
Kobayashi, Y. (2002) The role of gender in foreign language learning attitudes: Japanese female students' attitudes towards English learning. *Gender and Education* 14 (2), 181–197.
Kobayashi, Y. (2011) Global Englishes and the discourse on Japaneseness. *Journal of Intercultural Studies* 32 (1), 1–14.
Kohut, M.R. (2008) *Understanding, Controlling, and Stopping Bullies and Bullying at Work.* Ocala, FL: Atlantic Publishing Group.
Kramsch, C. (1993) *Context and Culture in Language Teaching.* Oxford: Oxford University Press.
Kramsch, C. (1997) The privilege of the non-native speaker. *Publications of the Modern Language Association of America* 112 (3), 359–369.
Kramsch, C. (1998) The privilege of the intercultural speaker. In M. Byram and M. Fleming (eds) *Language Learning in Intercultural Perspectives: Approaches through Drama and Ethnography* (pp. 16–31). Cambridge: Cambridge University Press.
Kubota, R. (1998) Ideologies of English in Japan. *World Englishes* 17 (3), 295–306.
Kubota, R. (1999) Japanese culture constructed by discourses: Implications for applied linguistic research and English language teaching. *TESOL Quarterly* 33 (1), 9–35.
Kubota, R. (2001) Discursive construction of the images of US classrooms. *TESOL Quarterly* 35 (1), 9–37.
Kubota, R. (2002a) The author responds: (Un)raveling racism in a nice field like TESOL. *TESOL Quarterly* 36 (1), 84–92.
Kubota, R. (2002b) 'The Impact of Globalisation on Language Teaching in Japan'. In D. Block and D. Cameron (eds) *Globalisation and Language Teaching* (pp. 13–28). London and New York: Routledge.
Kubota, R. (2004) Critical multiculturalism and second language education. In B. Norton and K. Toohey (eds) *Critical Pedagogies and Language Learning* (pp. 30–52). Cambridge: Cambridge University Press.
Kubota, R. (2006) Critical approaches to culture in English language teaching. In B. Beaven (ed.) *IATEFL Harrogate Conference Selections* (pp. 213–223). Canterbury: IATEFL.

Kubota, R. (2011a) 'The politics of school curriculum and assessment in Japan'. In Y. Zhao, J. Lei, G. Li, M. He, K. Okano, D. Gamage, H. Ramanathan and N. Magahed (eds) *Handbook of Asian Education: A Cultural Perspective* (pp. 214–230). New York: Routledge.
Kubota, R. (2011b) Questioning linguistic instrumentalism: English, neoliberalism, and language tests in Japan. *Linguistics and Education* 22, 248–260.
Kubota, R., Bashir-Ali, K., Canagarajah, S., Kamhi-Stein, L., Lee, E. and Shin, H. (2005) Race and (non)nativeness in English language teaching: A brief report. *NNest Newsletter* 7 (1). Online document: http://www.tesol.org/s_tesol/article.asp?vid=1 51&DID=4637&sid=1&cid=718&iid =4633&nid=2982.
Kubota, R. and Lin, A. (eds) (2006) Race and TESOL (special topic issue). *TESOL Quarterly* 40 (3), 471–660.
Kubota, R. and Lin, A. (eds) (2009) *Race, Culture, and Identities in Second Language Education: Exploring Critically Engaged Practice.* New York: Routledge.
Kubota, R. and McKay, S. (2009) Globalization and language learning in rural Japan: The role of English in the local linguistic ecology. *TESOL Quarterly* 43 (4), 593–619.
Kumamoto District Court (2002) Decision regarding demands for confirmation of status, Case No. 641, 1–33. Online document: http://www2.kumagaku.ac.jp/teacher/~masden/mamorukai/hanketsu/index.html.
Kumaravadivelu, B. (2003) Problematizing cultural stereotypes in TESOL. *TESOL Quarterly* 37 (4), 709–719.
Kumaravadivelu, B. (2006) Dangerous liaison: Globalization, empire and TESOL. In J. Edge (ed.) *(Re)locating TESOL in an Age of Empire: Language and Globalization* (pp. 1–26). London: Palgrave.
Kumaravadivelu, B. (2007) *Cultural Globalization and Language Education.* Yale: Yale University Press.
Kumaravadivelu, B. (2012) Individual identity, cultural globalization and teaching English as an international language: The case for an epistemic break In L. Alsagoff, W. Renandya, G. Hu and S. McKay (eds) *Teaching English as an International Language: Principles and Practices* (pp. 9–27). New York: Routledge.
Labour Standards Law of Japan (1947) Online document: http://www.ilo.org/dyn/natlex/docs/WEBTEXT/27776/64846/E95JPN01.htm.
Labov, W. (2006) *The Social Stratification of English in New York City.* Cambridge: Cambridge University Press.
Ladson-Billings, G. and Tate, W. (1995) Toward a critical race theory of education. *Teachers College Record* 97 (1), 47–68.
Lasagabaster D. and Sierra J.M. (2002) University student's perceptions of native andnon-native speaker teachers of English. *Language Awareness* 11 (2), 132–142.
Lebra, T.S. (1985) *Japanese Women.* Honolulu: University of Hawaii Press.
Lentin, A. (2008) Racism, anti-racism and the Western state. In G. Delanty, R. Wodak and P. Jones (eds) *Identity, Belonging and Migration* (pp. 101–119). Liverpool: Liverpool University Press.
Levine, R. and Campbell, D. (1972) *Ethnocentrism: Theories of Conflict, Ethnic Attitudes and Group Behaviour.* New York: John Wiley & Sons.
Lie, J. (2000) The discourse of Japaneseness. In M. Douglass and G.S. Roberts (eds) *Japan and Global Migration: Foreign Workers and the Advent of a Multicultural Society* (pp. 70–90). London: Routledge.
Lie, J. (2001) *Multi-Ethnic Japan.* Massachusetts: Harvard University Press.

Lin, A., Kubota, R., Motha, S., Wang, W. and Wong, S. (2006) Theorizing experiences of Asian women faculty in second- and foreign-language teacher education. In G. Li and G. Beckett (eds) *'Strangers' of the Academy: Asian Women Scholars in Higher Education* (pp. 56–82). Sterling, VA: Stylus.

Lin, A., Grant, R., Kubota, R., Motha, S., Sachs, G.T., Vandrick, S. and Wong, S. (2004) Women faculty of color in TESOL: Theorizing our lived experiences. *TESOL Quarterly* 38 (3), 487–504.

Lin, N. (1982) Social resources and instrumental action. In P.V. Marsden and N. Lin (eds) *Social Structure and Network Analysis* (pp. 131–145). Beverly Hills, CA: Sage.

Lippmann, W. (1922) *Public Opinion*. New York: Macmillan.

Lister, R. (1997) *Citizenship: Feminist Perspectives*. London: MacMillan.

Llewelyn, J. and Hirano, J. (2009, 30 November) Importing human capital: Contemporary Japanese attitudes to immigration. *Electronic Journal of Contemporary Japanese Studies*. Online document: http://www.japanesestudies.org.uk/articles/2009/Llewelyn.html.

Llurda, E. (ed.) (2005) *Non-native Language Teachers: Perceptions, Challenges, and Contributions to the Profession*. New York: Springer.

Lubit, R.H. (2004) *Coping with Toxic Managers, Subordinates . . . and Other Difficult People*. Upper Saddle River, NJ: Pearson Education.

Mackie, A. (2003) Race and desire: Toward critical literacies for ESL. *TESL Canada Journal* 20 (2), 23–37.

Mahboob, A. (2010) *The NNEST Lens: Non Native English Speakers in TESOL*. Newcastle upon Tyne: Cambridge Scholars Publishing.

Maher, J.C. and Yashiro, K. (eds) (1995) *Multilingual Japan: An Introduction*. Clevedon: Multilingual Matters.

Maher, J. and Macdonald, G. (eds) (1995) *Diversity in Japanese Culture and Language*. London and New York: Kegan Paul International.

Major, R.C., Fitzmaurice, S.M., Bunta, F. and Balasubramanian, C. (2005) Testing the effects of regional, ethnic and international dialects of English on listening comprehension. *Language Learning* 55 (1), 37–69.

Maner, J.K., DeWall, N., Baumeister, R.F. and Schaller, M. (2007) Does social exclusion motivate interpersonal reconnection? Resolving the 'porcupine problem'. *Journal of Personality and Social Psychology* 92 (1), 42–55.

Markus, H. and Nurius, P. (1986) Possible selves. *American Psychologist* 41 (9), 954–969.

Matsuda, A. (2002) The ownership of English in Japanese secondary schools. *World Englishes* 22 (4), 483–496.

Matsuda, A. (2003). Incorporating world Englishes in teaching English as an international language. *TESOL Quarterly* 37, 719–729.

Matsuura, H., Chiba, R. and A. Yamamoto (1994) Japanese college students' attitudes towards non-native varieties of English. In D. Graddol and J. Swann (eds) *Evaluating Language* (pp. 52–61). Clevedon: Multilingual Matters.

Matt, B.F. and Shahinpoor, N. (2011) Speaking truth to power: The courageous organizational dissenter. In D.R. Comer and G. Vega (eds) *Moral Courage in Organizations: Doing the Right Thing at Work* (pp. 157–170). Armonk, NY: M.E Sharpe.

Maybin, J. (2000) The New Literacy Studies: Context, intertextuality and discourse. In D. Barton, M. Hamilton and R. Ivanic (eds) *Situated Literacies: Reading and Writing in Context* (pp. 197–209). London and New York: Routledge.

McConnell, D. (2000) *Importing Diversity: Inside Japan's JET Program*. Berkeley, CA: University of California Press.
McKenzie, R.M. (1996) An examination of language attitudes to the Glasgow vernacular. Unpublished MSc dissertation, University of Edinburgh, UK.
McKenzie, R.M. (2003) Attitudes of Japanese nationals resident in Scotland towards standard and non-standard varieties of English. *Saga University Economic Review* 35 (5/6), 137–150.
McKenzie, R.M. (2004) Attitudes of Japanese nationals towards standard and nonstandard varieties of Scottish English speech. *The East Asian Learner* 1 (1), 16–25.
McKenzie, R.M. (2008a) Social factors and non-native attitudes towards varieties of spoken English: A Japanese case study. *International Journal of Applied Linguistics* 18 (1), 63–88.
McKenzie, R.M. (2008b) The complex and rapidly changing sociolinguistic position of the English language in Japan: A summary of English language contact and use. *Japan Forum* 20 (2), 267–286.
McKenzie, R.M. (2008c) The role of variety identification in Japanese university students' attitudes towards English speech varieties. *Journal of Multilingual and Multicultural Development* 29 (2), 139–153.
McKenzie, R.M. (2010) *The Social Psychology of English as a Global Language*. New York/Berlin: Springer.
McMillan, B.A. and Rivers, D.J. (2011) The practice of policy: Teacher attitudes towards 'English-only'. *System* 39 (2), 251–263.
McLaren, P. (1993) *Schooling as a Ritual Performance: Towards a Political Economy of Educational Symbols and Gestures*. London: Routledge.
McVeigh, B. (1996) Cultivating 'Femininity' and 'Internationalism': Rituals and routine at a Japanese women's junior college. *Ethos* 24 (2), 314–349.
McVeigh, B. (2002) *Japanese Higher Education as Myth*. Armonk, NY: M.E. Sharpe.
McVeigh, B. (2004) Foreign language instruction in Japanese higher education: The humanistic vision or nationalist utilitarianism? *Arts and Humanities in Higher Education* 3(2), 211–227.
Medgyes, P. (1983) The schizophrenic teacher. *ELT Journal* 37 (1), 2–6.
Medgyes, P. (1992) 'Native of non-native: Who's worth more?' *ELT Journal* 46 (4), 340–349.
Medgyes, P. (1994) *The Non-Native Teacher*. London: Macmillan.
Medgyes, P. (2004) Native speaker. In M. Byram (ed.) *Routledge Encyclopedia of Language Teaching and Learning* (pp. 426–438). London: Routledge.
Menard-Warwick, J. (2008) The cultural and intercultural identities of transnational English teachers: Two case studies from the Americas. *TESOL Quarterly* 42 (4), 617–640.
Mesthrie, R. (2010) New Englishes and the native speaker debate. *Language Sciences* 32 (6), 594–601.
MEXT (n.d.) Higher education in Japan. Online document: http://www.mext.go.jp/english/highered/1302653.htm.
MEXT (1989) *Chuugakko Gakushuu Shiduo Yourou* [Course of study for junior high school]. Tokyo: Okurasho Insatsu Kyoku.
MEXT (1991) *Zainichi kankokujin nado nihon kokuseki o yûshinai mono no kôritsu gakkô no kyôin eno ninyô nitsuite*. [Regarding appointment of Koreans living in Japan, who do not have Japanese citizenships, as public school teachers]. Online document: http://www.pref.kanagawa.jp.
MEXT (1996) *Chapter 2: Kokusaika to kyouiku. 21 seiki o tenbou shita wagakuni no kyouiku no arikata ni tsuite* [Chapter 2. Internationalization and education, Japan's education for

the 21st century]. Online document: http://www.mext.go.jp/b_menu/shingi/12/chuuou/toushin/960701n.htm.

MEXT (1998) *Shougakko gakushuu shidou youryou* [Course of study for elementary school]. Tokyo: Okurasho Insatsu Kyoku.

MEXT (2002) *'Eigo ga tsukaeru Nihonjin' no ikusei no tameno senryaku kousou no sakutei ni tsuite* [Formulating a strategy plan to develop 'Japanese who can use English']. Online document: http://www.mext.go.jp/b_menu/shing/chousa/shotou/020/sesaku/020702.htm.

MEXT (2003) *'Eigo ga tsukaeru Nihonjin' no ikusei no tameno kodo keikaku* [Action plan to develop 'Japanese who can use English']. Online document: http://www.e-jes.org/03033102.pdf.

MEXT (2006) *Neitibu supîkâ to ICT no tokuchô no rei* [Examples of characteristics of native speakers and ICT]. Online document: http://www.mext.go.jp/b_menu/shingi/chukyo/chukyo3/015/siryo/06020613/010.ht m.

MEXT (2008a) *Gakushuu shidou youryou kaitei no pointo (shougakko gaikokugo katsudou)* [The major points of reference in the revised Course of study (elementary school foreign language activities)]. Online document: http://www.hyogo-c.ed.jp/~gimubo/kyouikukatei/syo/syo12gaikokugokatudo_point.pdf.

MEXT (2008b) *Heisei 19 nendo shougakko Eigo katsudou jisshi joukyo chousa shuukei kekka* [A summary of the state of implementation of the elementary school English activities for Heisei 19]. Online document: http://www.mext.go.jp/b_menu/houdou/20/03/08031920/002.htm.

MEXT (2008c) *Shôgakkô gakushû shidô yôryô kaisetsu: Gaikokugo katsudô hen* [The guideline for the course of study for elementary schools: Foreign language activities]. Tokyo: Tôyôkan.

MEXT (2009a) Chapter 4: Foreign language activities [The course of studies for elementary schools]. Online document: http://www.mext.go.jp/component/a_menu/education/micro_detail/__icsFiles/afield file/2010/10/20/1261037_12.pdf.

MEXT (2009b) *Gikokugo shidô joshu no ukeoi keiyaku niyoru katsuyô nitsuite (tsûchi)* [Regarding the use of ALTs through contract agreement: Notice]. Online document: http://www.mext.go.jp/a_menu/kokusai/gaikokugo/1304104.htm.

MEXT (2009c) *Heisei 20 nendo monbu kagakushô hakusho* [2008 MEXT white paper]. Tokyo: Saeki Insatsu.

MEXT (2009d) Launching new project for promoting universities activity in implementing internationalization as well as exchange with Asia and the United States. Online document: http://www.mext.go.jp/english/highered/1303569.htm.

MEXT (2010a) Launching the project for establishing core universities for Internationalization. Online document: http://www.mext.go.jp/english/highered/1302274.htm.

MEXT (2010b) *Kôtôgakkô gakushû shidô yôryô kaisetsu: Gaikokugo hen / eigo hen* [The course of study for senior-high schools guideline: Foreign languages/English]. Tokyo: Kaiseidô shuppan.

MEXT (2011a) *Nihongoshido ga hitsuyou na gaikokujin jidouseito no ukeire joukyou nado ni kansuru chousa (H.22) no kekka nitsuite* [A report on the survey of the state of how the foreign students who require instruction in Japanese are received etc. (Heisei 22)]. Online document: http://www.mext.go.jp/b_menu/houdou/23/08/1309275.htm.

MEXT (2011b) The Course of study for elementary school [foreign language activities]. Online document: http://www.mext.go.jp/component/english/__icsFiles/afieldfile/2011/03/17/1303755 _011.pdf.

Michael-Luna, S. (2008) *Todos somos blancos*/We are all white: Constructing racial identities through texts. *Journal of Language, Identity, and Education* 7 (3/4), 272–293.
Michaels, W.B. (2006) *The Trouble with Diversity*. New York: Holt Metropolitan Books.
Miller, J., Kostogriz A. and Gearon, M. (2009) *Culturally and Linguistically Diverse Classrooms, New Perspectives on Language and Education*. Bristol: Multilingual Matters.
Miller, L. (1995) Crossing ethnolinguistic boundaries: A preliminary look at the *gaijin tarento* in Japan. In J. Lent (ed.) *Asian Popular Culture* (pp. 189–202). Boulder: Westview Press.
Miller, R.A. (1982) *Japan's Modern Myth: The Language and Beyond*. New York: Weatherhill.
Miller, R.L. (2003) The quiet revolution: Japanese women working around the law. *Harvard Women's Law Journal* 26, 163–215.
Milroy, J. (1999) The consequences of standardisation in descriptive linguistics. In T. Bex and R.J. Watts (eds) *Standard English: The Widening Debate* (pp. 16–39). London: Routledge.
Milroy, J. (2001) Language ideologies and the consequences of standardization. *Journal of Sociolinguistics* 5 (4), 530–555.
Miyazato, K. (2003) Anxiety or admiration?: Japanese EFL learners' perceptions of native speaker teachers' classes. *JALT Conference '02 Proceedings* 42 (49). Tokyo: JALT.
Miyazato, K. (2009) Power-sharing between NS and NNS teachers: Linguistically powerful AETs vs. culturally powerful JTEs. *JALT Journal* 31 (1), 35–62.
Modiano, M. (2009) EIL, native-speakerism and the failure of European ELT. In F. Sharifian (ed.) *English as an International Language: Perspectives and Pedagogical Issues* (pp. 58–81). Clevedon: Multilingual Matters.
MOFA (1980) *Gaimushô gaikô seisho 1980 nendo ban* [MOFA blue book 1980]. Online document: http://www.mofa.go.jp/mofaj/gaiko/bluebook/1980/s55-contents.htm#index.
MOFA (2010) *Heisei 22 nendo gaimushô gyôsei rebyû kôkai purosesu dai 2 nichi me* [2010 MOFA Review of governmental projects: Open process day 2]. Online document: http://www.mofa.go.jp/mofaj/annai/yosan_kessan/kanshi_kouritsuka/pdfs/gijiroku_houdou_g1.pdf.
Moloney, B.M. (2009) Language attitudes in Japan: stereotypes of Australians and the Australian accent. Unpublished PhD dissertation, University of Melbourne, Australia.
Moon, D.G. (2008) Concepts of 'culture': Implications for intercultural communication research. In M.K. Asante, Y. Miike and J. Yin (eds) *The Global Intercultural Communication Reader* (pp. 11–26). New York: Routledge.
Moussu, L. and Llurda E. (2008) Non-native English-speaking English language teachers: History and research. *Language Teaching* 41 (3), 315–348.
Murphey, T. (2004) Participation, (dis-)identification, and Japanese university entrance exams. *TESOL Quarterly* 38 (4), 700–710.
Nakane, I. (2007) *Silence in Intercultural Communication*. Amsterdam: John Benjamins.
Namie, G. and Namie, R. (2009) *The Bully at Work: What You Can Do to Stop the Hurt and Reclaim Your Dignity on the Job*. Naperville, IL: Sourcebooks.
Nation, P. (2003) The role of the first language in foreign language learning. *Asian EFL Journal* 5 (2), 1–8.
Nayar, B. (2002) Ideological binarism in the identities of native and non-native English speakers. In A. Duszac (ed.) *Us and Others: Social Identities Across Languages, Discourse and Cultures* (pp. 463–480). Amsterdam: John Benjamins.

Nemtchinova, E. (2005) Host teachers' evaluations of nonnative-English-speaking teacher trainees: A perspective from the classroom. *TESOL Quarterly* 39 (2), 235–261.

NHK (2011, 23 May) *Kyôdan ni tatsu nowa dare? Shôgakkô eigo hisshûka no hamon* [Who stands on the teaching platform?: The consequence of compulsory English in elementary schools]. TV programme.

Noguchi, M. (2001) Bilingual and bicultural children in Japan: A pilot survey of factors linked to active English-Japanese bilingualism. In M. Noguchi and S. Fotos (eds) *Studies in Japanese Bilingualism* (pp. 237–244). New York: Multilingual Matters.

Noguchi, M. and Fotos, S. (2001) *Studies in Japanese Bilingualism*. New York: Multilingual Matters.

Noriguchi, S. (2006) English education leaves much to be desired. *Asahi Shimbun*. Online document: http://www.asahi.com/english/Herald-asahi/TKY200609150129.html.

Nosaka, J. (2007) Racism in ESL and EFL: Constructing action plans. Workshop presented at the 33rd Annual International Conference of Japan Association of Language Teachers, Tokyo, Japan.

Oda, M. (2007) 'Globalisation or the world in English: Is Japan ready to face the waves?' *International Multilingual Research Journal* 1 (2), 119–126.

Ogoshi, K. (2003) *Academic Harassment in Japan: How to make a Harassment-Free University*. Online document: http://www.naah.jp/kenkyu/canada.pdf.

Okuno, H. (2007) *Nihon no gengo seisaku to eigo kyôiku* [Japan's language policies and English education]. Tokyo: Sanyûsha.

Onishi, N. (2008, 14 August) As its work force ages, Japan needs and fears Chinese labor, *The New York Times*. Online document: http://www.nytimes.com/2008/08/15/world/asia/15labor.html.

Paikeday, T. M. (1985) *The Native Speaker is Dead!* Toronto: Paikeday Publishing.

Pavlenko, A. and Lantolf, J. (2000) Second language learning as participation and the (re)construction of selves. In J. Lantolf (ed.) *Sociocultural Theory and Second Language Learning* (pp. 155–177). New York: Oxford University Press.

Payne, J. (2000) The unbearable lightness of skill: The changing meaning of skill in UK policy discourses and some implications for education and training. *Journal of Educational Policy* 15 (3), 353–369.

Pennycook, A. (1989) The concept of method, interested knowledge, and the politics of language teaching. *TESOL Quarterly* 23 (4), 589–618.

Pennycook, A. (1994) *The Cultural Politics of English as an International Language*. London: Longman.

Pennycook, A. (2000) Development, culture and language: Ethical concerns in a postcolonial world. Proceedings of the 4th International Conference on Language and Development. Online document: http://www.languages.ait.ac.th/hanoi_proceedings/hanoi1999.htm.

Pennycook, A. (2006) *Critical Applied Linguistics: The Encyclopedia of Language and Linguistics*. Amsterdam: Elsevier.

Pennycook, A. (2010) English and globalization. In J. Maybin and J. Swann (eds) *The Routledge Companion to English Language Studies* (pp. 113–121). Abingdon: Routledge.

Petition to European Commission High Level Panel (1996, 24 June) chaired by Simone Veil, in the possession of David Petrie.

Petition to President of the European Parliament, Romano Prodi (2000, 6 July) in the possession of David Petrie.

Petrie, D. (2011, January 25) David Petrie petitions the European parliament. Online document: http://www.youtube.com/watch?v=2uCLLx_GCXA.

Phillipson, R. (1992) *Linguistic Imperialism*. Oxford: Oxford University Press.
Phillipson, R. (2003) *English-Only Europe*. London: Routledge.
Pickering, M. (2001) *Stereotyping: The Politics of Representation*. New York: Palgrave.
Piller, I. and Takahashi, K. (2006) A passion for English: Desire and the language market. In A. Pavlenko (ed.) *Languages and Emotions of Multilingual Speakers* (pp. 59–83). Clevedon: Multilingual Matters.
Prefectural University of Kumamoto (1996) *LEAP! Ima kimi ga kagayaku tama ni* (VHS video) [LEAP! A place where you can shine]. Fukuoka: Nishi Nihon Eizo Kabushiki Gaisha.
Price, S. (2000) Natifs contre indigènes: pour une troisième mi-temps [Native speakers against indigenous speakers: For a third half-time]. *Les Langues Moderns* 4, 8–10.
Rajagopalan, K. (2006) Non-native speaker teachers of English and their anxieties: Ingredients for an experiment in action research. In E. Llurda (ed.) *Non-Native Language Teachers: Perceptions, Challenges and Contributions to the Profession* (pp. 283–303). New York: Springer.
Rampton, M.B.H. (1990) Displacing the 'native speaker': Expertise, affiliation, and inheritance. *ELT Journal* 44 (2), 97–101.
Reid, S., Spencer-Oatey, H. and Stadler, S. (2009) The global people landscaping study: Intercultural effectiveness in global education partnerships. *Warwick Occasional Papers in Applied Linguistics,* 1. Online document: http://www.globalpeople.org.uk/, http://www.warwick.ac.uk/al/.
Richards, J.C, Platt, J. and Platt H. (1992) *Longman Dictionary of Applied Linguistics*. Harlow: Longman.
Richardson, J.E. (2007) *Analyzing Newspapers: An Approach from Critical Discourse Analysis*. New York: Palgrave Macmillan.
Rivers, D.J. (2010a) National identification and intercultural relations in foreign language learning. *Language and Intercultural Communication* 10 (4), 318–336.
Rivers, D.J. (2010b) Implicating the role of Japanese national identification: National vitality, community appeal and attitudes toward English language learning in context. *Studies in Linguistics and Language Teaching* 21, 101–122.
Rivers, D.J. (2011a) Politics without pedagogy: Questioning linguistic exclusion. *ELT Journal* 65 (2), 103–113.
Rivers D.J. (2011b) Strategies and struggles in the ELT classroom: Language policy, learner autonomy and innovative practice. *Language Awareness* 20 (1), 31–43.
Rivers D.J. (2011c) Japanese national identification and English language learning processes. *International Journal of Intercultural Relations* 35 (2), 111–123.
Rivers, D.J. (2011d) Intercultural processes in accented English. *World Englishes* 30 (3), 375–391.
Rivers, D.J. (2011e) Evaluating the self and the other: Imagined intercultural contact within a 'native-speaker' dependent foreign language context. *International Journal of Intercultural Relations* 35 (6), 842–852.
Rivers, D.J. (2012) Modelling the perceived value of compulsory English language education in undergraduate non-language majors of Japanese nationality. *Journal of Multilingual and Multicultural Development*, 33 (3), 251–267.
Rivers, D.J., Houghton, S.A. and Petrie, D. (2012, April) Explorations of native-speakerism in foreign language education. Panel presentation at CALPIU'12: Higher Education Across Borders: Transcultural Interaction and Linguistic Diversity. Roskilde University, Denmark.
Rivers, D.J. and Ross, A.S. (forthcoming) Uncovering stereotypes: Intersections of race and English native-speakerhood: In S.A Houghton, Y. Furumura, M. Lebedko and L. Song

(eds) *Developing Critical Cultural Awareness: Managing Stereotypes through Intercultural (Language) Education*. Newcastle upon Tyne: Cambridge Scholars Publishing.

Rodney, L. and Garscadden, N. (1998) *Charisma Man*. Online document: http://www.charismaman.com.

Rots, I., Sabbe, E. and Aelterman, A. (2002, September) The feminization and the social status of the teaching profession. Paper presented at the European Conference on Educational Research, University of Lisbon. Online document: http://www.leeds.ac.uk/educol/documents/00002147.htm.

Russell, J. (1991) Race and reflexivity: The Black Other in contemporary Japanese mass culture. *Cultural Anthropology* 6 (1), 3–25.

Ryan, J. and Louie, K. (2007) False dichotomy? 'Western' and 'Confucian' concepts of scholarship and learning. *Educational Philosophy and Theory* 39 (4), 404–417.

Said, E. (1978) *Orientalism*. New York: Vintage.

Sakai, N. (1988) Modernity and its critique. *South Atlantic Quarterly* 87 (3), 475–504.

Saraceni, M. (2009) Relocating English: Towards a new paradigm for English in the world. *Language and Intercultural Education* 9 (3), 175–186.

Saraceni, M. (2010) *The Relocation of English: Shifting Paradigms in a Global Era*. London: Palgrave Macmillan.

Scheurich, J.J. (1997) *Research Method in the Postmodern*. London and Washington, DC: Falmer Press.

Schmidt, K. (1995) Use of Japanese in the EFL classroom: Which way to go? *ETAPS Journal* 2 (6), 25–35.

Schultz Lee, K., Tufis, P. A., and Alwin, D. F. (2010) Separate spheres or increasing equality? Changing gender beliefs in postwar Japan. *Journal of Marriage and Family* 72, 184–201. Online document: DOI:10.1111/J.1741-3737.2009.00691.X.

Scollon, R. and Scollon, S.W. (2001) *Intercultural Communication: A Discourse Approach*. Malden, MA: Blackwell.

Seargeant, P. (2009a) *The Idea of English in Japan: Ideology and the Evolution of a Global Language*. Bristol: Multilingual Matters.

Seargeant, P. (2009b) Ideologies of English in Shakespeare's Henry V, *Language and Literature* 18 (1), 25–44.

Seibert Vaipae, S. (2001) Language minority students in Japanese public schools. In M. Noguchi and S. Fotos (eds) *Studies in Japanese Bilingualism* (pp. 184–233). Clevedon: Multilingual Matters.

Sekiguchi, T. (2002) Nikkei Brazilians in Japan: The ideology and symbolic context faced by children of this new ethnic minority. In *Exploring Japaneseness: On Japanese Enactments of Culture and Consciousness* (pp. 197–222). Westport, Connecticut: Ablex.

Shakespeare, W. (2002) *Richard II* (ed.) Charles R. Forker, London: Arden Shakespeare.

Shakespeare, W. (2006) *Henry V* (ed.) Gary Taylor. Oxford: Oxford University Press.

Shao, T. (2005) Teaching English in China: NNESTS need not apply. *NNest Newsletter* 7 (2). Online document: http://www.tesol.org/s_tesol/article.asp?vid=151&DID=4663&sid=1&cid=718&iid =4633&nid=2982.

Shipper, A. (2008) *Fighting for Foreigners: Immigration and its Impact on Japanese Democracy*. Ithaca, NY: Cornell University Press.

Shuck, G. (2006) Racializing the nonnative English speaker. *Journal of Language, Identity and Education* 5 (4), 259–276.

Siegal, M. (1995) The role of learner subjectivity in second language sociolinguistic competency. *Applied Linguistics* 17 (3), 356–382.

Simon-Maeda, A. (2004) The complex construction of professional identities: Female EFL educators in Japan speak out. *TESOL Quarterly* 38 (3), 405–436.
Singh, R., D'souza, J.D., Monahan, K. and Prabhu, N.S. (1995) On 'new/non-native' Englishes: A quartet. *Journal of Pragmatics* 24, 283–294.
Singh, R. (ed.) (1998) *The Native Speaker. Multilingual Perspectives, Language and Development* 4. London: Sage.
Skutnabb-Kangas, T. (1988) Multilingualism and the education of minority children. In T. Skutnabb-Kangas and J. Cummins (eds) *Minority Education: From Shame to Struggle* (pp. 9–44). Clevedon: Multilingual Matters.
Smart, R. (2010, 4 May) Eikaiwa on the ropes after fall of Geos. *The Japan Times.* Online document: http://search.japantimes.co.jp/cgi-bin/fl20100504zg.html.
Smil, V. (2007, 19 April) The unprecedented shift in Japan's population: Numbers, age, and prospects. *The Asia-Pacific Journal: Japan Focus.* Online document: http://www.japanfocus.org/-Vaclav-Smil/2411.
Snow, N. (1998) *Propaganda Inc., Selling America's Culture to the World.* New York: Seven Stories.
Solórzano, D.G. and Yosso, T.J. (2002) Critical race methodology: Counter-story telling as an analytical framework for education research. *Qualitative Inquiry* 8 (1), 23–44.
Spears, A. K. (1999) Race and ideology: An introduction. In A.K. Spears (ed.) *Race and Ideology: Language, Symbolism, and Popular Culture* (pp. 11–58). Detroit: Wayne State University Press.
Stallybrass, P. and White, A. (1986) *The Politics and Poetics of Transgression.* Ithaca, NY: Cornell University Press.
Stanlaw, J. (2004) *Japanese English: Language and Culture Contact.* Hong Kong: Hong Kong University Press.
Sunderland, J. (2000) Issues of language and gender in second and foreign language education. *Language Teaching* 33 (4), 203–223.
Sung-Yul Park, J. and Wee, L. (2009) The three circles redux: A market-theoretic perspective on World Englishes. *Applied Linguistics* 30 (3), 389–406.
Swain, M. and Lapkin, S. (2000) Task-based second language learning: The uses of the first language. *Language Teaching and Research* 4 (3), 251–274.
Tabuchi, H. (2009, 23 April) Japan pays foreign workers to go home. *The New York Times.* Online document: http://www.nytimes.com/2009/04/23/business/global/23immigrant.html?pagewante d=all. Tachibanaki, T. (2006) Inequality and poverty in Japan. *The Japanese Economic Review* 57 (1), 1–27.
Tachibanaki, T. (2006) Inequality and poverty in Japan. *The Japanese Economic Review* 57 (1), 1–27.
Taguchi, T., Magid, M. and Papi, M. (2009) The L2 motivational self system among Japanese, Chinese, and Iranian learners of English: A comparative study. In Z. Dörnyei and E. Ushioda (eds) *Motivation, Language Identity and the L2 Self* (pp. 66–97). Bristol: Multilingual Matters.
Tahlin, M. (2006) Skill change and skill matching in the labor market: A cross-national overview. *State-of the-art, EQUALSOC Network.* Swedish Institute for Social Research (SOFI), Stockholm University. Online document: http://www2.sofi.su.se/~mta/docs/Skill_change_-_a_cross-national_overview.pdf.
Tajino, A. and Tajino, Y. (2000) Native and non-native: What can they offer? *ELT Journal* 54 (1), 3–10.
Takahara, K. (2008, 5 January) Assistant language teachers in trying times. *The Japan Times.* Online document: http://search.japantimes.co.jp/cgi-bin/nn20080105f1.html.

Tanabe, Y. (2004) What the 2003 MEXT action plan proposes to teachers of English. *The Language Teacher* 28 (3). Online document: http://jalt-publications.org/tlt/articles/730-what-2003-mext-action-plan-proposes-teachers-english.

Tanaka, S. (2007) *Kokka senryaku toshite no 'daigaku Eigo'* ['University English' as a national strategy] Tokyo: Sanshuusha.

Tang, C. (1997) The identity of the nonnative ESL teacher: On the power and status of nonnative ESL teachers. *TESOL Quarterly* 31 (3), 577–580.

TESOL Directory of Degree and Certificate Programs (n.d.). Online document: http://www.tesol.org/s_tesol/seccss.asp?CID=1770&DID=9326.

Thau, S., Aquino, K. and Poortvliet, P.M. (2007) Self-defeating behaviors in organizations: The relationship between thwarted belonging and interpersonal work behaviors. *Journal of Applied Psychology* 92 (3), 840–847.

The Independent (2010, 25 September) Family fiefdoms blamed for tainting Italian Universities. Online document: http://www.independent.co.uk/news/world/europe/family-fiefdoms-blamed-for-tainting-italian-universities-2089120.html.

THES (1998a, 9 January) Clan mentality rules in Italian universities. Online document: http://www.timeshighereducation.co.uk/story.asp?sectioncode=26&storycode=1053 39.

THES (1998b, 13 February) Euro-MP tells union to back foreigners. Online document: http://www.timeshighereducation.co.uk/story.asp?sectioncode=26&storycode=1058 79.

THES (2008, 8 May) Second Class Colleagues. Online document: http://www.timeshighereducation.co.uk/story.asp?sectioncode=26&storycode=4017 83.

The University of Edinburgh (2007, 1 March) Law seminar. Faculty of Law, Edinburgh University, UK.

The University of Tokyo (2004) *Tokyo Daigaku tokutei tanjikan kinmu yuuki koyou kyoushokuin no syugyo ni kansuru kitei* [The University of Tokyo regulations concerning the working conditions of staff who are hired in part-time non-tenured positions]. Online document: http://www.ne.jp/asahi/tousyoku/hp/syuki/25_frame.htm.

The University of Tokyo (2009) *Tokyo Daigaku no kokusai katsudou o sasaeru taisei genjou to kadai* [The support system for international activities at the University of Tokyo: Present state and challenges]. Issued by the University of Tokyo, Tokyo.

The University of Tokyo (2010a) *Tokyo Daigaku no koudou shinario*, Forest 2015, pamphlet [The action scenario for the University of Tokyo, Forest 2015, pamphlet]. Online document: http://www.u-tokyo.ac.jp/scenario.

The University of Tokyo (2010b) *Tokyo Daigaku Kokusaika Hakusho (Bukyokuhen)* [The University of Tokyo white paper on internationalization (for the departments)]. Issued by the University of Tokyo, Tokyo.

The University of Tokyo (2010c) *Tokyo Daigaku no gaiyo shiryohen* [The University of Tokyo Guidebook: Sources, 2010]. Tokyo: University of Tokyo.

The University of Tokyo (2011a) *Kokusai kouryu kankei tokei shiryou (gaikokujin ryugakuseisuu)* [International Exchange-Related Statistical Sources (the number of foreign international students)] Online document: http://www.u-tokyo.ac.jp/res03/d03_02_02_j.html.

The University of Tokyo (2011b) Background to the ALESS course. Online document: http://aless.ecc.u-tokyo.ac.jp.

Thiesse, A.M. (1999) *La création des identités nationales, Europe XVIIIè-XXè siècles* [The Creation of National Identities in Europe between the Eighteenth and Twentieth Centuries]. Paris: Seuil.

Tollefson, J. and Tsui, A.B.M. (2004) *Medium of Instruction Policies*. Mahwah, NJ: Lawrence Erlbaum Associates.

Torikai, K. (2010) *'Eigo kôyôgo' wa naniga mondai ka* [What's wrong with 'English as the official language'?]. Tokyo: Kadokawa.
Torpey, M.J. (2006) A case study of conflict in an educational workplace: Managing personal and cultural differences. *Teachers College Record* 108 (12), 2523–2549.
Train, R. (2003) The (non) native speaker: Standard language in foreign language education, a critical perspective. In C. Blyth (ed.) *The Sociolinguistics of Foreign Language Classrooms: Contributions of the Native, Near Native and Non-Native Speaker* (pp. 8–25). Boston: Thomson Heinle.
Triandis, H.C. (2006) Culture and conflict. In L.A. Samovar and R.E. Porter (eds) *Intercultural Communication: A Reader* (pp. 22–31). Belmont, CA: Wadsworth.
Trudgill, P. (2008) Native-speaker segmental phonological models and the English lingua franca core. In K. Dziubalska-Kolaczyk and J. Przetlacka (eds) *English Pronunciation Models: A Changing Scene* (pp. 77–100). Berlin: Peter Lang.
Tsai, Y. and Houghton, S. (eds) (2010) *Being Intercultural: Inside and Outside the Language Classroom*. Newcastle upon Tyne: Cambridge Scholars Publishing.
Tsuda T. (2006) Localities and the struggle for immigrant rights: The significance of local citizenship in recent countries of immigration. In T. Tsuda (ed.) *Local Citizenship in Recent Countries of Immigration* (pp. 3–36). Lanham, MD: Lexington Books.
Tsuda, Y. (1990) *Eigo shinai no kouzou: Nihonjin to ibunka komyunikeishon* [The structure of English domination: Japanese and intercultural communication]. Tokyo: Daisan Shokan.
Tsuda, Y. (1997). Hegemony of English vs ecology of language: Building equality in international communication. *World Englishes 2000* 14, 21–32.
Tsuido, K. (2007) *Nihon no Eigo kyouiku kaikaku ni kansuru ichi kousatsu: JET program o chuushin ni* [A thought on educational reform in Japan: Focusing on the JET program]. *Hiroshima Gaikokugo Kyouiku Kenkyuu* 10, 1–16.
Tsuneyoshi, R. (2005) Internationalization strategies in Japan: The dilemmas and possibilities of study abroad programs using English. *Journal of Research in International Education* 4 (1), 65–86.
Tsuneyoshi, R. (2010) The 'New' foreigners and the social reconstruction of difference: The cultural diversification of Japanese education. In R. Tsuneyoshi, K.H. Okano and S.S. Boocok (eds) *Minorities and Education in Japan: An Interactive Perspective* (pp. 149–172). New York: Routledge.
Turner, B.S. (2002) Cosmopolitan virtue, globalization and patriotism. *Theory, Culture and Society* 19 (1–2), 45–63.
Twenge, J.M., Baumeister, R.F., Tice, D.M. and Stucke, T.S. (2008) If you can't join them, beat them: Effects of social exclusion on aggressive behavior. In J. Feinberg (ed.), *Cultural Animal Reader for Baumeister and Bushman's Social Psychology and Human Nature* (pp. 160–188). Belmont, CA: Thomson Wadsworth.
Twenge, J.M., Zhang, L., Catanese, K.R., Dolan-Pascoe, B., Lyche, L.F. and Baumeister, R.F. (2007) Replenishing connectedness: Reminders of social activity reduce aggression after social exclusion. *British Journal of Social Psychology* 46, 205–224.
Uemura, S. (2008) Salaries of *oyatoi* (Japan's foreign employees) in early Meiji. *Ryuutsuu Kagaku Daigaku Ronshuu* 21 (1), 1–24. Online document: http://www.umds.ac.jp/kiyou/r/21-1/r21-1uemura.pdf.
Usui, C., Rose S. and Kageyama, R. (2003) Women, institutions, and leadership in Japan. *Asian Perspective* 27 (3), 85–123.
Usher, R. and Edwards, R. (1994) *Postmodernism and Education: Different Voices, Different Worlds*. London: Routledge.

Van Dijk, T.A. (1993) Principles of critical discourse analysis. *Discourse and Society* 4 (2), 249–283.
Van Dijk, T. (1984) *Prejudice in Discourse*. Amsterdam: John Benjamins.
Van Dijk, T. (2001) Critical discourse analysis. In D. Schiffrin, D. Tannen and H. Hamilton (eds) *The Handbook of Discourse Analysis* (pp. 352–371). Malden, MA: Blackwell.
Van Gennep, A. (1960) *The Rites of Passage*. Chicago: Chicago University Press.
Van Gorder, A.C. (2008) Educating students in North American Christian higher education from privilege toward social justice. In J.K. Stronks (ed.) *Teaching to Justice: Christian Faculty Seek Shalom in Different Disciplines* (pp. 7–29). Online document: http://www.cccu.org/filefolder/teaching_to_justice_final_short1.doc.
Van Leeuwen, T. (1996) The representation of social actors. In R.C. Caldas-Coulthard and M. Coulthard (eds) *Texts and Practices: Readings in Critical Discourse Analysis* (pp. 32–70). London: Routledge.
Van Lier, L. (1996) *Interaction in the Language Curriculum: Awareness, Autonomy and Authenticity*. London: Longman.
Vickers, M.H. (2001) Bullying as unacknowledged organizational evil: A researcher's story. *Employee Responsibilities and Rights Journal* 13 (4), 205–217.
Walby, S. (1994) Is citizenship gendered? *Sociology* 28 (2), 379–395.
Walby, S. and Olsen, W. (2002) *The Impact of Women's Position in the Labour Market on Pay and Implications for UK Productivity*. Women and Equality Unit. London: DITI Publications.
Wallis, K. and Poulton, J. (2001) *Internalization*. Oxford: Oxford University Press.
Warhurst, C. and Thompson, P. (2006) Mapping knowledge in work: Proxies or practices? *Work, Employment Society* 20, 787–800.
Waters, A. (2007) Native-speakerism in ELT: Plus ca change…? *System* 35 (3), 281–292.
Wenger, E. (1998) *Communities of Practice: Learning, Meaning, and Identity*. Cambridge: Cambridge University Press.
Weschler, R. (1997) Use of Japanese in the English language classroom. *TESL Journal* 3 (1), 1–12.
Widdowson, H.G. (2000) The monolingual teaching and bilingual learning of English. In R.L. Cooper, E. Shohamy and J. Walters (eds) *New Perspectives and Issues in Educational Language Policy* (pp. 7–18). Amsterdam/Philadelphia: John Benjamins.
Wilhelm, K., Dewhurst-Savellis, J. and Parker, G. (2000) Teacher stress? An analysis of why teachers leave and why they stay. *Teachers and Teaching: Theory and Practice* 6 (3), 291–304.
Willis, D.B. and Rappleye, J. (2011) *Reiminging Japanese Education: Borders, Transfers, Circulations, and the Comparative*. Oxford: Symposium Books.
Wordell, C. (1993) Politics and human relations in the Japanese university. In P. Wadden (ed.) *A Handbook for Teaching English at Japanese Colleges and Universities* (pp. 145–155). Oxford: Oxford University Press.
Worthington, C. (1998) Counterarguments and conclusions: The Union vs. the University. *PALE Journal of Professional Issues* 4 (3). Online document: http://www.debito.org/PALE/.
Worthington, C. (1999) Combating discrimination at a Japanese university. *JPRI Working Paper* 58. Online document: http://www.jpri.org/publications/workingpapers/wp58.html.
Wu, Z. (2005) *Teachers' Knowing in Curriculum Change: A Critical Discourse Study of Language Teaching*. Beijing: Foreign Language Teaching and Research Press.
Yamamoto, M. (2001) Japanese attitudes towards bilingualism: A survey and its implications. In M. Noguchi and S. Fotos (eds) *Studies in Japanese Bilingualism* (pp. 24–44). Clevedon: Multilingual Matters.

Yamanaka, N. (2006) An evaluation of English textbooks in Japan from the viewpoint of nations in the Inner, Outer, and Expanding Circles. *The JALT Journal* 28 (1), 57–76.

Yngve, V.H. (1981) The struggle for a theory of native speaker. In F. Coulmas (ed.) *A Festschrift for Native Speaker* (pp. 29–49). The Hague: Mouton Publishers.

Yonezawa, A. (2007) Japanese flagship universities at a crossroads. *Higher Education* 54, 483–499.

Yonezawa, A. (2009a, June). International attractiveness of Japanese universities: Perspectives of Japanese and non-Japanese faculties [PowerPoint slides]. Presented at the 45th General Conference, Tokyo Gakugei University, Japan.

Yonezawa, A. (2009b) The internationalization of Japanese higher education: Policy debates and realities. Tohoku University: Center for the Advancement of Higher Education 9, 199–219. Online document: http://www.cshe.nagoya-u.ac.jp/publications/journal/no9/13.pdf.

Yonezawa, A. (2010) Much ado about ranking: Why can't Japanese universities internationalize? *Japan Forum* 22 (102), 121–137.

Yoshikawa, H. (2005) Recognition of World Englishes: Changes in Chukyo University students' attitudes. *World Englishes* 24 (3), 351–360.

Yoshino, K. (1992) *Cultural Nationalism in Contemporary Japan: A Sociological Enquiry*. London: Routledge.

Zarate, G., Lévy, D. and Kramsch, C. (2011) *Handbook of Multilingualism and Multiculturalism*. Paris: E.A.C.

Zarate, G. and Liddicoat, A. (2009) La circulation internationale des idées en didactique des langues [International Circulation of Ideas in Language Teaching/Tearning]. *Le Français dans le Monde, R & A,* 46.

Index

administration, 143
   school/university, 46, 53, 60, 96, 100, 103, 110, 140, 143, 154, 155, 189, 215
agency, 110, 114, 132, 147
African American Vernacular English (AAVE), 224
alignment, 113–115
Australian English, 224
authenticity, 78, 79, 81, 89, 98
autonomy, 21, 22, 64, 72, 76, 150

backlash, 70, 71, 169, 176, 210
beliefs, 195, 198, 200, 211, 238, 241, 249, 252
belongingness hypothesis, 107
biopolitics, 174
birthrate, 172
bullying, 110, 111, 216
burnout, 112

Charisma Man, 152
citizenship, 79
   substantive, 148–149
collective bargaining, 9, 62–63
collective imagination, 113
commodification, 186
communicative method, 109
contamination, 81
counter-storytelling, 196–197, 198
Critical Race Theory, 13, 196–199
cultural competence, 250
cultural models/references, 247
culture, 122
   dominant and non-dominant, 132
   dual layers, 157
curriculum reform, 52–55, 63–65

deconstructing, 210–213, 255
discrimination, 3, 9, 18, 31, 32, 199–200
dis-identification, 114
   cultures, 190
doxa, 246

economics, 170, 247
   neoclassical, 171
empowerment, 66
engagement, 108–111
entrance exams, 102, 103, 109
equality, 83, 148
   barriers to, 148
   of opportunity, 83
essentialism, 135
ethnicised, 254
ethnocentric discourse, 79, 247
ethnocentrism, 3, 4, 14, 191
exchange, 25, 35–36, 94, 161, 175
exoticism, 13, 78, 82, 98, 104, 194, 202

firewall, 177
financial instability, 153
foreign labour markets, 132, 134, 149
formal qualifications as proxies, 133, 135
four skills, 64, 67
full-time, 44, 46–48, 51, 58, 127, 134

gaikokujin, 47, 56, 60, 170, 175
   kyoushi, 47, 52, 60–63, 68, 170
   kyouin, 60, 61
gender, 149–150
   gap, 40, 148, 161, 167–168
   gender-based attitudes, 155, 156, 222
General American (GA), 219
Glasgow vernacular, 224, 225
global spread of English, 14, 220, 235, 237
grammar-translation, 8, 55, 109, 192, 210
guest workers, 171

habitus, 221, 248
harassment, 111, 151, 157
   academic, 151
   power, 111, 156, 157
   sexual, 11, 156, 157
health care and pension, 148–149
hegemony, 69, 73, 192, 210

hijoukin, 44, 48–52
homophily, 147–157
human rights organizations, 62, 111
hybridity, 173

identity, 6, 10, 14, 55–57, 88-89, 94–95
imagination, 111–113
immigration, 172, 173
insularity, 178, 191, 192
International Convention on the Elimination of All Forms of Racial Discrimination, 62
International Covenant on Social, Economic and Cultural Rights, 62
intersectionality, 198, 206
isolation, 10, 11, 81, 82, 106, 153, 157, 192, 204, 215, 233

English in Japan, 13, 94
    English language policy, 191, 226
    higher education, 125–126, 227
    Japanese English, 207, 225, 226
    Japanese language, 12, 70, 140, 225
    Japan Exchange and Teaching (JET) Programme, 8, 94, 99, 108–109, 160, 161, 162, 239

Kumamoto General Union, 42, 43, 52

labor dispute, 43
language as battleground, 21, 67–72
language attitudes, 14, 220
    and native speakers, 222
    attitude change, 219–220
    future research, 226
    status vs. solidarity, 225
    towards English in Japan, 222–225
language ability/competence, 11, 67, 70
    Japanese, 11–12, 63, 67
language,
    as proxy, 135
    market, 243, 253
    model, 98
    policy, 12, 13, 71, 78, 80, 82, 165, 191, 210, 215, 216, 226
    variation, 220, 222, 223, 226, 229

law suit, 32, 40
leaders, 55, 83, 148
    women, 148, 151
learning,
    cultures, 23
    model, 100, 245
legitimacy, 244, 245, 251
lettori, 30–41
linguicism, 66–67, 71
linguistic, 104, 134, 184, 235
    competence, 250, 251
    continuum, 221
    market, 243, 253
    imperialism, 17, 68–69, 196, 247

mediation, 143
mentorship, 112–113
monolingual paradigm, 255
multiculturalism, 20, 175

nationality, 1, 11, 29, 30, 57, 99
native-speaker,
    native-English speaker teacher, 12, 246
    adaptation to institutional norms, 80, 90, 190
    adopting a critical perspective, 75–76
    badges of authenticity, 78, 79, 81
    classroom efforts packaged as research, 87
    commodity, 90, 101
    conditioning, 88
    contamination, 81
    definition, 82, 104, 220, 221
    designer mannequin, 82, 187
    disenfranchisement, 77
    economic value, 81
    edutainment, 80
    expendable commodities, 90
    ghettoized expatriate professoriate, 82
    guilt reaction, 83
    hallucinatory foundations, 79
    ideology, 142, 225, 226, 229
    limited term contracts, 30, 33–38, 42, 44, 47, 52–54, 57, 61, 63, 77, 87, 133, 134, 137, 139, 174, 248
    management, 77, 79, 80, 82–85, 88

mass employment, 61–63
non-existence, 89
performance typology, 88
positionality, 206
professional frustration, 142
role capability, 81
role in research, 87
self-confidence, 109
self-depreciation, 105
vanquished status, 80
versus non-native speaker, 220–221
native-speakerism,
  benefactors, 89
  conflict with authority, 10, 43, 76, 86
  conformity, 83–86
  conveyor belt mentality, 77
  definition, 1–14
  dissent and resistance, 8, 9, 10, 75, 85, 90
  dress code, 81, 82, 186, 187
  educational disservice, 90
  endless optimism, 90
  exploitative mentality, 84
  fear, 10, 41, 72, 86–88, 89–90, 157
  figures of salvation, 88
  global citizens & citizenship, 79
  grapevine culture, 88
  groupthink mentality, 90
  human collateral, 90
  institutionalization, 75, 245
  internationalization, 13, 120, 121, 125, 126, 130, 188
  minority voices, 75
  oppressive social structures, 80, 86
  personal experience, 85–88, 102
  power and privilege, 75
  psychological impact, 70
  threats to employment, 110
  variants of English, 219–220, 222, 223, 229
Nihonjinron, 200, 201
Nikkei, 170, 172–173, 177

oppression, 13, 71–72, 75, 80, 84, 93, 171, 197, 198, 205, 206
orientalism, 4
othering, 3, 13, 19, 25, 66, 98, 194, 201, 202, 204

outsider, 101, 169
outsourcing, 171

part-time, 44, 46–48, 58
plurilingual/pluricultural paradigm, 246
polarities, 175
policies, 173, 207, 211, 216, 247
professional,
  legitimacy, 245
  vision, 193
professionalism, 22, 168, 189, 195
power, 3, 72, 88, 120, 159–160
prejudice, 3, 7, 14, 70, 198
promotion, 2, 51
  of foreigners, 60–61
pronunciation, 97, 164
publishing,
  politics of, 76
purity, 176

qualifications versus skills, 135, 141

race, 13, 78, 185, 197, 204, 240
racial discrimination, 62, 206
racism, 3, 4, 14, 20, 196, 198
rational-choice theory, 170
Received Pronunciation (RP), 219
revolving door, 174, 178, 179

Scottish Standard English (SSE), 224, 225
self-fulfilling prophecy, 65
sennin, 49–52, 57
sexism, 3, 4, 14
Shakespeare, 192, 233, 234
slippage, 122, 123, 173
social welfare benefits, 147–148
sociology of knowledge, 170
Southern United States English, 225
speech community, 229, 233, 237
standard English versus non-standard English,, 222
standard language ideology, 222, 225
stereotypes, 65, 112
stereotyping, 3, 68
stigmatism, 71, 109, 200, 201, 254
strategies, 99, 114, 141

structures
  ideological, 152–154
  social, 154–157

teacher development, 68, 81, 109
teaching cultures, 247
teaching competence, 246, 251
teaching field of English as a Foreign
  Language, 244–246, 249
teaching model, 228, 244
tenure, 11, 12, 30, 33, 34, 39, 62, 63, 67, 68, 70,
  77, 88, 114, 133, 134, 137, 139, 140, 152,
  156, 157, 184
Teaching English as a Second Language
  (TESOL), 2, 5, 92, 95, 104, 147
  male dominated in Japan, 77, 148, 150, 151

Test of English for International
  Communication (TOEIC), 64, 68, 70

variationist sociolinguistics, 226, 230
variety recognition, 225
vertical segregation, 143

White supremacy, 169
women, 144, 147, 151, 155
workforce, 77, 143, 169, 172
World Englishes model, 219, 220

xenophobia, 171, 174, 192

For Product Safety Concerns and Information please contact our EU Authorised Representative:

Easy Access System Europe

Mustamäe tee 50

10621 Tallinn

Estonia

gpsr.requests@easproject.com

www.ingramcontent.com/pod-product-compliance
Lightning Source LLC
Chambersburg PA
CBHW070554300426
44113CB00010B/1252